THE ENGLISH
COUNTRYWOMAN

THE ENGLISH COUNTRYWOMAN

Her life in farmhouse and field
from Tudor times to the Victorian age

G. E. & K. R. FUSSELL

ORBIS PUBLISHING · LONDON

First published in Great Britain by
Andrew Melrose Limited, London 1953;
reprinted by Orbis Publishing Limited,
London 1981

© G. E. & K. R. Fussell 1953, 1981

Printed in Singapore

ISBN: 0-85613-336-1

The authors are grateful to the *Farmer's Weekly*
for giving them permission to use certain
material which had already appeared in that
publication.

CONTENTS

List of Illustrations   *Page* vii

Introduction   xi

Chapter I   The Elizabethan Countrywoman   17

II   Cavalier and Puritan Countrywomen   43

III   In the Days of The Restoration   74

IV   The Georgian Country Housewife, 1712–1760   103

V   The Country Housewife under George III   131

VI   Regency and Early Victorian Countrywomen   157

VII   The Late Victorian Countrywoman, 1860-1900   185

Appendix: authorities used   212

Index   217

LIST OF ILLUSTRATIONS

The following illustrations appear between pages 48 and 49

1. Harvest work, 1577
2. Marketing in 1598
3. Maid brushing away flies, 1556
4. Open fire in Tudor hall
5. Old fireplaces—late Tudor times
6. A Tudor hall
7. Elizabethan lady riding pillion
8. The Hall of Eltham Palace
9. "A new French cook to devise kickshaws. . . ."
10. A cottage chimney-corner
11. Public washing grounds, 1582
12. The Duke and Duchess of Newcastle
13. An open chimney
14. Mrs. Caudle's "curtain lectures"
15. Lady and gentleman hawking in early Stuart times
16. Milking scene, seventeenth century
17. Cooking, 1618
18. "The Cruell Shrow . . ." a ballad of 1610

The following illustrations appear between pages 96 and 97

19. Garden lay-out in 1618
20. The Bee-hive house, 1618
21. Surface drainage pond
22. The milkmaids' May Day dance, 1698
23. Farmhouse kitchen
24. Woman at work in kitchen, seventeenth century
25. The Squire's family, 1691
26. "The woman works, the shepherd snores"

27. Work in the still-room, 1691

28. "The woman reaps, the man sleeps"

29. An enclosed plot, 1691

30. Beating flax or hemp

31. A formal garden, 1717

32. Open-air musical party

33. The pleached alley, 1730

34. Illustration to *PAMELA*

The following illustrations appear between pages 128 and 129

35. Busy dairymaid, 1736

36. Milk delivery, eighteenth century

37. Ducking chair

38. Proper dress, 1730

39. The farmer's door, 1790

40. The squire's door, 1790

41. A parlour fire, mid-nineteenth century

42. Eighteenth century kitchen

43. "A matron old, whom we Schoolmistress name..."
1812

44. Eighteenth century mop fair

45. The farmyard, 1790

46. The tithe pig, 1793

47. Old pump, Hammersmith (London)

48. The village pump at Fressingfield

49. Dr. Syntax and the dairymaid, 1812

50. Making oatcake, Yorkshire, 1814

51. Hand-spinning, Yorkshire, 1814

The following illustrations appear between pages 176 and 177

52. The cottage fireside, c. 1810

53. A cottage interior, c. 1805

54. The dairy, c. 1810

55. An outing, 1825

56. Riding pillion, 1822

57. To market by boat, 1822

58. Dairymaid, c. 1860
59. The butter-making competition, Windsor, 1889
60. Women hoeing, 1899
61. Washing clothes in stream
62. Sweet hay-makers, 1899
63. Making straw ropes, 1885
64. The corn harvest, 1885
65. The gleaners, 1885
66. "Mrs. Pyecroft makes a pudding," 1905
67. A nineteenth century mop fair

INTRODUCTION

The small but virile population that flourished or failed under the sovereign lordship of Henry VIII lived in a very different country from the England we know. There were only three or four million of them scattered over the countryside, a great deal of which was almost empty and uninhabited.

The scene in its plains and hills, mountains and valleys was, of course, the same as it is today, but it was not tamed. Wide areas of forest, moor and fen bounded the narrow area of cultivation. Three-quarters of a million acres of marsh and fen were in their native state in the eastern counties. Flood water often swamped the land to the verges of Cambridgeshire and Huntingdon. From Peterborough to King's Lynn, from Mildenhall and Ely to Boston and Lincoln was an area inhabited mainly by fowlers and fishermen who ran a few cattle on the drier summer grazing, and who drank poppy juice to combat the ague that constantly afflicted them. On the other side of the country Sedgemoor and its neighbouring marshes, though not adequately drained, was dry enough to graze cattle in the summer. Romney Marsh and Pevensey Marshes hugged the south-east coast.

Forests of oak, scrub and timber, often matted with undergrowth, covered much of the Weald of Kent and Sussex. The New Forest, Waltham Forest and Alice Holt covered much of Hampshire. Windsor Forest stretched from Wokingham to Windsor. There were many others, Epping Forest, the Forest of Bere, Woolmer, Rockingham, Selwood, Hatfield, Cranbourne, Knaresborough among them.

At the end of Queen Elizabeth's reign Thomas Wilson estimated that there were nine hundred forests, chaces and parks in the country-side. Many of these were very extensive and covered thousands of acres.

They were not all dense jungles, and there was some minute degree of settlement in and about them, but much of their areas was known only to a few. Travellers regarded them with fear, because the paths and tracks were difficult to follow, and the wild wood was the haunt of masterless men, footpads and robbers, or vagrants who would take what they could not beg, if their gang was strong enough. The forests, too, were likely to be haunted with witches, warlocks and other fantasies of a rich and superstitious imagination.

Besides the fen and the forest, heaths stretched for miles across the country. The coast of Suffolk was a wild waste of heath some miles wide. From Bagshot Heath the wilderness stretched all across the sandy wastes that are now suburbia, through the Devil's Punchbowl to Hindhead and the marshes round Thursley, through Surrey to Westerham in Kent. Nearer London, Hounslow and Hampstead Heaths were much more extensive than they are now. A few people lived in one or two small villages, quite unlike the massed and serried streets we know. Farther away still the Quantock Hills, Exmoor, Dartmoor and Bodmin Moor were desolate and uninhabited. Through the west midlands other similar country was to be found, notably Cannock Chase.

The South Downs were the haunt of the wailing curlew and huge flocks of now long-vanished bustards, that provided fine sport. A few lonely shepherds wandered after the bell wethers that led their flocks. The same solitude was characteristic of the Berkshire and Marlborough Downs and of Salisbury Plain. Far to the north the wastes of Northumberland and the high hills from Derbyshire to the border were the homes of an isolated and fierce population ready to take up arms against the robbers and reivers from across the Tweed. Cumberland vales were scantily inhabited by a sturdy race of small landowners known as statesmen. The Yorkshire Wolds were the habitat of the famous hares, and a few lonely flocks. Lincoln Heath and Cliff were deserted.

England was an almost empty land, though a belt of villages stretched across the midland plain, and scattered more sparsely elsewhere. Wilson estimated that there were only 641 market and shire towns. There were perhaps, 9,000 parishes, some of which were "in compass 40 English miles" of fruitful ground, but having only one church. Of these, examples were, he said, to be found in Yorkshire and Norfolk. Few of the market towns had more than a thousand or so people living in them; many of the villages only a hundred or so. Quite a lot of people lived out their whole lives only having seen two or three hundred different persons. They were born, lived and died in the same house, and in the same tiny community.

Of the three or four million people living in England, there were only sixty-one noble and titled families in 1600. In addition there were twenty-six bishops, or spiritual lords, as they were called. Five hundred knights were less in number than the present House of Commons. The 16,000 esquires completed the tale of the landed gentry. The yeomen of England were a larger body, but included two very different classes. Ten thousand of them were rich men with incomes ranging between £300 and £500 a year, the salary of a very minor bureaucrat today. Eighty thousand poor yeomen brought up their families on small holdings, and were such as possessed from six to eleven milk kine, five or six work horses, some young beasts and a few sheep apiece. Wilson's estimate of the situation of these men is amply confirmed by contemporary inventories, but he was unable to make any estimate of the lower classes.

They were mainly copyholders who held some small parcel of land and a tenement of some lord, or a parcel of the demesne at the will of the lord. They earned their living chiefly by day labour at country work. They were paid in meat and drink and some small wage. How many of these men there were no one knows. The possibility of invasion in 1588 led to a general muster of all men between sixteen and sixty who were capable of bearing arms. Excluding the nobles, who would be the natural leaders, and sufficient countrymen to till the ground, some 300,000 were placed upon the strength. They were not actually enrolled in a standing army and segregated from the rest of the population; but were organized mainly in their own neighbourhood. Possibly there was some such number of copyholders, since it would not be unreasonable to conjecture that the total number of males in the country did not amount to more than a million. Their wives and children of both sexes would complete the population.

This is but a wild surmise, but would give a class distribution of something like this. Nobility, knights, esquires and yeomen just over 100,000; copyholders 300,000; cottagers, who were not copyholders, at least equal to them, i.e. 300,000; making a total of 700,000 heads of families. The remaining 300,000 heads of families, if there were so many, would be artisans of one kind and another, shopkeepers in London, builders, carpenters, smiths, wrights, cloth workers, miners and so on. In this number must be included, too, the mass of vagrom men, wanderers and gipsies about whom so many romances have been written. No especial virtue is claimed for these assumptions which are indeed nothing more than speculation that may be probable.

Only one indication of the value of money has so far been given. The richer yeomen were worth £300 to £500 a year in 1600. This was after a rise in prices that took place during the preceding century. Just before this time, in 1593, the Yorkshire magistrates fixed the wages of labourers in husbandry at 5d. a day in summer and 4d. a day in winter. Mowing hay was to be paid by the piece at 10d. an acre, reaping corn at 8d. and the men were expected to cut an acre a day. The price of wheat in that year was 18s. 4½d. a quarter, of oatmeal 29s. 4d. and of malt 12s. 3½d. An old horse might be worth £1, better ones slightly more. A good cow would sell at £1 to £3, and a steer perhaps the same. Sheep were valued at from 4s., and mature hogs and sows at 13s. 4d. upwards. The maxima were not much higher. Money was scarce and a good deal of what trading was done must have been carried out by barter. Grain and cheese, livestock and wool, of course, went to London, and this was for the time big business, dealt with by travelling or resident factors and merchants. Small sales of butter and cheese, eggs and poultry were made by the country housewives in the local market. The annual or semi-annual fairs dealt in larger quantities.

Many people, we have said, did not see more than three or four hundred people in the course of their lives. Travelling was a luxury, but an uncomfortable and difficult pleasure, if pleasure it could be called. The dirt roads were a sea of mud in winter and deep in dust in the summer. Floods were the least of obstacles. The highways, such as they were, were infested with robbers and footpads, and beggars and vagrants would turn their hands to any dishonesty if a good opportunity offered. A country housewife going only a few miles to market might easily be molested and robbed on her way home, if her day had been successful. The side lanes leading to remote villages were mere tracks, distinguishable only to those who knew them well. Everything combined to make the country population stay at home; there was nothing to encourage them to fare forth and risk getting lost in the woods, or upon the lonely heaths, or perhaps to be drowned in the swamps and marshes.

And they were too busy to have the leisure for travel. Their lives were spent in producing their living. Their work, when crowned with the joy of a plentiful harvest, was their pleasure. Outdoor work made heavy demands upon them with their simple and inadequate means and methods of food production. What they garnered they consumed through the year. The net product for sale in a bad year was often a minus quantity. All that they had been able to produce barely saved them from starvation. Indeed, famine was only too often the blood brother of feasting.

When they were not able to work out of doors they had plenty to occupy them indoors. Most necessities were made at home. Tools and clothing were home-made, so were the many household necessities. Quite a large proportion of the things that today are bought at the village shop were unknown. Those that were known were made at home because there was no village shop, and, if there had been, people would have had little or no money to spend there. All this kept people busily employed at home, men and women alike.

The family was a unit that worked in a partnership, usually voluntary and accustomed, but none the less forced upon them by the circumstances in which they lived. Their condition was little different from that of the settlers that sailed in the *Mayflower* and settled in New England. It was a rough and ready kind of life, lacking in convenience and comfort but not joyless.

The father and husband was the acknowledged and accepted head of the family. The wife and mother, though actively employed in assisting to win the family livelihood with her dairy and poultry, her spinning and weaving, her preserving and distilling, accepted her subjection to her husband. It was what she expected, but it was very real. She was the inferior but not unhappy partner in the matrimonial venture, and she did not revile or revolt against her lot. No doubt she had her ways of making her wishes felt, though ostensibly under the control of that superior being, man.

The role of the country housewife was her destiny. She was brought up to no other idea. Her ambition was to make a success of the job, and very notably many a housewife succeeded.

The Tudor housewife was a pattern for future ages. But as time passed and society gradually grew more wealthy her condition changed. Now conveniences were invented, manners changed as did the relation of the classes, and the duties that devolved upon the housewives were modified. It is these changes that we have tried to tell in the following pages.

Throughout the four centuries from 1500 to 1900 people have left behind them diaries of their daily doings from which we can reconstruct the life they led. Earnest persons have always written pamphlets and books condemning others for the way they lived, and incidentally reporting how people did live. The woman question is not new. It has always been discussed. Other pamphleteers and politicians have discussed the wrongs inflicted by one class upon another. Even Acts of Parliament tell us something of how people were believed to have lived.

Plays and stories have been written about the daily life of ordinary people, and poets exercised their licence to praise country life and living throughout the whole time. All of these describe one or other facet of daily life, and it is from such sources that we have gathered together the threads of our story. Drawings and paintings too tell us a good deal. From all of these sources we hope that we have been able to collect a true description of the way in which the country housewife lived and spent her days.

The Elizabethan Countrywoman

MEN HAVE always been quite convinced that they could tell women how to manage their household affairs. They felt just the same when Master Thomas Tusser wrote his *Points of huswifery united to the comfort of husbandry* in the reign of Queen Elizabeth. Of course in those times few women wrote books, and if they did all the work Tusser recommends to their attention this is not at all surprising. He did not spare the farmer in his *Points of Husbandry*, and he probably saw no reason to spare the farmer's wife. She certainly worked hard and long, and must know many things.

The isolation of the villages made all this strictly necessary. The modern countrywoman, almost everywhere in touch with a bus service, infrequent though it may be, would find it difficult to realize that many people in Tudor England were born in a village, lived in it all their lives, and died there without ever going farther, if as far, as the neighbouring village a couple of miles or so away. A contemporary says there was many a squire whose "travel is seldom farther than the next market town". The roads were mere dirt tracks and did not encourage travel; trade was in its infancy, and the local markets dealt only in locally produced goods. The housewife must wait until the annual or semi-annual fair to buy foreign goods, such spices, and knick-knacks as were then provided; for the rest she was dependent upon the produce of her village; indeed very often upon her own.

17

"All the corn we make our bread of," declared the country gentleman of the time, "groweth on our own demesne ground; the flesh we
eat is all (or the most part) of our own breeding; our garments also
or much thereof, made within our house. Our own malt and water
maketh our drink." The countrywoman had a part to play in all this,
and it was by no means a small part.

Naturally enough a book of housewifely advice, even one written
by a man, must be addressed to those who could read it, and reading
was a scarce accomplishment in Elizabethan days. Only the well-to-
do could read, the mass of the people being quite illiterate, so that
Tusser's book was for the well-to-do farmhouse wife, the squire's lady
and so on. This is made quite clear by the instructions what to do
at dawn.

Most important, she must be up and doing herself to set a proper
example to the maids; a little slackness on her part will be the ruin of
all, the very best servants included. And she must roust them out of
bed in no unequivocal fashion. The maid is warned of what is likely
to happen, and a sidelight on sleeping habits thrown by the distich:—

> "Past five a clock holla, mayde, sleeping beware,
> lest quickly thy dame do uncover thy bare."

Once up all were to get to work. There was no mawkish hanging
about for breakfast. Only the slovens went to the larder for food and
drink before setting about the day's tasks, and these tasks were manifold. House cleaning was obviously an everyday job, and for health's
sake "sluttes corners" must be avoided. Next in importance was food
preparation and preserving. The milk had to be churned, the pottage to
be boiled, malt ground, brine to be prepared for pickling, hemp and
flax carded and spun, rushes peeled for making the wicks of rushlights
used to illuminate the evening's work dimly.

Everything and everybody being started, the lady of the house
served breakfast. This was to be a snack and no more, and no time was
to be wasted in idle chatter while eating it. Each man and maid
got a dishful of pottage and a morsel of meat, but this meal was
only provided for those who deserved it. It was not to be accepted
out of hand as the usual thing. Truly the Elizabethan countrywoman
believed in the proverbial wisdom, who would eat must work, and was

prepared to abide by it. Another part of wisdom was to keep her own
counsel as to what food she had in store. It was quite unnecessary for
the servants to know. All they need know was what job they were
to do; they would be only too ready to help themselves to extra food
if they got the chance, and economy in the use of household stores
was one of the ways to get rich. Therefore the dairy must be forbidden
to cats; open windows must be watched for "two-legged" cats, the
wandering vagabonds who will pilfer anything left handy to them.
"Foresight is the stopper of many a gap."

These were the duties of the farm housewife and the lady of title
alike, though the latter delegated most of them. Everyone was a
countryman in Tudor days. Even the London "cits" had the fields at
their doors. They did not farm them, and were, no doubt, townified
enough. Of other great cities there were none. Norwich was a large
country town. Most other places were little, if any, more than villages.

The great ladies of the sixty or so families and their hangers-on who
formed the Court were, like their husbands, always in attendance upon
the Queen, but they had great estates and their wealth came from the
land. Below them were the numerous landed proprietors and their
families who rarely left their country homes. The richest of them
managed their own estates, and their wives their households, just like
countrymen and women of every degree down to that of the poor
farmer, who was only tenant of an acre or two.

Life was a pleasant thing to the better off. Standards of behaviour
had improved. The passionate but formal romance of the days of
chivalry, the long ages of adoration of the Virgin Mother in the
medieval church, had given the lady a place in the sun. It was artificial
enough. Much of the formal courtesy disappeared when the ownership
of an estate or estates was in question; but in ordinary times the lady
received a homage that was emphasized by the fantastic theatricality
Elizabeth demanded from her courtiers. This could not but have
influenced the behaviour of all men to all women. It was in fact a
substitution of the worship of the Virgin Queen for the earlier adoration
of the Virgin Mother; a devotion that had been common to all classes
of men. In proportion to their degree of courtesy or uncouthness, it
was reflected in their bearing towards their wives, daughters, female
relations and other women. The wealthy English country lady was
no longer a domestic drudge nor kept in strict seclusion as her social

equals still were in Spain. At all banquets and feasts they were given the greatest honour and were served before the men. They wasted little time playing outdoor games though some of them, including the Queen herself, hunted and hawked. These could gallop with hawks or after hounds and shoot with the crossbow. They walked and rode, played cards, discussed sermons, did a great deal of fine needlework and embroidery, curtains, carpets, quilts and cushions. Sometimes they read books. Amongst the higher ranks were many who knew the classical and modern languages, and were learned ladies who could almost emulate the Queen in the wide range of their accomplishments; but these were a small minority and rather above the class that spent their whole life as countrywomen.

From babyhood the country girl of whatever degree, had been brought up to understand that her obvious and normal destiny was to manage a home. Everything else gave place to that. No one could teach her this better than her mother, or in the very highest class, some great lady to whom she was sent to be taught.

An Italian visitor thought this practice showed a great want of affection for children in the English. He was, of course, writing of the great families, the nobles and first gentry. He had never noticed anyone in love in this country. The English, for him, were incomprehensible, and might be incapable of love. Nevertheless they kept a jealous guard over their wives "though anything might be compensated in the end by the power of money".

It was the practice of putting out children that most appalled him. This showed how little English parents cared for them. The children were kept at home till they were seven years old, or a little older, nine at the utmost, when both boys and girls were sent to hard service in the houses of other people. This was the unhappy lot of all but very few, for everyone, however rich, sent away his children to the houses of others, whilst he, in return, received those of strangers into his own home. Actually, of course, the children were usually sent to friends or relatives because in the small population of the day the well-to-do were very much acquainted with and related to each other.

The Italian had been told that this system was employed to teach the children better manners, a type of boarding school in fact; but he believed it was done for cold-bloodedly selfish reasons. The parents wanted all the comforts for themselves, and thought they would be better served by other people's children than their own. If they did, they were probably right enough.

Even worse was to come. "Besides which," he wrote, "the English being very great epicures and very avaricious by nature, indulge in the most delicate fare themselves and give their household the coarsest bread and beer and cold meat baked on Sunday for the week, which however they allow them in great abundance." If their own children were kept at home these gluttons would have to give them the same food as they ate themselves, but they need not feed other people's children any better than the rest of the household.

A last criticism was that the girls often married from their patron's home, and the boys made the best marriages they could, so that none of the children ever returned home again permanently.

The lesser lights were drilled in catechism and Bible story, taught to take a graceful part in all the popular dances of the day, and to play the virginals and the lute. The little girl, who now would be at school, industriously learned the details of household management, especially the doings of the kitchen, laundry and dairy. In like places of her own she expected to reign supreme when the happy day of her marriage came. In her eyes the fate of an old maid was the worst that could befall her, and she would not dream of anything so horrid happening to her until she was at least twenty. She feared nothing more.

At fifteen she had helped in every department of the household and was ready to marry. She was fully trained as we might say. She had had it bred in her bones that however well dowered her marriage might be her first duty was to be a good housewife. She must be able to govern the greater or lesser galaxy of lady's maids, laundresses, needle-women and dairy maids, goose girls and hen wives, who were all submitted to her charge.

Most of them she must have known well. They came from the families of the lesser tenants and cottagers of the village, who knew of no other employment for their strong young bodies than the household of the lord of the manor. And they were needed. Everything that is done today by electricity, gas or public water supply was then done by hard manual labour. Water had to be carried; wood for kindling and fuel collected, brought home, sawn and chopped; the office of baker and butcher had to be supplied on the estate; whatever sanitary measures were taken were manual, though Sir Joshua Harington had invented a water closet.

Large households of this kind required large houses. At Upcot, Broadwood, Devon, in the reign of Henry VII the hall was small but a huge fireplace decorated, if it did not warm it. Above stairs there was but a single large dormitory. Possibly there was a separate room for Squire Upcot and his wife over the parlour that was rebuilt at a later date. In the dormitory slept all the unmarried ladies of the family and the maid servants. All the men, gentle and simple, slept about the fire in the hall on the straw, fern and broom that was strewn on the stone-paved floor.

These crude arrangements were improved upon a little later. Several bedrooms were made, all communicating with each other. Squire Upcot and his wife slept in a room opening out from the top of the stairs. All the other rooms were only accessible through their room. These were in two sets, one for the men and boys, the other for the women and girls. The maids slept in the most distant rooms and had to pass through both the master's room, and those next to it where the young ladies slept. The same arrangement was made for the boys. The sons of the house slept in the rooms nearest the squire, the serving men in those farthest.

"When the party in the house retired for the night, a file of damsels marched upstairs, domestic servants first, passed through the room of the master and mistress, then through those of the young ladies, and were shut in at the end; next entered the daughters of the house to their several chambers, the youngest lying near the room of the serving maids, the eldest most outside, near that of her father and mother. That procession disposed of, a second mounted the stair, consisting of the men of the house, the stable-boy first, and the son and heir last, and were disposed similarly to the females, but on the opposite side of the staircase. Then finally, the squire and his wife retired to roost in the chamber that commanded those of all the rest of the household." This arrangement is said to have still been known in 1895.

One careful father made it a provision of his will that his daughter Joan should "have free *ingress, egress* and *regress* to the bedd in the chamber where she now lieth, so long as she continueth unmarried", in order to secure her comfort when his son Thomas inherited the estate, which he did in 1672.

Long before the end of the Elizabethan age a better arrangement
had been made in some of the great houses. Many houses in that time of
prosperity were being rebuilt or extended, and in these a grand corridor
was constructed upstairs, out of which opened all the doors of all the
bedrooms. This corridor, often called the gallery, was used for dancing,
music and games. It soon became the recreation place for wet and
wintry days. The children could play here, skip and jump, chase
the blind man and indulge in many other noisy games. Sparsely
furnished, there was plenty of room, and our ancestors did not suffer
from nerves that forbid the children to make a noise. They were
fond of company. They always lived in intimate and daily, even hourly,
contact with each other, and would have been lonely otherwise.

The housewife at the head of such an establishment ruled her own
particular world. Her job was to manage the household, and to second
the men's outside interests. She governed with a strong but sympathetic
guiding hand, and did not hesitate to use corporal punishment if she
considered it necessary. The welfare of her family and dependants,
and of the whole neighbourhood was her first thought. They may not
always have thought so, especially when she was unusually severe,
but it was the woman's function, as it still is, despite all the so-called
emancipation, to care for the needs of others. She knew the way to
humour people. Consideration of the freedom of everybody within
reasonable and defined limits, sympathy with all the affairs of those
she dealt with, keeping people in an agreeable mood, was part of her
training, and had become largely instinctive. As ever she was absorbed
in tangible things, the commonplace, a homely sense of life going steadily
on in the present moment. This is, indeed, the unique feminine
quality.

This was natural enough. Then living was the business of life.
The great manor was a factory for the production of food and clothing.
Wood for fuel and water for use was used on almost a factory scale, and
must be got by heavy manual work. Some measure of the quantities of
fuel and water used can be imagined for a household that frequently
sheltered more than a hundred people, all of whom had to be fed. In
the greater houses the number was even larger.

The mistress herself did not take any actual part in the cooking
of the daily meals. She did in the work of the still-room. There was no
need for her to engage in the arduous and unpleasant work of cooking

before the open fire set in the wall, that smoked and blazed, and smoked again.

Heat and dirt was the lot of the cooks, scullions and kitchen wenches. They knew nothing of the care of the hands. Broken finger-nails engrimed with soot, hands cracked, scorched, burned and chapped, hair grimed with the soot of the wood fires, and the grease of roasts cooked on spits, and general discomfort such as no modern kitchen worker could dream of were commonplace. Such cooks and scullions had to be forbidden to work mother-naked for the sake of hygiene, and to practise such elementary cleanliness as was possible. An unfortunate kitchen maid might spend the whole of her working day bending over a stone sink, when she was not carrying water, until she found a happy release in marriage to some cottager or yeoman, if she were lucky.

The mistress took no personal part in this scene of bustle, smoke and grease. She did in the daintier operations of the still-room, where she behaved handsomely in preserve and cordial making, candying flowers and fruit, making quince and damson marmalade, almond butter and marchpane, and all the unnumbered delicacies we have forgotten how to use. Truly this was more dainty work, but most of it was done over an open fire and scorched faces and hands, if no worse, must have been usual accompaniments of this pleasant occupation. Herbal ointments, unguents and medicines, too, were compounded, and stocks of dried herbs maintained against the onslaught of sickness.

Country doctors were few. Country apothecaries may have been a little more plentiful, but there was not likely to have been one in every village. There is not a chemist in every village today. Even if there was an apothecary, he was usually a sort of white witch, and everybody preferred to consult the great lady, if his own wife had no simple cupboard from which to draw her nature's remedies. If no more, she was called upon to cure the aches and pains of her own family, and very likely the families of the numerous villagers, both male and female, employed about her household. The household alone might be quite a job.

Small accidents must have always been happening. Cuts and bruises, bites and stings, in the winter chilblains, in the summer heat rashes, sties on the eyes, boils, were the least of all these. The lady of the manor, or a proper substitute, perhaps a poor relation, some young widow or undowered spinster, must have spent a regular hour or so daily in handing out salves, herbs and lotions. Of these she had a special and esoteric knowledge. Many of the prescriptions were secrets carefully handed down from mother to daughter by word of mouth rather than in writing.

With all their large store of practical accomplishments, the great majority of country gentlewomen were not terribly literate, and it was easier for them to memorize than to refer to written authority. A minority of those in the most exalted families were learned like the Queen herself, and it was for their delectation that the new popular literature was composed. John Lyly wrote *Euphues and his England* for them. "Euphues," he wrote, "had rather lye shut in a lady's casket than open in a scholar's studie." Sidney's *Arcadia* also appealed to the ladies. These works and others like them mark the birth of the literature of the drawing-room, though there were then no drawing-rooms. The ladies, who wanted to appear cultured, wanted books they could talk about. They could hardly do that with the somewhat licentious works of writers like Boccaccio, free though manners and conversations were, but, of course, the circle who could appreciate Lyly, Sidney and Nash was small, and confined almost entirely to the Court.

It was amongst these that Shakespeare found his immortal examples. They provided a great variety of interesting women for his portrait gallery. There were "learned women like Lady Russell, clever stateswomen as Lady Raleigh and Lady Warwick; vengeful women like Lady Shrewsbury; a devout one in Lady Hoby and a devoted one in her sister-in-law, Lady Sidney. Beautiful and vivacious Lady Rich, impetuous Lady Northumberland; humble wives, gentle and docile wives like Lady Southampton and Lady Essex". And all of these played the part of the lady of the manor on their country estates at some time during their lives despite their courtly attendance, duties, and pleasures.

All these people gave each other costly presents, and presents of food. Gifts of venison, poultry, cheese and game and wine passed between them much more frequently than letters. Some of the food suffered in transport, especially when it was sent from remote or distant counties, to London. The Duke of Suffolk sent presents of two great flagons and two great pots of silver and gilt as christening gifts to Jane

Seymour's son by Henry VIII, that son who afterwards became the unfortunate boy King, Edward VI. A partridge pie was also sent, and John Hussee said in a letter that he thought "the ladies liked the partridge pie, though its fashion was marred by the ship which brought it lying almost a tide under water in the Thames". It was thankfully taken though it came not best conditioned, something it is easy to believe. Perhaps it was not so bad after all. The Thames then was not the muddy river of today. It was the poet's silvery Thames in spite of the shocking garbage that flowed into it from the Fleet River and other reeking open drains of the City. The London of those days would have seemed quite a small town to us. Outside the walls there were few houses. From Temple Bar to Westminster Palace the Strand was the only street. Covent Garden was really a garden, and St. Martins was really in the fields.

These great ladies had some pleasant toilet accessories. Many recipes for sweet-scented toilet soap are included in the household treatises like Sir Hugh Plat's *Delightes for Ladies*. These, like the coarser soaps used for washing clothes, often no more than a lye made from wood ash, were home made. So were most of the perfumes and cosmetics used. Monday mornings were not set aside for the weekly wash as they are today. It was an irregular upheaval and often lasted several days, but only once or twice a year.

It is not certain when tooth-brushes were first used, but fragrant mouth washes were common, and the teeth were rubbed with cloth. A somewhat cynical American historian, Mr. E. Parmalee Prentice in his book *Hunger and History*, 1939, says that these mouth washes were necessary to disguise evil-smelling breaths. These were the result, he thinks, of using food that would today be considered uneatable, perhaps like the famous partridge pie. As he says, there was no refrigeration, and the need for sterilizing cooking utensils had never been conceived.

Baths were not taken frequently. They were too much trouble. All the water had to be drawn from the well, heated over the fire in iron or copper vessels, and then poured into a wooden bath placed before the fire. And there was little privacy in which this rigmarole could be carried out.

Latten or pewter ewers and basins for washing are mentioned in some inventories of goods, and the very wealthy had them made of silver, but not many are noticed, and we think they must have been unusual. Thomas Sackville, Lord Buckhurst, had 220 persons daily on his check roll for twenty years at Knole, Kent. He was Lord Treasurer to Elizabeth and the first Earl of Dorset, but when he wanted to supply a visiting cardinal with a basin and ewer he had to lend his own. It was the only one in that great house.

These great ladies of the countryside and the Court were the English-women whom Thomas Plattner, a German tourist, so much admired when he visited this country in 1599. They were mostly handsome and had fine complexions. Most had blue grey eyes and were fair and pretty he repeats. They had neither carts nor coaches, but travelled on horseback preceded by footmen, and followed by maids of honour. Many rode pillion behind a husband or groom. Our women had "great liberty of action". They did very much what they liked subject to the correction of the ducking stool, the wooden cage that "put some curb upon their pranks and machinations".

Platter may have been misled by a freedom of manners that the foreigners greatly enjoyed. Erasmus, one of the great scholars of the Renascence a hundred years before, admired and appreciated the affectionate habit of kissing at meetings and partings of friends and relations. He liked kissing the lovely English women, and this courtesy gave him a great many opportunities he would not otherwise have had. In a letter he told a friend that our ladies were

"divinely beautiful, the kindest and most fascinating creatures in the world. . . . There is besides a custom it is impossible to praise too much. Wherever you go everyone welcomes you with a kiss, and the same on bidding farewell. You call again when there is more kissing. If your friends call upon you they kiss you. You meet an acquaintance anywhere and you are kissed till you are tired. In short, turn where you will, there are kisses, kisses everywhere. And if you were once to taste them, and find how delicate and fragrant they are, you would certainly desire, not for ten years only, like Solon, but till death to be a sojourner in England".

This pretty picture of amiability was all very well, and we have remarked upon the adoration of women expressed in the formal manners and the poetry and prose of the time. But there was a great deal of drinking that led to bad behaviour when it was added to the rough and ebullient spirits of some of the more unruly young men.

Lady Margaret Hoby, that quiet, deeply religious woman, had an unfortunate experience of such behaviour. A party of young men out hunting on the wild moors sent a footman to beg the hospitality of Sir Thomas and Lady Hoby at Hackness, a few miles from Scarborough. This was quite a customary request, and no gentleman householder of the time would have dreamed of refusing house-room and food to his equals. They were received with the usual warm and courteous welcome by Sir Thomas, though Lady Hoby was ill in bed.

They behaved very badly. As soon as they arrived they began playing cards in the great chamber, something their hosts greatly disapproved of. There was a good deal of drinking at supper time, but Sir Thomas did not join in very heartily. He visited his sick wife, and then saw to it that his guests' rooms were made ready for them.

At evening prayers some of the young men's servants, copying the bad manners of their masters, interrupted by making a great noise and laughing. Some of the guests themselves sang ribald tunes during the psalms. The following morning their behaviour was no better. They drank a good many healths, and wasted wine by spilling it in the rushes on the floor. They shouted and hallooed, disturbing their sick hostess. A request for better and quieter behaviour was met only with insults, and rudest of all, a demand for the charge for the meat and drink consumed. The whole scurvy crowd then declared they could hold the chamber they were in against any attempt to put them out by force, but one of them who saw some men coming towards the house thought the country had been raised against them. There was a struggle with Nettleton, one of Sir Thomas's servants, who was hurt. But at last these tiresome guests took themselves off, tearing up a couple of stiles before they went, and damaging a newly laid courtyard by galloping up and down across it. They, like the babies they were, smashed some windows by throwing stones at them. Not unreasonably, Sir Thomas brought a suit against them for damages.

The Hoby's establishment at Hackness was not large. There were only ten men servants and four women, but Lady Hoby had great estates, and was as earnest in their management as she was in her behaviour and devotions. She was a fine example of the simplicity and industry of the wealthy countrywoman of the later years of Queen Elizabeth's reign, though she was exceptionally religious.

She spent a great deal of each day at her prayers and in reading books of sermons and exegesis, Fox's *Book of Martyrs,* and so on, but not to the neglect of more mundane affairs. She kept careful control of her household and estates, she kept accounts herself, and checked those she made her servants keep. She practised medicine and minor surgery in her home and amongst the villagers, and she did her best to encourage and sustain religious principles in her servants and neighbours. Her pleasures were those of the countryside, playing bowls, boating and fishing, and playing a musical instrument, the alpherion. Less serious ladies found pleasure in lighter literature, and one of the pleasures of winter evenings was to listen to some scholar, perhaps the chaplain or tutor, read *Guy of Warwick, The Ship of Fools,* or *The Book of Riddles.* In all her ordinary routine she was like others of her class and time. Lady Berkeley, for example, who "living at Yates, Callowden and her other Country houses, would betimes in Winter and Somer mornings make her walkes to visit the stable, barns, hay house, poultry, swine-troughs and the like".

At the other end of the country from Lady Hoby, Leonard Mascall, a writer of farming textbooks, lived at Plumpton in Sussex. Marcus Woodward in *The Countryman's Jewel,* a work based on Mascall's books and other contemporary writings, makes his hero ask his ward whether there had been alarms and excursions in his absence upon a journey. "No raids?" he said, semi-jocular.

"Not even an attempt to carry me off. Life indeed has been dull," was the reply in the same vein.

This light-hearted banter concealed and discussed a very real danger to unattended young women of fortune and beauty in the lonely manor houses. To capture an heiress was the proper ambition of every young landed gentleman, and some of them were not at all scrupulous about their methods.

Sir William Darrell, who owned great estates at Littlecote, Uffington, Berkshire, and Wanborough, Wiltshire, was guilty of running away with, if he did not actually kidnap a young woman, though she was not a landed proprietor, and other more definite cases of rapine and forced marriages are known. Ordinarily marriage was arranged by the parents with or without the consent of the young people.

Many a prosperous yeoman had a household as large as Lady Hoby. From such a scale the households descended to those of the copyholder who worked his minute holding with the help of his family. These people were the middle class in the country. The housewife was the controlling influence in such homes as she was in the large ones of the nobility and gentry. The moral of this class was much the same as it is today. The husband was expected to earn the income; the wife must use it carefully for the comfort of the family. Her character and ability decided the success and happiness of her household. "If she was a railing shrew, an extravagant, gossipy or faithless creature, the domestic efficiency and happiness so earnestly desired by every worthy husband could be jeopardized." The virtues this class expected of their wives, and equally those the wives looked for in their husbands, were the biblical virtues. Treatises of domestic relations like Becon's *The Boke of Matrimony* were expressions of the common sense of the day supported by the precepts of the Bible.

Thomas Tusser put his finger on the spot in one of his doggerel verses:—

"For husbandrie weepeth,
Where huswiferie sleepeth,
And hardly he creepeth,
Up ladder to thrift."

Whether the *ménage* was large or small she had to manage it. The maids, whether one or two or a whole retinue, must be kept cheerfully busy at all the multifarious household tasks. By far the most important of these was the preparation of the daily meals. Nothing can be done by people who are not fed.

To turn out an appetizing and filling meal for midday was the crown and seal of the yeoman housewife's day. Dinner was the main meal, usually the only substantial meal of the day. Breakfast was a drink and possibly a snack, supper a light meal. When times were good dinner was composed of bread, beef and beer with heavy pies and tarts. None of the fripperies and kickshaws to be found on the tables of the nobility were included. One thing we depend upon so much, the potato, was not generally known, was not grown and therefore not used. A variety of herbs took their place.

Bread was, of course, the main constituent of all meals, and it was of various kinds. Pure wheat bread, known as manchet, was used only by the wealthy or on great occasions. The most common bread used was made of rye, or rye and wheat mixed. In some households pea and bean meal was mixed in and others used barley. If the harvest was poor all sorts of substitutes were sought.

Beef, mutton and pork were all used, the last or bacon, being eaten most often. Rabbits and hares and wild birds were killed and eaten. Besides domestic poultry of all kinds, blackbirds, rooks, even larks, were made into pies. Near the sea and rivers fresh fish provided sport in the catching and a change in the diet. Salt fish, known as stockfish, the red herring, and other dried and smoked fish were eaten in inland counties.

Cheese, butter and cream produced on the farm provided a supply of what was known as white meats.

Recipes were jealously guarded and some became famous. Great ladies made notes of them for use in their houses. Lady Dorset thought it well worth the while to include in her cookery note book "Goodwife Wells, her runnet"; "Goodwife Rivers, her liver cakes"; and "Goody Cleaves receipe for Hog's Cheeke", by the side of Lady Gore's "How to make Angelica staulkes" and "How to make Brisket bread Mistress White's way".

The yeoman's wife did not work in the fields. She had plenty of other work proper to her station to keep her busy from dawn to dark. It was socially correct for her to be hard at it all day in the kitchen, the dairy, the garden and about the poultry. But driving the plough team, or doing other tasks of that kind were beneath her, proper work as it was for the wives and daughters of labourers, or of the occupier of one of the minute holdings that were everywhere to be found.

One resentful young woman, the daughter of a Berkshire yeoman, brought her stepfather before the Court of Star Chamber after a dispute about her proper duties. She complained that he "had given her very base service to do about the husbandly and household affairs in keeping cattle, swyne and sheep" that were "uncomely offices" for a young girl of her class. Doubtless she was infected with the poison of snobbery, but to an Elizabethan her complaint would seem very proper. Status was very closely defined and all classes accepted it, with a very clear idea of their own worthiness. This young woman would not have had the slightest objection to working in the garden where she would have been happy in growing the herbs for the table and for medicine.

Elizabethan country housewives did not believe in running to the apothecary or the doctor. Their apothecary's shop was a garden full of pot herbs and well they knew how to use it, as we have said. The very first book on gardening ever printed in English is full of details of the use of herbs in medicine. It was written by a Londoner, Thomas Hyll, in 1563, and its title is *A Most Briefe and Pleasant Treatyse, Taechyne howe to Dress, Sowe and Set a Garden*. A typical farmhouse garden of Tudor days was full of lush fruit, gooseberries and currants and raspberries. There was a strawberry plot and a neighbouring orchard contained apples, pears, cherries, damsons, quinces and bullaces. The old-fashioned flowers, roses, carnations, wallflowers, geraniums, that country housewives have always cherished, filled it with sweet scents, and Thomas Tusser took it for granted that this was the special province of the housewife. In his book *The Points of Huswifery united to the comfort of Husbandry* he provided excellent practical instructions about digging, weeding and sowing seeds. His opinion was that it was her duty to collect her own seeds, and to exchange with her neighbours. There were few seedsmen, and that was the only way to extend her crops or to secure a change of seed. He wrote:—

> "Good huswives in Somer will save their own seedes,
>   Against the next year, as occasion needes,
>   One sede for another, to make an exchange,
>   With fellowlie neighbourhood seemeth not strange."

This was not a new idea: it was well established when Tusser wrote these lines. Half a century before, Fitzherbert had written in 1523, "And in the begynninge of Marche or a lyttall afore, is time for a wife to make her garden and to gather as many good sedes and herbes as she canne, and specially such as be good for the potte and to eate; and as ofte as nede shall requyre it must be weded, for els the wedes will over growe the herbs."

If they did, the wife was roundly condemned. Barnaby Googe, a Lincolnshire gentleman writing in 1577, said that the state of her garden was an old yardstick by which to judge a wife. "Herein were the olde husbandes very careful and used always to judge that where they founde the Garden out of order, the wyfe of the house (for unto her belonged the charge thereof) was no good huswyfe."

Though many modern writers have greatly praised Tudor gardens, some of the things grown would not be very readily bought for use by a modern townswoman, and a countrywoman who grew them would be very disappointed. She would not be likely, for example, to exhibit in her local flower show strawberries like those the Elizabethans grew. The Elizabethan wife and gardener gathered wild strawberry roots and planted them under gooseberry, raspberry and rose bushes. These Thomas Hyll thought had been improved by selection, and had become so large as hedge blackberries. Strawberries of this size would hardly be acceptable to the customers of a modern barrow boy, but they were a good deal larger than the tiny wild berry.

Many things were cultivated that have disappeared from the modern garden. Skirrets have fallen into undeserved disuse. Our salads are the poorer by cowslips, violets, primroses, longwort, liverwort, and purslane that was used as an anti-scorbutic. The kitchen garden and cook book alike no longer include harefoot, blood-wort or bloody dock, penny-royal, marigolds, sea-blite, burnet, cat mint or tansy. The physic border is no longer cultivated, and the plants that adorned it, eringoe (sea-holly), mandrake, blessed thistle, wormwood, plantain and valerian do not concern the modern gardener.

On the other hand some things we grow were unknown to our ancestors of three hundred and fifty or four hundred years ago. They had no asparagus, kidney beans, scarlet runners, cardoons, horse radish, or, as we have said, potatoes.

The common garden plants included artichokes, cabbages, turnips, broad beans, Rounceval peas, pumpkins, skirrets, radishes, carrots, parsnips, onions, garlic, leeks, endive, spinach, common sorrel, lettuce, parsley, mustard, cress, sage, tarragon, fennel, thyme, mint, savory, rhubarb as well as the numerous herbs used in the still-room and as medicine.

Rhubarb, for example, was used only as a drug, but saffron was a drug, a condiment too, and a scent. Saffron cakes were famous eating, but it was also used to colour "warden" pies, a dainty usual at the sheep-shearing feast. Warden pies were made with "Warden" pears that had been grown originally at the Cistercian Abbey of Warden in

C

Bedfordshire. They were used for stewing, and the name soon became common for all cooking pears. Apples, besides being eaten raw and cooked, were mixed with hog's lard and rosemary to make a pomatum.

Besides apples and pears a fairly large number of fruits are named in Shakespeare's plays, though some of them like purple figs, pomegranates and almonds, may have been poetical rather than the fruit of English gardens. For the rest there were plums, medlars, mulberries, quinces, apricots, rubied cherries, strawberries and gooseberries, blackberries, dewberries, and blue bilberries. Raspberries and melons are not named. Currants were imported.

Many other things besides herbs were used medicinally; some that we should find rather disgusting. Some were only queer. For example "an old cheese all mouldie, braied and mixed with the decotion of a salt gammon of bacon, and applied in forme of a cataplasme doth soften all the hard swellings of the knees". This was certainly one way to dispose of all cheese that was more or less bad, but its efficacy is as doubtful as the disease is peculiar.

Different writers thought different jobs the most important that a housewife should pay attention to. Richard Surflet thought "the ordering of pullen . . . the chiefest thing that a good housewife is to regard", and he gave her very full and detailed instructions how to look after the poultry of all sorts. These included hens and chickens, geese, ducks, teal, water hens, swans, cranes, storks, pheasants, peacocks, turtle doves, partridges, quails, stockdoves and thrushes and a dove house.

A common verse ran:—

> "The egge is good and for delight
> That's long and new and white in sight."

Eggs should be kept warm upon straw in winter and cool in bran in summer. Surflet was not too sure that this was the best way to keep them, nor was he in great favour of packing them in salt or in brine, but he does not suggest any better way. He had the odd idea that, "The hen will hatch chickens of divers colours, if she sit upon eggs drawn with divers or painted colours, as also she will hatch pullets of very pleasant colour to behold if you make her tread by male pigeons or partridges or feasants".

In the summer the yeoman's wife was busy with her dairy.

"From April beginning, till Andrew be past,
So long with good huswife her dairy doth last,
Good milch cow and pasture, good husbands provide,
The res'due good huswives know best how to guide
Ill husewife, unskilfull to make her own cheese,
Through trusting of others, hath thus for her fees,
Her milk pan and cream pot, so slabber'd and sost,
That butter is wanting and cheese is half lost."

This sort of exhortation was all very well, but no one pair of hands could compass all the tasks these pundits laid down for the housewife. She had to delegate some either to maids or to her daughters; but, of course, those who employed maid servants must see to it that they worked hard and did not pilfer. Indeed maids were treated much the same as children and lived in fear of beating with a holly wand, though carrying one must often have been as effective as using it.

What sort of a person was such a maid? One important thing about her was that her wages had been regulated in Henry VIII's reign by an Act of Parliament passed in 1515. No woman servant was to be paid "above xs. by yere and for her clothing iiijs. with mete and drynke", and children were to be paid even less, 6s. 8d. a year and 4s. for clothing with meat and drink. This, of course, means living in. Hours of outdoor work were laid down by another Act of the same year. They were from 5 a.m. until 7 p.m. or 8 p.m. from mid-March till mid-September, and from dawn till dusk the rest of the year. The winter evenings were occupied with indoor tasks by the light of the fire, or a glimmering rushlight. Meal times were allowed at half an hour for breakfast, the same for "nonie" (noon) meat, or elevenses, one hour for dinner, and this could be extended by half an hour for a sleep.

By the end of the century money wages had risen: so had prices generally. In the meantime the Statute of Apprentices had ordered more control, and women as well as men servants had to look for work at the Statute Fair, or Mop Fair, as it was sometimes called. Cooks wore a red ribbon and carried a basting spoon to show what they were. Housemaids wore a blue ribbon and carried a broom. A milkmaid carried a pail.

The Statute Fair was called by the Chief Constable and for obvious reasons of convenience was often on the same day as the local fair for other purposes. It was attended by the Petty Constables, unpaid officials selected by the Vestry and serving in rotation. They could be expected to know the servants from their own villages. The employers came and the workers, ready to be discharged and re-engaged for another year, perhaps in the same household. Provided the employer agreed and the Chief Constable would sign a certificate, a worker could leave her employment and seek a new master. When an agreement was reached a "fastening penny" was paid, and both mistress and maid betook themselves to such pleasures as the fair could afford. Some of them were, unluckily, none too innocent.

Maids at the end of Queen Elizabeth's reign were paid from 10s. to 40s. a year plus board and lodging, and on this contrived to impress contemporaries with their worth. Like her mistress the overseer of all her tasks, both indoor and outdoor, she was a skilled worker. She was a happy creature. Matthew Parker in *The Milkmaid's Life* describes her zestful living:—

> "The bravest lasses gay
> Life not so merry as they,
> In honest civil sort
> They make each other sport,
> As they trudge upon their way,
> Come fair or foul weather,
> They're fearful of neither—
> Their courages never quail;
> In wet or dry
> Though winds be high
> And dark's the sky
> They ne'er deny
> To carry the milking pail.

> *   *   *   *   *

> If grass will grow
> Their thanks they show,
> And frost or snow
> They merrily go
> Along with the milking pail." etc.

Naturally when so much of her work exposed her to all kinds of weather she did not possess the daintiness of the Court lass. Her attraction was more buxom and robust. And it had some flaws. Her lips were red with health, but might be a little chapped at some seasons of the year. Her complexion was good and ruddy—peaches and cream is the modern phrase—but exposure to sun and wind might cause peeling; at least these are the merits and defects ascribed to her by Thomas Churchyard in his poem *The Spider and the Goat*. More than her nice appearance, industry and skill made the maidservant a pleasing character. She was up with the lark, working at house-cleaning with petticoats tucked up, and a handkerchief to protect her hair— quite the modern fashion. She was a good cook and made the lightest of pastry. Churchyard's quatrain in praise of her cakes and bread is:—

> "As soon as the flour came from the mill,
> She made the goodliest cakes thereof,
> And baked as fair a household loaf
> As e'er was set on any board."

Good cookery was an essential quality of the good woman. She must be able to bake bread without too much crust and without the bread going mouldy before it was eaten. And the cook was expected to brew as well.

> "Good cook to dress dinner, to bake and to brew
> Deserves a reward, being honest and true."

Brewing at home was an economy, not only because the ale was good and cheap, but because pigs could be fattened on the grains. The care of the dairy was another part of the country housewife's business.

Besides preparing flax and hemp for spinning and weaving, the housewife must spin and weave wool into cloth, and all these materials were used for making the household goods and the family's clothing. There were no shops where these things could be bought. If a man wore a pair of leather breeches, the leather was often of his own tanning, and, by the same token, if his wife wore a woollen gown, a flannel petticoat or a linen kerchief, these goods were home grown. Wives were expected to be content with comely garments that would preserve health as well as adorn the person. The maids were quite simply clad.

In Jack of Newbury's clothing factory, one of the earliest examples of capitalist organization, many young women were employed. Deloney in his admiring poem, said there were hundreds.

> "An hundred women merrily
> Were carding hard with joyful cheer,
> Who singing sat with voices clear.
> And in a chamber close beside
> Two hundred maidens did abide
> In petticoats of stammel red,
> And milk white kerchiefs on their head;
> Their smock sleeves like to winter snow."

These young women doubtless got their pretty clothes from the factory, but few other people could do so.

> "A gown made of the finest wool
> Which from our pretty lambs we pull . . .
> A belt of straw and ivy buds
> With coral clasps and amber studs"

completely satisfied the ordinary housewife or maid.

Jack of Newbury's enterprise was quite an isolated one at that date. Making cloth and linen was one of the many evening jobs. Then while the men mended tools, made handles and so on, the women of the household "plaited straw or reed for horse collars, stitched and stuffed sheepskin bags for cart saddles, pulled rushes for wicks and made candles. Spinning wheels, distaffs and needles were never idle. Women spun, wove, dyed and cut out the cloth as well as malted the barley, brewed the ale and baked the bread for the family". Home-made coverlets kept the winter nights' chill at bay.

Lighting was a simple matter. Perhaps for great occasions a tallow or wax candle might be used, but if the firelight did not suffice for the evening's tasks, or the mutual entertainment by singing and games, then the humble rushlight, made at home, had to do. This was no more than a peeled rush dipped in molten mutton fat, and allowed to cool. Special holders were used. Many examples can be seen in local museums. The light they gave was very dim and flickering, but had to suffice. There were enough odd jobs to be done at all times of the year, besides the regular work of feeding the family and the men and maids, often amounting to a fairly numerous company.

Dinner, the midday meal, must be ready to time. It was better, and economical of working time, to "let meat tarry servant, not servant his meat". No time was wasted over the meal. "Dispatch hath no fellow, make short and away." The necessity for good meals for the workers was recognized, but they should not be overfed. Indeed the remarks on this subject sound rather like instructions for feeding working horses. If underfed they cannot work well, if overfed they get slothful, is what it comes to.

After this meal the farm wife, or squire's lady, should visit any sick employee and see to his or her welfare, "grutching" him nothing. If the invalid was suffering from a disease beyond the housewife's treatment, a doctor should be called in—and his advice treated with respect. The Elizabethans did not like physic, but they acknowledged that it sometimes saved lives, though they had a stout idea that good food was probably the best medicine of all.

The rest of the afternoon was spent in keeping the maids hard at their various tasks. Amongst these was butter and cheese making, both highly skilled jobs. Cheeses must be made of curd properly broken and worked. If it was not, the cheeses would have Argus eyes to the shame of Cisley the dairymaid, or would be hollow and puffy. It must not be too heavily salted, nor be adorned with hairs won while Cisley was combing and decking herself in the dairy—a habit condemned later as inexcusable filthiness.

> "If gentils be scrawling, call maggot the pye,
> If cheeses have gentils, at Ciss by and by."

Elizabethan taste did not care for overripe cheese. If it was wormy it was only fit for the magpie, and Cisley should be punished for letting the cheese get too warm, and to be attacked by blowflies. It was important and profitable to care for the dairy properly.

> "Good dairy doth pleasure,
> Ill dairy spends treasure.
> Good housewife in dairy, that needs not be told,
> Deserveth her fee, to be paid her in gold."

Active dairy work was a summertime task. The milk yield began to fall as winter drew on, and soon dried up completely. Fresh milk disappeared from the Elizabethan menu then, but salted butter and cheese were used until the supply was exhausted. This often happened before the merry spring came bringing with it the sweet young grass, the frolicsome calf and lamb and a new supply of milk.

The multitude of tasks went on all through the day, but at last the evening came,

> "When hens go to roost, go in hand to dress meat
> Serve hogs and to milking and some to serve meat."

Everything must be finished, the poultry shut up, the cattle fed and bedded, all clean clothes collected from the garden, and all the doors bolted "ere supper began". This was a jolly though light meal, when the whole household was gathered together and made merry. It was, in fact, a small daily feast, and a few moments of relaxation before the end of the day. Perhaps there was a little singing and instrumental music when the next morning's work had been laid out, and each person given instructions. Then, the evening dishes washed, and the morning table laid, "lock doors and to bed, a good huswife will say".

The countrywoman's day in the yeoman, squire and peer's household was a continuous round of hard work, but in these establishments the women were not called upon to do some of the more arduous and dirty tasks that the small farmer's wife had to make part of her duties. None of these women escaped the continual childbearing. They took this in their stride as part of the normal lot of women. Ceremonious visits of gift-bearing relatives were some consolation to the woman in childbed as were the religious formalities and festivities that accompanied them. At the christening feast sugar and biscuits, comfits and carraways, marmalade and marchpane, and all kinds of sweet suckets, a great failing of our ancestors, were consumed with unbounded gusto.

On the smaller farms the women had to help with the field work in addition to all their other tasks, much like the daughters of cottagers and labourers, who did field work for wages.

Fitzherbert pronounced the happy opinion that the first and principal business of a wife "was to love her husbande, above father

and mother, and above all other men", according to the precept of
Holy Writ. It was decidedly only her principal business. He laid down
a long list of secondary jobs.

A good wife said her prayers on waking in the morning. "And,"
he exhorted her, "when thou arte up and ready, then first swepe thy
house, dresse up thy disheborde, and sette all thynges in good order
within thy house; milke thy kye, seele thy calves, sye up thy milke,
take up thy chyldren and arraye them, and prouyde for thy husbandes
brekefaste, dinner, souper, and for thy chyldren and servants and take
thy parte with them. And to ordeyne corne and malte to the myll, to
bake and brue withall whanne nede is." Be careful to see that the
miller did not cheat. Millers were notoriously sharp. "Thou must make
butter, and cheese when thou maist, serve thy swyne both mornynge
and evenyne and gyve thy poleyn meate in the mornynge and whan
tyme of year commeth, thou must take hede howe thy hennes, ducks
and geese do lay and to gather up theyr egges." They must be cared
for when broody.

In March as well as laying out the garden the farmer's wife must
sow flax and hemp. When harvested there were many processes to
win the fibre in preparation for making sheets, board cloths, towels,
shirts, smocks and other textile goods. The distaff must always be kept
ready for a pastime if this busy woman ever had an idle moment. She
must be ready to make cloth of her husband's sheep wool, or at the
least to make clothes or blankets out of the locks of wool gathered
from the hedgerow or the bramble bush. Besides all this, it was the
wife's part to winnow all manner of corn, to make malt, to wash and
wring, to make hay, to shear corn, and in time of need to help her
husband to fill the muck-wain, or dung cart, drive the plough, load hay,
corn and such other. And to go or ride to market, to sell butter, cheese,
eggs, chickens, capons, hens, pigs, geese and all manner of corn.
And also to buy all manner of necessary things for the household, and
to make a true reckoning and account to her husband what she hath
paid.

At the present day women in public offices, even the highest, are
no curiosity, but to the believer in recent feminine emancipation it
will come as a surprise to learn that four or five hundred years ago
countrywomen were elected to the office of churchwarden. The office
was then much more onerous than it is today, and its duties well

defined. The churchwarden played an important part in local government, and we may imagine that the women fulfilled the duties no less successfully than men.

A few examples are Alice Cooke and Alice Pypedon who were wardens at St. Patrick Ingestre in 1426–7. Nothing is known of their social status. At Kilmington, Devon, a woman warden was appointed occasionally between 1560 and 1580.

The Elizabethan countrywoman, like her menfolk, worked hard whatever her station in life was, but she had the satisfaction of doing productive work even if the produce only vanished in the appetites of her family; and there were many breaks in the year's work when a riotous time was had by all. Easter, Whitsun and Christmas were the occasions of great festivity when strong drink flowed in more than usual plenty, food was consumed in quantity, and customary proceedings were carried on amidst laughter and jollity. There was as much music and dancing as there was eating and drinking, and that is no light saying. Again, May Day, Midsummer Day, sheep-shearing and harvest provided other opportunities for indulging in the same pleasures. It must never be forgotten that such festivals and feastings were occasional. Feasting, it has been said, trod upon the heels of famine, and many must have been the days of short commons without the saving grace of fasting as a religious observance. Life was not a continual round of work, although hours worked were long and tasks were numerous and skilled; it was very far from being a continual round of pleasure. Many things that we consider necessary were lacking, but these things were not wanted because they had not yet been heard of—and so long as the harvest was sufficiently plentiful to provide the family with food for the year, there was a good deal of contentment with their lot, clearly reflected in contemporary literature, amongst our feminine as well as our masculine ancestors of three and a half centuries ago.

CHAPTER TWO

Cavalier and Puritan Countrywomen

A CHANGE OF dynasty would not be likely to have much effect on
the lives of everyday people today; three hundred and fifty years ago
things were very different. The manners and opinions of the king could
influence all the people, because the Court was the government, and
the population was so small (only about $4\frac{1}{2}$ million) that all were, so to
say, in contact with each other.

James I was a great contrast with Elizabeth. She had been able to
govern with much of the bluff heartiness of her father, Henry VIII;
James was a foreigner, and he was unable or unwilling to adapt himself
to what was a time of change. He was conceited, peevish and he found
it difficult to make decisions. None of these qualities endeared him to
his subjects, and the quarrels about religion that had prevailed in
Elizabeth's reign grew steadily worse. They were complicated by
unwise taxation and royal claims to authority that merchants and
country gentry of increasing wealth would not tolerate. These quarrels
ended in civil war in his son, Charles I's, reign.

While all this led to uncertainty and insecurity in society it did
not and could not affect the natural country round. The seasons
changed, the crops were sown, grew ripe and were harvested, if not
destroyed in the hazards of war. Both sides, of course, requisitioned
local supplies. Since there was no large-scale national trade in grain, or
indeed any very great surplus above local requirements, this action led

43

to hardship and complaint. Anne Manning, for example, makes Mary Powell (Milton's wife) record in her diary that in April 1646 Milton received a demand from Oxford, where the King was besieged, for a larger quantity of winnowed wheat, than, with all his loyalty, he liked to send.

The war turned some of the great ladies of the day into warriors who defended their husband's castles against the opposing faction. For this the normal life, much the same but differing in scale, of the country housewife in castle, manor house, grange, or farmhouse had provided some measure of experience—for each of these domiciles was itself largely a self-supporting unit where food production, and its ancillary occupations, and the making of clothes, etc., from the local raw materials was the ordinary business of the day.

When the more ambitious country ladies persuaded their husbands to take them to London, so that they might parade in their fineries and gay dresses in Hyde Park—their husbands, meantime, finding their pleasures in the notorious pleasure houses across the river—the Court took umbrage at this rural attempt to break into the select preserves of the aristocrats. The Royal Proclamation made by Charles I—and enforced by fines in the Star Chamber—soon drove these pioneers back to their rural homes and duties. (G. M. Trevelyan, *England under the Stuarts*, 1904, p. 5.)

In all this hurly-burly of country business, the housewife, like her Tudor forbears, played her part. Perhaps the noble lady managing the internal affairs of a great castle did not actually do so much with her own hands as the farmer's wife; it would have been unreasonable to expect it simply because of the magnitude of her task, but she knew how to do the work, and was a very good judge of when it was well done. George Herbert set out the character that was considered essential for the wife of a country clergyman. No doubt this was an example of the best type of country lady. First, she must be able at training up of her children and maids in the fear of God; secondly, at curing and healing of all wounds and sores with her own hands, which skill she either brought with her (at marriage), or acquired whatever she could learn from some religious neighbour. Thirdly, providing for her family in such sort as that they neither want a competent sustentation, nor her husband be brought in debt. It was a pattern taken from his own beloved mother, whom he celebrated in these verses:—

"But after modest braiding of her hair,
Such as becomes a matron wise and fair,
And a brief bath, her freshen'd mind·she brought
To pious duties and heart-healing thought,
Addressing to the Almighty Father's throne
Such warm and earnest prayers as He will own,
Next she goes round her family, assigning
What each may need for garden, distaff, dining,
To everything its time and place are given;
Then are called in the tasks of early even.
By a fixed plan her life and house go on,
By a wise daily calculation;
Sweetness and grace through all her dwelling shine,
Of both first shining in her mind the sign."

This was a pleasant exordium. Other masculine writers were more emphatic about wifely duty. There were indeed no feminine writers of domestic treatises yet, and consequently most of the housewives accepted the conditions of life as they found them. They were busily occupied, and found little leisure to argue about their equality with men. They shared in the life of the family in a very real way. Often they were the hub round which the wheel revolved, and though some of them rebelled against the common round of domestic duty, most of them were content enough to do whatsoever their hands found to do.

Gervase Markham, who may have been a Nottinghamshire gentleman, was a voluminous writer about country affairs from horse coping to house keeping, and he did not fail to set out a pattern for the perfect *English Hus-wife* in his book of that title published in 1615.

"The inward and outward vertues that ought to be in a compleat woman" was the simple, but comprehensive total he aimed to describe. His admonitions were no doubt addressed to the lady for her guidance, but they may have been equally useful as a lead to a young man seeking a wife. He could learn the impossible perfection that he ought to look for, that is, if he, or more likely his parents, were looking for anything more than a successful and profitable matrimonial alliance.

The perfect housewife, according to Markham, must be skilful in physic, cookery, banqueting stuff, distillation, wool, hemp, flax, dairies, brewing, baking and all things that belonged to the household.

She must be of great modesty and temperance as well inwardly as outwardly—a shrewd touch that. She must shun all violence of rage towards her husband, "coveting less to direct than be directed". She must be pleasant, amiable and delightful.

To this list of carefully cultivated personal qualities, Markham thought it competent to add his ideas about the proper fashion of women's clothes. His own words are: "Let the hus-wife's garments be comely, clean and strong, made as well to preserve the health as adorn the person altogether without toyish garnishes or the gloss of light colours and as far from the variety of new and fantastic fashions as near to the comely imitations of modest Matrons. . . ." He even laid down rules about food. "Let her diet be wholesome and cleanly, prepared at due hours and cooked with care and diligence . . . let it be rather to satisfy nature than our affections and apter to kill hunger than to renew appetite . . . let it proceed more from the provision of her own yard than the furniture of the markets, and let it be rather esteemed for the acquaintance she hath with it rather than for the strangeness and rarity it bringeth from other countries."

After this diversion Markham felt that he had not yet laid down quite definitely what the housewife must be in her personal character, and he does not show the slightest hesitation in emphasizing what he thought she ought to be. Her numerous desirable virtues included chaste thought, and stout courage. She ought to be "patient, untired, watchful, diligent, witty, pleasant, constant in friendship, full of good neighbourhood, wise in discourse, but not frequent therein, sharp and quick of speech, but not bitter or talkative, secret in her affairs, comfortable in her counsel and generally skilful in all the worldly knowledge which do belong to her vocation". Markham's ideal was a very paragon, yet there must have been many housewives of early Stuart times who conformed very closely to it.

Those, who failed to do so, did not fail from want of exhortation, both from laymen like Markham and from divines. The writing of "characters" was a favourite occupation in the early seventeenth century, and the wife was so important (as she for ever is) that "The Good Wife" takes pride of place in Thomas Fuller's *The Holy and the Profane State*, first issued in 1642.

The character is purely abstract. It takes no colour from any living person, and must have been Fuller's ideal, just as his other studies were the ideal of such people as the yeoman, the gentleman, the king, the prince, the faithful minister and many others. Mr. William Addison, however, in his recent book, *Worthy Dr. Fuller*, 1951, has said that he feels that Fuller's first wife must have been in his mind when he wrote it, even though Mrs. Fuller may not have possessed all these manifold virtues in an identical degree. She had died only a year before the book was issued, and her death was a very real bereavement to the worthy Doctor. His mind could then have only idealized her virtues.

He had a formula for his characters. He set them in maxims. To delineate "The Good Wife" required no less than ten. They were:—

1. She commandeth her husband in any equal matter, by constant obeying him.
2. She never crosseth her husband in the spring tide of his anger, but stays till it be ebbing water. And then mildly she argues the matter, not so much to condemn him, as to acquit herself.
3. She keeps home if she have not her husband's company, or leave for her patent to go abroad. For the house is the woman's centre.
4. Her clothes are rather comely than costly, and she makes plain cloth to be velvet by her handsome wearing of it.
5. Arcana imperii (her husband's secrets) she will not divulge— especially is she careful to conceal his infirmities. If he be none of the wisest she so orders it that he appears on the public stage but seldom.
6. In her husband's absence, she is wife and deputy-husband, which makes her double the files of her diligence. At his return he finds all things so well that he wonders to see himself at home when he was abroad.
7. Her carriage is so modest that she disheartens wantons not only to take, but to besiege, her chastity. I confess, he adds, some desperate men will hope anything.
8. In her husband's sickness she feels more grief than she shows. Partly not to dishearten him and partly because she is not at leisure.
9. Her children, though many in number, are none in noise, steering them with a look whither she listeth. (This accomplishment has unfortunately been lost.)

10. The heaviest work of her servants she maketh light, by orderly and seasonably enjoining it. Wherefor her service is counted a preferment and her teaching better than wages.

Fuller's character of "The Good Husband" is as conventional as that of "The Good Wife". Both reflect the accepted opinion of his time. There is no question of equality between husband and wife. For this Biblical authority is cited. "Excellently doth the Apostle argue the doctrine and dignity of men above women from the end and intent of their creation."

In Bible, book and sermon, men of the Puritan age asserted the ordering of the family and the household under masculine dictatorship, with a kindly and comfortable subjection of the woman, who nevertheless knew very well how to secure her ends.

The Reverend Robert Wilkinson preached at Whitehall before King James I on 6th January, 1607, at the wedding of Lord Hay and his Lady. The sermon was directed far more to the lady than the lord, and was afterwards printed under the title, *The Merchant Royall*. It was a lengthy exordium, but a few extracts are illuminating. Wilkinson proclaimed that a lady's countenance and conversation are "ballased" with soberness and gravity. A wife is for pleasure, for profit, and (if she be good) to bring her husband to good too. She should exceed neither decency in fashion, nor the limits of her state and degree, but if she was not proud she could wear anything. It was commendable in a woman if she was able "of her wisdom" to instruct her children and give good counsel to her husband.

Not very politely or with elegance Wilkinson compares a good woman to a snail, "not only for her silence and continual keeping of her house, but also for a certain commendable timourousness of her nature". If she will have bread she must not always buy it, but she must sow it and reap it and grind it, and as Sarah did (Genesis xviii) she must knead it and make it into bread. Or if she will have cloth, she must not always run to the shop but begin at the seed, sowing flax, gathering it, spinning the thread, weaving the cloth and so come to her coat.

A wife who lived up to these high precepts must have been a very paragon. Some there may have been, and many modern writers have declared that there were many. Most marriages of that time, they say, were happy and the acceptance of this order of things made them so.

1. HARVEST WORK. From Holinshed's *Chronicle*, 1577

Picture Post Library

2. MARKETING in 1598: Engraved by Hoefnagel

Picture Post Library

3. MAID BRUSHING AWAY FLIES. From John Heywood's *The Spider and the Flie*, 1556

4. OPEN FIRE in centre of Tudor gentleman's hall: whole logs burning. The people in the musicians' gallery *must* have enjoyed the smoke! From a nineteenth-century engraving

5. OLD FIREPLACES adapted for burning coal—probably late Tudor times

6. A TUDOR HALL: fire in centre, long dining tables at either side, musicians' gallery at end

7. AN ELIZABETHAN LADY riding pillion: from Robert Kemp Philp's
The History of Progress in Great Britain, 1860

8. THE HALL OF ELTHAM PALACE used as a barn and threshing floor in the early nineteenth century. From E. W. Brayley's *Graphic and Historical Illustrator*, 1834

9. "A new French cook to devise kickshaws and toys"—showing a stove for cooking. The smoke escaped the roof or a vent in the wall. From Knight's *Old England*, c. 1840

10. A COTTAGE CHIMNEY-CORNER in a house in Henley Street, Stratford-on-Avon. From Knight's *Old England*, c. 1840

11. PUBLIC WASHING GROUNDS, 1582. From *Harleian MS. 3469*

Thus in this *Semy-Circle* wher they *Sitt*,
Telling of *Tales* of pleasure & of wilt.
Heer you may read without a *Sinn* or *Crime*,
And how more innocently pafs your tyme

12. The Duke and Duchess of Newcastle and their family.
From the frontispiece to the Duchess' works

13. An OPEN CHIMNEY fitted with a Sussex fire-back and andirons. From a drawing made by J. J. Hissey in 1887

14. A Jacobean version of Mrs. Caudle's "curtain lectures".
From a contemporary broadsheet

15. LADY AND GENTLEMAN HAWKING in early Stuart times. From an early nineteenth-century engraving

16. MILKING SCENE: seventeenth century

17. Cooking. By Jan Dirk de Bry, 1618

18. "The Cruell Shrow, or the Patient Man's Woe." A ballad of 1610

There is certainly some truth in this idea, but to offset it there is in contemporary ballad literature a good deal about the shrewish wife. She, too, has long adorned the stage in Shakespeare's immortal *Taming of the Shrew.*

On a humbler scale a clever artist anticipated *Mrs. Caudle's Curtain Lectures,* a word that has become proverbial, and many another used the same theme. The "shrew" had all the unpleasant qualities which have always been condemned by uneasy husbands and fearful bachelors. One such invites the attention of all the male world to share his misery.

"Come Batchelors and Married Men,
 and listen to my song;
And I will show you plainly then,
 the injury and wrong
That constantly I doe sustain
 by the unhappy life,
The which doth put me to great paine,
 by my unquiet Wife.

She never linnes her bawling
 her tongue it is so loud,
But alwaies she'll be railing,
 and will not be contrould;
For she the britches still will weare,
 although it breeds my strife,
If I were now a Batchelor,
 I'de never have a Wife.

Sometimes I goe in the morning
 about my dayly worke,
My wife she will be snorting
 and in her bed she'll lurke,
Untill the chimes doe goe at Eight,
 then she'll begin to wake,
Her mornings draught well spiced and straight
 to clear her eyes she'll take.

D

As soon as she is out of bed,
    her Looking Glass she takes,
So vainly is she dayly led,
    her mornings work she makes,
In putting on her brave attyre,
    that fine and costly be,
Whil'st I work hard in durt and mire,
    alacke what remedy."

And so on for ten more stanzas.

This great poet was by no means singular in his choice of a subject. The scribblers of broadsheets return to it again and again, so it must have been popular. Perhaps the truth is that happiness is not very vocal. It is content with its lot. Misery, or the lesser affliction, annoyance, takes refuge in a storm of protest.

Some housewives must have deserved these lampoons. Often they must have found their life of unremitting labour and child-bearing irksome in the extreme, and the men realized this only by their complaints. They did not take much heed of the complaints. They took occasion to suppress them by severe and public punishments.

One thing used to punish a scold was a kind of iron mask and muzzle called the brank. This was a framework made of iron that fitted over the head like a knight's helmet. The mouthpiece was made so that an iron tongue was inserted into the mouth and the rest of the instrument clamped the jaw shut. It was really an instrument of torture, and a woman who was forced to wear it often had her mouth and lips torn and bleeding. Many a woman must have been afraid to speak her mind for fear of it. Another thing was the ducking stool. A notorious scold was seated in this either roped or shackled to it. The stool hung from a pivoted pole over a stream or pool, and the unfortunate woman was plunged into the water until her ardour was cooled. If the jest was carried too far she may well have been half drowned. Occasionally she was ducked in the village well. That was just as bad for her, but it cannot have been good for the water supply. Personal hygiene was in its infancy, and the bottom of the well may have concealed many things that it was undesirable to disturb. Against all this must be set the patience recommended by Old Fuller. He said that even if one's wife were "of a *servile* nature such as may be bettered by beating", it was best to hold one's hand and bear with her because she is the weaker vessel.

It is not very likely that any of the wives of the nobility and gentry ever suffered such punishments, however unconventional they may have been. The whole number of titled families, including knights, was less than a thousand, though there was a larger number of gentry, but in all they were but a fraction of the population. Moreover the women of this class had been educated for the profession of matrimony and housewifery, and were probably able to secure their ends by more subtle methods than mere railing, scolding and bad temper.

Formal education of the upper-class women had reached a very high standard during the Elizabethan age. The wives of the nobility in general were only too anxious to follow the example of their learned sovereign. Different influences, more particularly that of the Puritans, combined to reduce that standard of acquirement in the early Stuart age. Only a few exceptional women maintained it, and these were inordinately vain of their attainments, expressing whole-hearted contempt for the easy-going domesticity of the majority.

Lucy Hutchinson, the wife and well-known chronicler of her husband, Col. Hutchinson, was one. The Duchess of Newcastle was another.

Mrs. Hutchinson, though she admired the orthodox behaviour of her mother, had not the least desire to follow her amiable example. Lucy's only interest was her book. She was a linguist, and outstripped her brothers in the study of Latin, despite her contempt for that pitiful dull fellow, her brother's tutor, who was her instructor. Proudly she wrote of herself, "Play among the children I despised, and when I was forced to entertain such as came to visit me, I tired them with more grave instructions than their mothers, and plucked all their babies (dolls) to pieces, and kept the children in such awe that they were glad when I entertained myself with elder company". She was an insufferable little prig, in fact, but she is remembered when the children whose dolls she tore to pieces are forgotten, except for that memorable event.

In one thing she showed herself a very woman of her day. Her mother's attention to her sick father had aroused her emulation to this extent. When her father was ill her mother attended him with the greatest assiduity. She was cook, nurse and physician in one. Lucy, too, was capable of forgetting her learning in a pinch, and was equally assiduous in attending the wounded of both sides during the siege of Nottingham.

The Duchess of Newcastle was even more unconventional than Lucy Hutchinson. Poet, playwright and writer of memoirs, she was quite deficient in housewifely virtues. Her neighbours disliked this departure from the common pattern. They told her that her maids were spoilt with idleness because she always forgot to give them orders, and that by ordinary she neglected her proper housewifely cares. Stirred by these strictures the Duchess sent for her gentlewoman and gave orders for a supply of flax and spinning wheels to be bought. She would, she declared, sit with her maids and spin. The gentlewoman gently replied that the Duchess would spoil more flax than she would get cloth by her spinning. Nature made her mistress a spinster in poetry, but education had not made her a spinster in housewifery.

This rather daunted the Duchess, who must have been of quite a singular wit and patience to accept this reproof, and to record it against herself. She refused to be absolutely discomfited, and told the gentlewoman to buy a stock of varicoloured silks. She had determined to take up the embroidery of flowers, and so on, that was a popular recreation with the other ladies of her class. The gentlewoman assured her that such toys as silken flowers could be bought in the shops much cheaper and better than she could make them.

Still the Duchess would not give up. It was the season of the year when the fruit hung ripe upon the trees. She thought she would undertake preserving it. But it was not to be. Again she was confronted with the unanswerable argument that she never gave banquets. More she could keep a half a score of servants for the cost of the sugar and coal used in preserving a few sweetmeats.

This was the *coup de grâce*. The Duchess abandoned her ambition to become a conventional housewife, and continued with her writing. Her husband remained a frugal man instead of becoming a host at noble banquets. He ate but one meal a day, with two good glasses of small beer and a glass of sack (sherry) in the middle of his dinner. For breakfast he had only a glass of sack and a morsel of bread. His supper was an egg and a draught of small beer.

The Duchess complained that for three or four days her thoughts, but not her actions, had been so busily employed about housewifery that she could think of nothing else.

With such examples in their minds it is little wonder that some of the gentry, like Ralph Verney, warned their daughters and goddaughters to beware of acquiring too much book-learning. They had plenty of other more practical things to occupy them, both usefully and for recreation.

Childhood did not last long when a young woman was ready to marry at the age of fifteen, and no time could be wasted. As soon as they could walk they were set to learn their letters from the Horn Book. This was a printed card fixed in a frame rather like a lady's hand mirror, and protected from fingering by a sheet of horn. The little girl learned to sew a sampler just as soon. This was the more important task. On the sampler the child became expert in all the intricate stitches she would use after marriage to adorn curtains, bed quilts, hangings and chair covers, and the little caps for her babies.

Lady Fanshawe, another lady who has left us a record of her adventurous life, was educated at home "with all the advantages that time afforded, both for working all sorts of fine works with my needle, and learning French, singing, lute, virginals and dancing". But she was a wild one, who "loved riding in the first place, running and all active pastimes, in short I was what we graver people call a hoyting girl". It was well for her that she was. The hardihood gained from her outdoor exercises enabled her to endure the hardships and perils to which she was exposed in the Civil War, not the worst of which she discovered at Oxford when she went there to join her husband, Secretary of War to Prince Charles, who became Charles II. There the only accommodation she could find was a baker's house in an obscure street. She slept on a very bad bed in a garret, had only one dish of meat, and that not the best ordered, no money, for they were as poor as Job, and no clothes more than a man or two brought in their cloak bags. Later on she travelled on horseback all the way to Cornwall, and did not find this appalling journey overwhelming.

The resourcefulness that Lady Fanshawe possessed was by no means unique. It was a common possession of the great ladies, and was developed by their training and their active partnership with their husbands in the business of life. The same lengthy list of jobs as Tusser, the Elizabethan writer, laid down for her was still described as the woman's lot in the early Stuart housewife's textbooks. Indeed, country life, the only life lived by most people, made the same demands on the Continental countrywoman as on the Englishwoman. A translation from a French book, the *Country Ferme*, makes this clear.

"The condition and state of a huswife is that countrie women looke unto the things necessarie and requisite about kine, calves, hogs, pigs, pigeons, geese, duckes, peacockes, hennes, feasants, and other sorts of beasts, as well for the feeding of them as for the milking of them: making of butter and cheese; and the keeping of lard to dresse the labouring men their vittails withal. Yet furthermore they have the charge of the oven and cellar; and we leave the handling of hempe unto them likewise; as also the care of the making of webs, of looking to the clipping of sheepe, of keeping their fleeces, of spinning and combing of wooll to make cloth to cloath the familie, of ordring of the kitchen garden; and keeping of the fruites, herbes, rootes and seedes, and moreover of watching and attending the bees. (Buying and selling and paying of wages belongs to the man.) But the surplussage to be imploied and laid out in pettie matters, as in linnens, cloathes for the household, and all necessaries of household furniture, that of a certaintie belongeth unto the woman. (She must be) given to store up and keepe things sure under lock and key."

Things should be kept in their proper place, and the housewife must be kind or severe to the servants and the children as the occasion demanded; and she must always be first at work. She must not listen to talebearers. And she must look to her profits.

Another thing was that she must be "skilfull in natural phisicke, for the benefite of her owne folke and others when they shall fall out to be ill".

She must also govern her bread well—a delightful way of putting it—that it is used carefully; "and in time of dearth (never very far away in those days) let her cause to be ground amongst her corne beanes, peas, fetches or sarrasins corne in some small quantitie, for this mingling of these flowers, raiseth the paste, maketh the bread light, and to be of greater bulke".

Such a variety of duties developed resource and the initiative necessary to cope with the unexpected. Overseeing large numbers of men and maids in the bigger establishments bestowed a sturdy measure of self-reliance on the great ladies. No wonder that in the absence of their husbands so many of them were able to defend their houses and castles against the troops of the husband's political opponents. Lady Banks defended Corfe Castle for the Royalists, even physically. On the occasion of one assault she and her daughters with five soldiers employed themselves in heaving stones and burning embers on the enthusiasts who tried to climb the scaling ladders. These efforts effectually defeated the attackers. But of course Corfe Castle fell at last, like most of the stubbornly defended strongholds of the time. Lathom House, another fortified castle, was as bravely defended by Charlotte, Countess of Derby, for two years. Anne Murray emulated Lucy Hutchinson in her accomplished attention to the casualties of war. When she was staying at Dunfermline with Lady Fyvie she cared for "the sicke and wounded persons" that came to her, care that she herself says "the Lord was pleased to bless".

These ladies were not alone in their resolute character. The records of the time provide the names of many such another. One of the Verney ladies managed the estate in the absence of her husband, and her only regret, besides his absence, was that she did not make it pay better so that she could send him more money for the cause. Lady Falkland was another who endured all this. She lost her husband and son in the fighting, but through all the troubles she managed the estate for her younger son, looked after the household and the neighbouring poor, for she was a very religious lady, and resisted the exhortations of the Parliament. All this she did in face of her failing health. No doubt these exertions were partly responsible for her early death of consumption at the age of thirty-five.

The Civil War and its consequences made the duties of the great country ladies more onerous and difficult, but it was not unusual for them to manage estates both before and after the wars, either in the absence of their husbands, or if they were widowed. Lady Coke, for example, managed affairs at home when that ambitious man, Sir John Coke, Lord Chief Justice, was absent in London. She wrote to him reporting progress on the building of Longhall in 1606, and remarked "The weather hath hindered our teams from ploughing and other work they would have done".

Lady Anne Clifford, daughter of George, Earl of Cumberland, a maiden "innocent of any unnecessary diffidence", first married Richard, the third Earl of Dorset. Dorset died young, however, and she is better known to us as the Countess of Pembroke by her second marriage to the fourth Earl of Pembroke. As a young girl she was taken to see the new King, James I, and made the appealing record that "we were all lousy by sitting in the chamber of Sir Thomas Erskine". Her mother travelled all the way from Appleby in Cumberland to Knole in Kent to be present at the birth of her first child, a journey to appal anyone in the conditions then. At the end of her life this Lady lived in the north, and occupied herself in "building brew houses, wash houses, bake-houses, kitchens, stables at her half dozen castles . . . endowing alms-houses", ruling all about, tenants, almspeople, children, grand and great grandchildren alike, with a rod of iron.

She read a curious collection of books. Montaigne's *Essays* was one that is still read. *The History of the Netherlands* is forgotten. She read books of devotion. Other books she had read to her, one so odd for a lady as Mr. Sandy's book about the government of the Turks.

Books of sermons and devotion were favourite reading. Judith, Lady Isham, lent Anne Washington no less than ten such works in 1625. Lady Washington also borrowed a French A.B.C. and the French garden, and from Doctor Cozens a copy of Bacon's *Essays*. These somewhat mitigated the austerity of her choice of reading matter.

One lady of that time has left us an outline of her daily activities. Dorothy Osborne's life at Chicksands in Bedfordshire in 1653 must be very like that of many country ladies both just before and after the Civil War. She told her lover that what she did that day she might do daily for seven years, if she stayed there so long. She rose reasonably early in the morning, and "before she was ready" went round the house, presumably overlooking the maids, till she wearied of that. Then she went into the garden until it grew too hot for comfort. While sitting there she doubtless occupied herself in embroidery, or fine sewing, or in reading of the lighter type which she preferred. About ten o'clock (this sounds as if it was latish in the day) she thought of making herself ready. When that was done, she visited her father in his room and afterwards went to dinner, then the midday meal, and often served so early as eleven o'clock in the morning. She sat in great state with her cousin at a table "that would hold a great many more". After dinner they sat and talked, but the "heat of the day" was spent in reading and working, and about six or seven o'clock she went for a walk on a neighbouring common "where a great many young wenches (the daughters of small farmers and cottagers) keep sheep and cows and sit in the shade singing of ballads. I talk to them and find they want nothing to make them the happiest people in the world but the knowledge that they are so. Most commonly when we are in the midst of our discourse, one looks about her and spies her cows going into the corn, and then away they all run as if they had wings at their heels. I . . . stay behind and when I see them driving home their cattle, I think 'tis time for me to retire too. When I have supped, I go into the garden and to the side of a small river that runs by it, where I sit and wish you with me".

Dorothy Osborne was an exceptional young woman. She chose to fall in love with a man of her own choice. This was no part of the business of the ordinary young woman. A less strong-minded young woman would be married between the ages of thirteen and eighteen to an equally youthful suitor of fifteen to twenty-eight whose financial and social qualifications—a subject on which Dorothy Osborne jests continually—had been carefully examined by the parents who had selected him. Oddly enough these marriages, arranged so unromantically, turned out well, if we can believe contemporary correspondence and memoirs.

Occasionally, of course, there was a bit of double dealing and chicane. John Chamberlain, in a letter written on 11th October, 1617, declared that Lord Rich was:

"in greate perplexitie, or rather crased in braine, to see himselfe overreached by his new wife who hath so conveyed her estate that he is little or nothing the better by her, and if she overlive him like to carry away a great part of his; her sister the Lady Bowes hath dealt cleane contrarie, being lately married to Lord Darcy of the North, and bringing a great estate whole and entire, and refusing any jointure or other advantage, saying it is sufficient for her to have the honour without any hindrance to the house."

Marriage was recognized among all classes as a way to mend family fortune or improve it. William Powell in his pamphlet, *Tom of all Trades or the Plain Pathway to Preferment*, made this clear to the lesser gentry in 1631. He was emphatic on the need for the practical education of daughters.

"I would have their breeding like to the Dutch woman's clothing tending to profit only and comeliness.

Though she never have a dancing school master, a French tutor, nor a Scotch Tailor . . . it makes no matter; for working in curious Italian purls or French borders, it is not worth the while. Let them learn plain wools of all kind; so they take heed of too open seaming. Instead of song and music let them learn cookery and laundry. And instead of reading Sir Philip Sidney's *Arcadia*, let them read the *Grounds of Good Huswifery*. I like not a female poetess at any hand. Let greater personages glory their skill in music, the posture of their bodies, their knowledge in languages, the greatness and the freedom of their spirits and their arts in arraigning of men's affections at their fluttering faces. This is not the way to breed a private gentleman's daughter."

It was far better for a daughter to be trained by her mother, or if there was more than one, they could be placed out in the house of some good merchant, or citizen of civil and religious government, or with a judge or lawyer or some other justice and country gentleman. In such households the daughter might expect to learn good things, sempstrey, confectionery, and all requisites of huswifery and she would be kept under a proper discipline. Moreover she would meet young men who would make good husbands. The girl at home would make a wife for some good yeoman's eldest son, whose father would be glad to crown his sweating frugality with alliance to such a house of gentry, so that both he and his wife would be inclined to pass over all respect of portion or patrimony.

Many of the lesser gentry were ostentatious to a degree that lowered their resources. They were over generous to servants, dependants, godchildren and the like. If they had marriageable daughters they could repair the damage by marrying them to a well-to-do yeoman's son. Prideful of their birth and caste as they were—the human stud book was the only one then kept—they could unbend in the presence of fortune.

Mrs. Jeffries of Hereford, for instance, indulged unwisely in what is now called conspicuous expenditure, and so impoverished herself. She gave costly gifts, more especially to her numerous godchildren. She gave gifts of money, and she made innumerable small loans to local knights, yeomen, gentry, farmers and tradesmen. Her accounts show that many of these were never repaid, and she must have had great difficulty in collecting interest charged at eight per cent. The very evident risk attached to these investments justified this high charge.

Besides these extravagances she kept more servants than were really necessary, and she clothed them in costly liveries. She herself had expensive garments. A tawny camlet coat and kirtle cost £10 17s. 5d., an enormous sum in those days, more than five times the 40s. per annum she paid to her coachman.

Her housekeeping, too, was on a grandiose scale. In summer she frequently had her own sheep killed, in autumn a fat heifer, and at Christmas a beef, and, perhaps, a pig were consumed in her house. She was a supporter of old customs, patronized the fiddlers at the sheep shearing, and gave to the wassail and the hinds on Twelfth Night. Valentine's Day was great fun for her, and made good gratuities to her valentines.

What her own extravagance began, the Civil War ended. Her house was torn down, and when she fled she was plundered of a great deal of household goods, some money, linen and clothes and two bay coach mares.

A great many of her class must have lived just as unwisely as Mrs. Jeffries, and come to the same sad end. Others were as careful as the yeomen to whom they so often allied themselves, and lived a life that was in no way distinguishable from the richer yeomen.

In their houses, one, or two, or three women servants were employed. The number was naturally greater or less according to the wealth of the husband, and similarly so was the amount of actual handwork the wife had to do herself. The more well-to-do housewife worked, if she actually worked at anything besides the daintier jobs of cooking and still-room, exclusively indoors. The poor husband's wife, like the cottager's, worked in the fields as well.

Maybe the wife did her baking herself; maybe she had a chief maid who was capable of making the bread and brewing the ale as well. Whichever did the work the bread was rarely of whole wheat. Manchet, or bread entirely of wheat, was a luxury for the very rich, or to be indulged in only on high days and holy days by others. Ordinary bread was made of a mixture of wheat and rye, or rye alone, or of some other mixture.

Henry Best, lord of the Manor of Elmswell in the East Riding of Yorkshire, sent two bushels of mixed wheat and rye at a time to the miller in winter. In summer he sent only one bushel at a time because the bread would not keep so long. This was to be ground for making bread for the family. For what he called brown bread he sent a bushel each of rye, of peas and of barley, ready mixed, for grinding. This was for the servants. For pies for the family a wheaten crust was used; for the "folks" puddings, barley, never rye, was considered good enough, and rye for pie crust. In harvest time they had their wheat puddings. Poorer farmers usually put a peck of peas to a peck of rye, and some mixed peas with the mixture of wheat and rye known as massledine.

Markham recommends oats for thickening potage, a dish that had long been a staple of the working husbandman, his family and employees. Oats were also used to make thick and thin oat cakes as Anacks, Janocks and such like, haggis and porridge. This was a favourite dish in the west country where it was called "wash-brew"; in Cheshire and Lancashire it was known as "flamery" or flummery. Fifty years ago it was called "frumity" in Dorset. It was eaten with some tasty addition, honey, wine, strong beer or ale, or milk. Markham, too, thought bread for the hinds should be made of a mixture of inferior grain: 2 bushels barley, 1 peck of rye or wheat and 1 peck of malt. This confirms Best's practice with a book's authority.

Among the "folk" for whom Best provided this inferior food were several women employees. During haymaking he always had one man or the best of the women to abide on the mow besides those with the waggons. The best men shearers (mowers) he paid 8d. a day. The women only got 6d. At peas harvest he employed eighteen to twenty-four pullers and arranged them in gangs of six to a land (ridges, the area between two water furrows), three men or three women and boys.

When this job was finished, he usually gave a harvest-home feast of puddings, bacon or boiled beef, flesh or apple pies, and then cream, brought in platters and every one a spoon. After this the feast was crowned with hot cakes and ale.

Other tasks women did on Best's farm were to go in deep furrows with wain rakes to gather the corn that had fallen in after it was cut. A thatcher always had two women to help him, one to draw thatch, and the other to serve the thatcher and make bands. Women and boys or girls spread muck and molehills for 2d. or 3d. a day.

These were probably women regarded as the "second-best sort". The chief woman servant was one who was hired "by a gentleman or rich yeoman whose wife doth not take the pains or charge upon her". She might be the bailiff's wife who was charged that she

"must always be with him that she may keep him from running at rovers and may help him in his labours; her age must be such as we required in the bailiff before (between thirty and forty), she must be painful, healthy, careful and honest, she must not be ill-favoured, lest she be loathsome to him, nor too beautiful, lest he doat too much upon her, and keep home when he should be abroad. She must in the meantime look to the kitchen and to other workes at home, governe the maids, and keep them at their worke, looke to their necessaries and give them their allowance"!

The bailiff's wife, or chief woman servant, whose wages were from 26s. to 40s. a year, must be just such another paragon as her mistress was expected to be. She was a woman who resembled her superiors in another way too. She could take charge when her husband was absent on his proper occasions, or improper, should he run at "rovers" and she might not unreasonably expect that one day she should share a small farm with him.

Many women did, and proved themselves capable of working it when need arose. Women farmers were not unknown in the early seventeenth century. The Salford Portmote Records mention several who were naughty enough to infringe the customs of that Mote. Isabell Horworthe was presented to the Court for keeping pigs unlawfully, and worse for letting them trespass in a neighbour's corn to feed. Katherine Davies failed to pave before her door according to the regulations; she did not keep her bit of the street clean, and raised a dunghill against her barn to the manifest annoyance of the neighbours, though their sense of smell could not have been easily offended. Isabell Dawson did the same. Mrs. Byrom, the wife of the neighbour whose corn Mrs. Horworthe let her pigs feed, was just as bad. She and some men let their pigs run unringed and trespass on other people's corn. These pigs were impounded, but they, Mrs. Byrom and the men, rescued the animals instead of leaving them there and paying the proper fine. They were fined for doing it, so they did not get out of being punished.

Other wives, or widows, are mentioned in the records of Guildford, Surrey, and Carlisle, Cumberland. These few lived in widely different parts of the country, and it is likely that there were many others. Some of them may have had husbands living, and only kept a few pigs to add to the joint income. Even the minor gentry, who as we have said, were in much the same financial position, were not too proud to sell farm and garden produce. They were "our Country Squires who sell Calves and Runts and their wives perhaps Cheese and Apples". mentioned in one of Howell's *Familiar Letters* of 1644.

Richard Braithwaite waxed poetical about his wife's virtues and industry.

> "Oft have I seen her from the Dayry come
> Attended by her maids, and hasting home
> To entertain some Guests of Quality,
> She would assume a state so modestly
> Sance affection, as she struck the eye
> With admiration of the stander by."

This was not at all unusual. Household work was often interrupted by the arrival of a guest and then the housewife would be kept busy helping the maid to prepare the sweet conserves and pasties while the cooks looked after the roast or boiled meats. When everything was in a fair way of being ready the housewife hastened away to her chamber to make herself presentable for her guests. She would put on her best kirtle and lace apron and veil, and descend upon them in all her self-composed dignity.

On such an occasion in another house an unexpected guest protested against giving trouble by his arrival. He did not want the Lady of the house to take too much trouble with his dinner. The wife of his host replied with some ceremony, "Not a whit, Sir, you must be contented with country fare. You shall have neither red Deere, Marchpaine, nor Sturgeon, nor any Courtier's fare; but an egge and a sallet, a Pullet or a piece of Lamb." This was to be washed down with "our Country wine", some home-made drink made from orchard or wild fruit or flowers.

It might have been mead or metheglin because keeping bees and the gathering of honey was one of the usual duties of a housewife. Honey was used extensively in cooking and medicine as well as for eating and for making drink. William Lawson, the Yorkshire author of *The Countrie Housewife's Garden,* 1617, admonished his dainty reader that he "will not account her any of my good Housewives that wanteth either Bees, or skilfullnesse about them". Often the honey was a very substantial asset if there were many bee-keepers like the Cornishman who paid eight gallons of honey as tithe. Bees, can of course, find some of their subsistence from wild flowers, heather and so on, but it is an advantage to have a flower garden for them to forage in.

Cavalier and Puritan lady alike, and the humbler folk who professed no great leaning to politics as well, all adored their gardens. Beautiful as they necessarily were it was the practical worth of their produce that was most valued.

Brother Francis sent Dorothea, Lady Coke, five artichokes for her garden. Henry Vyner brought bay berries into Warwickshire, and a wish for some of St. Thomas onion seed. Persimmon and pear grafts were sent down from the garden of the London House in the Strand, and the stock was enriched by plants from the Fellows Garden at Trinity College.

There was a generous appreciation of gardens by writers like Bacon and Marvel. The latter wrote:—

> "How well the skilful gardener drew
> Of flowers and herbs this dial new,
> Where, from above, the milder sun
> Does through a fragrant zodiac run
> And as it works, the industrious bee
> Computes its time as well as we!
> How could such sweet and wholesome hours
> Be reckoned but with herbs and flowers."

A professed preference for the delights of a country life was no less a character of the minor literature of the day than it is in the modern resurgence of rural writing, or has been in most ages of English writing. Nicholas Breton, a gentleman who spent most of his life in London, compared the *Court and Country* in 1618 to the vast advantage of what was not then called the simple life.

"Now for the delight your eyes, we have the May painting of the earth, with divers flowers of dainty colours and delicate sweets; we have the berries, the cherries, the peare and the beans, the plums and the coddlings, in the month of June; in July the peares and the apples, the wheate, the rye, the barley and the oats, the beauty of the wide fields, and the labourers with delight and mirth, and merry cheare at the coming home of the Harvest cart. We have againe, in our woods the birds singing; in our pastures the Cowe lowing, the Ewe bleating and the Foal neighing, which with profit and pleasure makes us better music than an idle note and a worse ditty. Againe we have young Rabbets that in a sunny morning sit washing their faces, while as I have heard beyond the Seas there are certaine old Conies that in their beds sit painting of their faces. . . .

Furthermore, at our meetings on the holydays between our Lads and the Wenches, such true mirth at honest meetings, such dancing on the green, in the market house, or about the May-poole, where the young folks smiling kisse at every turning, and the old folks checking with laughing at their children, when dancing for the garland, playing at stoolball for a Tansie and a banquet of Curds and Creame, with a cup of old nappy Ale, matter of small charge, with a little regard for the Piper. . . . Againe we have hay in the barne, horses in the stable, oxen in the stall, sheepe in the pen, hoggs in the stie, corn in the garner, cheese in the loft, milke in the dairy, creame in the pot, butter in the dish, ale in the tub, *Aqua vitae* in the bottle, beefe in the brine, brawne in the sowce, and bacon in the roofe, hearbs in the garden and water at our doors, whole cloths on our backs, and some money in our cophers, and having all this, if we serve God withall, what in God's name can we desire to have more?"

Anyone living in these conditions must have been happy enough, but such wealth was not to be secured without a deal of hard work, and did not invariably result from that.

In the summer garden of flowers and in the herb garden the wife and her maids worked hard at weeding. She was heartily advised to be present herself to oversee the job, and to teach her maids to know herbs from weeds. If she did so, she might produce a garden that was so much admired as that of Goodwife Cantry, a Northamptonshire yeoman's wife.

Goodwife Cantrey grew double and single larkspurs, double and single Sweet Williams, three kinds of spiderwort, lupin in four colours, purple and white scabious, marigolds, Life Everlasting, London pride, Hollyhocks and many other flowers. Besides these she cultivated medicinal flowers, fennell, an infusion of which was thought a good bath for weak eyes, camomile to cure headaches, white lilies to break the bile, goat's rue for an infusion to take against the plague, and double "fetherfew" against a shaking fever.

All country housewives whatever their status from great lady down the scale must grow herbs from which to make salves, drinks and medicines, both for man and beast. The list was long and expansive. It grew longer as more plants were brought home by the valorous overseas adventurers.

Markham with his usual elaboration set out a calendar of operations and, in his usual fragmentary manner, left it incomplete. He laid great emphasis on the necessity for planting the different herbs and flowers in the appropriate phase of the moon. Everybody agreed that it was necessary to take account of the moon, not only in gardening but in farming as well, and the woman gardener was glad of the advice that Markham gave. One month's example will suffice.

February was a busy month. When the moon was new a large variety of plants must be sown. They were spike (lavender) garlic, borage, bugloss, chervil, coriander, gourds, cresses, marjoram, alma Christi, flower gentle, white poppy, purslane, radish, rocket, rosemary, sorrel, double marigold and thyme. At full moon the gardener sowed aniseed, violets, cleets, skirrets, succory, fennell, parsley; and when the moon was old, holy thistle, cole cabbage, white cole, green cole, cucumbers, hartshorn, dyer's grayne, cabbage, lettuce, melons, onions, parsnips, larks-heel, burnet and leeks. This was a substantial programme, and it was maintained throughout the year.

The produce was not all consumed fresh picked. In her still-room the country housewife preserved and pickled sallets in salt and vinegar

E

for later use, as well as violets, primroses, cowslips, gillyflowers of all kinds, broom flowers "and all wholesome flowers of all kinds", few of which we should now consider worth the trouble.

The dairywoman was busy, too, and though she need not take note of the phases of the moon, she must take into account the days when the local market was held. If she was wise she would churn her butter twice a week, on Tuesdays and Fridays, so that it would be fresh to send to market on Wednesdays and Saturdays. Most country markets were held on those two days.

The gentlewoman, or well-to-do yeoman's wife, usually worked with her maids in the dairy. These maids were recruited from the families of the tenants, and both employer and employed looked forward to the same country life, present and future. Their interests were the same, if different in degree, a condition that was cheerfully accepted in that carefully stratified society. They had been known to and familiar with one another from childhood, and often a strong bond of mutual affection held them together. "The servants of this age received moral and even physical chastisement with as much meekness as the children, and returned the kindly if autocratic care bestowed upon them by their instructor with loyal devotion."

Of course there were some malcontents. They voiced their grievances in the hearing of such people as Nicholas Breton, who was quick to set them down in writing. At six o'clock in the morning "Now begins the curst Mistresse to put her Girles to their taskes, and a lazy Hylding will doe hurt among good workers. . . ." The lazy Hylding, if she really was lazy, complained:

"I must serve the Olde Woman, I must learne to spinne, to reele, to carde, to knit, to wash buckes, and by hande, brew, bake, make Mault, reap, bind sheaves, weede in the Garden, milke, serve Hogges, make clene theyr houses; within doors, make beddes, sweepe filthy houses, rubbe dirtie ragges, beate out the old coverlets, drawe up old holes; Then to the kitchen, turne the spitte, although it was but seldome, for we have not had roaste Meate often; then scoure Pottes, wash dishes, fetch in wood, make a fire, scalde milke Pannes, wash the Cherne and butter dishes, ring up a Cheese clout, set everything in good order. And, alas, to all this, was but another Maid and I."

This long list of duties does not leave much time for this young woman to be lazy. Her employer was evidently not wealthy, and it was on the small farms that the most various and arduous and day-long jobs were all done by the same person, just as they were in the houses of the husbandmen, the small farmers, into whose ranks the lesser yeomen imperceptibly merged.

The life of the peasantry, the lesser yeomen and the husbandmen, and of course their families, was idealized in verse and prose by enthusiasts that have flourished in every generation.

Thomas Campion sang:—

"Jack and Joan they think no ill,
  But loving live and merry still;
Do on their week days work and pray
Devoutly as the holy day;
Skip and trip it on the green,
And help to choose the summer Queen
Lash out, at a country feast,
Their silver penny with the best.

Well can they judge of nappy ale,
And tell at large a winter tale,
Climb up to the apple loft,
And turn the crabs till they be soft,
Tib is all the father's joy,
And little Tom the mother's boy.
All their pleasure is Content;
And care to pay their yearly rent.

Joan can call by name her cows,
And deck her window with green boughs;
She can wreaths and tutties make
And trim with plums a bridal cake.
Jack knows what brings gain and loss;
And his long flail can stoutly toss;
Makes the hedge while others break;
And ever thinks what he doth speak.

Now you courtly dames and knights,
That study only strange delights;
Though you scorn the home spun grey,
And revel in your rich array;
Though your tongues dissemble deep,
And can your heads from danger keep
Yet, for all your pomp and strain,
Securer lives the silly swain."

"The woman of the husbandman class," wrote Alice Clark in 1919, "was muscular and well nourished. Probably she had passed her girlhood in service on a farm, where hard work, largely in the open air, had sharpened her appetite for the abundant diet which characterizes the English farmer's housekeeping. After marriage much of her work was still out of doors, cultivating her garden, and tending pigs and cows, while her husband did his day's work on neighbouring farms. Frugal and to the last degree laborious were her days, but food was still sufficient and her strength enabled her to bear healthy children and to suckle them."

Rather too much emphasis is placed by this writer on the plentiful food that was available. Doubtless ample meals were prepared and consumed when the barns and store rooms were full, but there were many years of deficient harvest in the first half of the seventeenth century, and then everyone went short, the husbandman and the daily labourers shortest of all.

Besides their work out of doors these housewives had to do the work of the home as well, bed-making, scrubbing and cleaning, fire-lighting and cooking, dish washing, clothes washing and scullery work. The apparatus for all this was quite primitive. Water, for example, must be dipped from a pond or drawn from a well. Waste water and slops of all kinds were simply thrown out of the door and left to soak or drain away.

A recipe for cleaning pewter plate that was recommended by one of the Verney family was probably over elaborate for these overworked housewives but it shows how much work must be done to keep the plates clean.

"For your plaites if they be well washed every meal with water and bran soe hott as their hands can indewar it, then well rinsed in faire woater, and soe sett one by one befoare the fire, as they may drie quick, I am confident they will drie without spots, for I never knew any sawce staine soe except it be pickled rabbits, which stand upon the plaite awhile, soe they will staine them filthyly."

Ambitious, as they must have been, to acquire a service of pewter, most cottagers' and husbandmen's wives must have been quite pleased to use the wooden bowls and dishes that an ordinary soaking and scrubbing would cleanse. How careful they actually were to wash their dishes it is not possible to know. It is certain that people of their class were not especially dainty, to put it on a low note. A confirmation of this conclusion is that all the contemporary writers on dairying found it necessary to be quite unequivocal in their exhortations to cleanliness in utensils and in persons.

In their youth the women were very attractive. The old, old nursery tale makes a dairy maid tell an aspiring gallant, "My face is my fortune Sir". And Sir Thomas Overbury drew a happy picture of "A fair and happy milkmaid". For him she

"is a country wench, that is so far from making herself beautiful by art, that one look of hers is able to put all face physic out of countenance. She knows a fair look is but a dumb orator to command virtue, therefor minds it not. All her excellences stand in her so silently, as if they had stolen upon her without her knowledge. The lining of her apparel (which is herself) is far better than outsides of tissue; for though she be not arrayed in the spoil of the silkworm, she is decked in innocency, a far better wearing. She doth not, with lying long abed spoil both her complexion.... She rises therefore with chanticler, her dame's clock, and at night makes lamb her curfew. In milking a cow and straining the teats through her fingers, it seems so sweet a milk-press makes the milk the whiter or sweeter. The golden ears of corn fall and kiss her feet as she reaps them. She makes her hand hard with labour, and her heart soft with pity; and when winter's evenings fall early (she sits at her merry wheel spinning). She bestows her year's wages at next fair. . . . The garden and the bee hive are all her physic and chirurgery and she lives the longer for it. . . . She dares go alone and unfold the sheep in the night. . . ."

Milking in the light of a dim horn lanthorn or by rushlight on a freezing winter's morning would have given Overbury a different picture to paint, especially if the hardy milkmaid's sweet white or brown summer hands were broken with chaps or swollen with chilblains. Her winter evenings spinning was more comfortable. She sat by the fire and spun the wool she had collected lock by lock on the bramble and furze of the common during the long hot days of summer. The hardships of country life on what were no more or less than frontier conditions these amateurs of rural joy carefully omitted, but it is unlikely that the maids they praised so highly considered their lot too severe. What would now be unbearable was the common lot, the accustomed contrast of the burning sun of the harvest field and the bitter cold of winters more severe than we know. They were a hardy lot. They had to be to survive.

Before marriage, or rather while in service to more wealthy farmer or gentry, the women of the humbler grades of rural society lived fairly well, as well indeed as their employers could or would provide for them. After marriage their lot was not so happy. Most people were far from rich in those times, though much romantic nonsense has been written about the good old days. Even the famous and renowned roast beef of old England was as yet unknown. Cattle were small; 600 lb. was a good size, and they were often as half starved as their owners. The vast beasts of the latter part of the eighteenth century would have seemed elephants and giants indeed to the Cavalier and Puritan. Their beef, too, was often old cow beef, and we, to our sorrow, know only too well what that is. That poor stuff was not often, if ever, eaten by the rural day labourer and his family. They were lucky if they got an occasional dish of bacon. This is made abundantly clear in Quarter Sessions Records where a shocking state of starvation and misery among the working class is revealed in great and convincing detail. This was not caused by exceptional calamity, or infrequent disaster. It was the ordinary life of families of the wage-earning class. The men lived lives that were drab and monotonous, lacking pleasure or recreation and consumed by unceasing toil, but when they were working they often got at least one meal a day in their employer's house. Some of them lived in, and only visited their wives and families at the week-end, or on holydays.

The result was that the full impact of their poverty fell upon the housewives. It was caused by a misconception of the function of wages. The maximum rates of wages were determined by the Justices, but no minimum was laid down. The actual rate paid was fixed by chaffering between the employer and the man, and we may be sure that these rates were never in excess of the maximum. An employer would have been very foolish to break the law by paying more than that, and would have been ridiculously extravagant as well.

The maximum was not intended to provide full subsistence for the man and his family. Every cottager was supposed to have a legal minimum of four acres of land attached to his dwelling that he could cultivate to provide his own food supply. Unfortunately this enactment was not honoured. Some cottages may have had the legal four acres attached, but a very large number certainly did not. If there was a small strip of garden the occupier was lucky. Besides this, there were opportunities of grazing cows and pigs on the manorial common and waste land, if the cottager was able to scrape together enough to buy them. Theoretically this was very well, but it did not always work out in practice. The maximum rates of wages were fixed upon the assumption that it did, and that money wages were only a supplement to what the family could provide for itself out of these facilities.

Marriage was often undertaken with a reckless lack of foresight and with a bovine acceptance of conditions. Soon a family began to arrive with monotonous regularity. The event was annual, if not happy. Infant mortality in this class was even worse than in higher classes, and it was very serious amongst the very highest. It was worse amongst the poor because of under feeding, bad housing, and the continual undernourishment of the mother that was really semi, sometimes complete, starvation. When she had to share the children's food, it was natural for her to give her own share of the minute quantity in her larder to them.

"Vainly she gave her own food to the children for then she was unable to suckle the baby and grew too feeble for her former work.

The once lusty young woman who had done a hard day's work at harvesting with the men was broken by this life."

She seldom had enough to eat. She could only earn twopence a day and her food at harvest, and at the death of her husband, or desertion, because he could fly from his unendurable obligations, both she and the rare child that survived, fell upon the parish. Those who died in infancy were fortunate. "Of those who reached maturity many were crippled in mind and body, forming a large class of unemployables", and a social problem that was quite insoluble at that time. The life of these unfortunate women seems pitiable in the extreme to modern ideas, but all countrywomen worked so hard then as to make their endurance remarkable.

And they had a good opinion of themselves if a contemporary ballad reflects a self-portrait. It runs:—

> "Although I am a Country Lasse,
>   a loftie mind I beare a,
> I think myself as good as those
>   that gay apparell weare a,
> My coate is made of comely Gray,
>   Yet is my skin as soft a,
> As those that with the chiefest Wines
>   do bathe their bodies oft a,
>
> What though I keep my father's sheep
>   a thing that must be done a,
> A garland of the fairest flowers
>   shall shrewd me from the sun a,
> And when I see them feeding be
>   where grasse and flowers do springa,
> Close by a crystal fountain side
>   I sit me downe and sing a.
>
> In every season of the yeare
>   I undergoe my labour,
> No showre or Winde at all I fear,
>   my limbs I doe not favoure,
> If summer's heat my beauty stain
>   it makes me nere the sicker
> Sith I can wash it off againe
>   with a cup of Christmas liquor."

And much more to the same effect. It is notable that these jocund verses describe a young woman before marriage.

The housewives in noble and gentle families were employed in a ceaseless round of daylong occupation, though some of their work was pleasant and enjoyable, being recreational and satisfying. The richer yeomen's wives lived a similar life, and had servants to help in the work. The woman of the husbandman and wage earners lived harsh laborious lives. Even mothers, nearly always expectant, worked, especially at the harvest, putting their babies to play in the corner of the field. Again in their little leisure they were obliged to try to supplement their husband's wages by spinning yarn for the clothier in the nearest town, or in following some other domestic employment, straw plait, stocking knitting, or glove making in different parts of the country. Not for these women the pleasant times of leisurely contemplation, letter and memoir writing, ill-spelt though the product was, in which the more fortunate wives of the squirearchy, great and small, indulged, but a life of overlong work before the era of the much condemned factory system.

For their daughters this was broken up, as the ballad quoted above says, by tending beasts on the common and singing songs on a summer day, but the summer was all too short as were the few years spent in this enjoyable and easy task before the maiden daringly entered upon the state of matrimony.

CHAPTER THREE

In the Days of The Restoration

THE POPULAR idea of the English under Charles II is that every man was a rake, and every woman little better than a whore. This can never have been true of the whole population; most of them must have been too busy providing for their livelihood to indulge in Courtly vices. The Court, and the group of parasites that battened upon it, formed but a small proportion of the whole nation, and it was a closed circle to the great majority.

Only for this small exclusive group, with its sense of being the sole urbane section of society, would such a poem as *The Italian Husband* have been written by Ravenscroft in 1698. It was contemptuous of the bucolic life that was the lot of most people; its sneers were not urbane. It runs:—

> "Fond nymphs, from us true pleasure learn,
>   There is no music in a churn,
>   The milkmaids sing beneath a cow,
>   The sheep do bleat, the oxen low,
>   If these are comforts for a wife
>   Defend, defend me from a country life.
>
> The team comes home, the ploughman whistles,
>   The great dog barks, the turkey cock bristles,
>   The jackdaws caw, the magpies chatter,

Quack, quack, cry the ducks that swim in the water.
　　If these are comforts for a wife
　　Defend, defend me from a country life.

Then melancholy crows the cock,
And dull is the sound of the village clock;
The leaden hours pass slow away;
Thus yawning mortals spend the day.
　　If these are comforts for a wife,
　　Defend, defend me from a country life."

These sentiments could only have been subscribed to by those whose life centred round town dissipations, the tavern, the theatre, the growing number of coffee shops, tea gardens and clubs. These, though most remarked by foreign visitors to England, were limited to the capital, and the spaws, of which Bath was already the foremost with the fashionable world.

For the rest, the seventeenth-century English, men and women alike, were deeply religious in a way that we, as their descendants, find it difficult to understand. And religious scruples, coupled with a full life of varied employment by no means led to sensual freedom or excess like those that made the Court and the Town notorious. There were some naughty ones. The Earl of Clarendon, looking at them with an old man's nostalgia for the days of his youth, wrote:—

"The young women conversed without any circumspection or modesty and frequently met in taverns and common eating houses; they who were stricter and more severe in their comportment became the wives of preachers, or of officers of the army. The daughters of noble and illustrious families bestowed themselves upon the divines of the time, or other low and unequal matches. Parents had no manner of authority over their children, nor children any obedience or submission to their parents."

This complaint is ever new and eternally old. It is voiced today as it was before the birth of Christ, but there was some truth in it. A foreign traveller, Jorevin, who came to England in 1672, remarked adversely upon the freedom of the manners of the wives and daughters of innkeepers and others he came across when staying at such places.

"According to the custom of the country," he wrote, "the land-ladies sup with strangers and passengers, and if they have daughters they are also of the company, to entertain the guests at table with pleasant conceits, where they drink as much as the men. But what is to me the more disgusting in all this is, that when one drinks the health of any person in company, the custom of the country does not permit more than half the cup, which is filled and presented to him or her whose health you have drunk. Moreover, the supper being finished, they set on the table half a dozen pipes, and a packet of tobacco for smoking, which is a general custom as well among women as men, who think that without tobacco one cannot live in England, because, they say, it dissipates the evil humours of the brain."

These were humble people enough, but their occupation threw them into the company of a variety of people from travelling pedlars and tinkers, gipsies and the tribe of beggars, petty thieves and petty traders to great merchants, the members of Courtly families and their trains, and the rare foreign tourist, of whom Jorevin was one.

Divines are always favourites with the ladies. Clarendon deplored marital alliances between them and the daughters of noble families, but he could not have condemned the kindness some great ladies showed them. During the troubled times some ladies had hidden distressed clergy in their homes, or protected them from the persecution they would otherwise have suffered. Dorothy Sidney, the poet Waller's "Sacharissa", Countess of Sunderland, was one of these. When she was allowed to return to her husband's house at Althorp, Northampton-shire, she gave "many" of the numerous dispossessed clergy of the neighbourhood shelter in her house. To these men "her house was a sanctuary, her estate a maintenance, and the livings in her gift pre-ferment", as Dr. Lloyd wrote in his *Memorials of Loyalists*.

One of those who found a home at Althorp was Dr. Thomas Pierce, a fellow of Lord Sunderland's college, Magdalen, who had been ejected from Oxford by the Parliamentary Commissioners. He became tutor to the young Earl, and was given the Rectory of Brington when his pupil went to Oxford. Later this pious and learned divine became President of Magdalen.

Mary Rich, Countess of Warwick, sister of Robert Boyle, was

another example. She was an avid reader of devotional works, and practised an oppressive piety that was something of a contrast to the sweetness of "Sacharissa's" disposition.

These and many others, like Lady Hoby at the end of the Elizabethan age, were intimately and immediately concerned with the realities of their religion. For them, their Creator was quite omnipresent, omniscient, all seeing, a fact in their everyday lives that it was impossible to ignore. They spent their Sundays listening to sermons, during the week their leisure was often occupied with books of devotion. The leisure of the lesser country housewife was naturally more restricted than that of these great ladies.

Her lot was not an easy one, but her multiplicity of duties, though continuous and changing with the seasons and the unaltered round of farm work, were not so onerous as they would have been in a more rushing age. Life was regulated by the succession of the months and the turning of the year, placid but varying in its demands for different jobs to be done. The young woman of yeoman or gentle birth who anxiously looked forward to marriage, anticipated a better lot than that of a scullion, as Macaulay has drawn her lot.

The wife and daughter of many lords of manors, according to him, were in taste and acquirements below a housekeeper or a still-room maid of his own day (1848). They stitched and spun, brewed gooseberry wine, cured marigolds and made the crust for the venison pasty. They had these duties and many others, duties that were much the same for my Lady as for the village housewife, the farmer's or the cottager's spouse. Although there was so much to do once she was married—she had probably, nay certainly, learned many of the jobs in her parents' house—the prospect did not deter the Carolean young woman from wishing to marry. What formidable obstacles indeed there would have had to be, to do that!

Marriage was their business in life, and, though amongst all but the lowest classes of society, it was a matter of careful arrangements, accounting of the financial and other advantages of a particular union, and infrequently enough the result of mutual and spontaneous attraction between the parties, it was welcomed by both men and women. The latter grew up to fear the fate of an old maid, which amongst the gentry often led to that life of dependance on a richer relation, so much loathed by a dependant woman of that class. Probably there were few old maids in the working class, and these could earn a living as domestics, or in other ways that were not open to the gentle, but for almost all women any marriage was better than none.

The marriage of daughters of landed proprietors with penniless dependants or hirelings was frowned upon, and prevented whenever possible. Many of the returned exiles were extremely hard put to it for ready money, and had no taste for a daughter's marriage that did not at once, or in prospect, help to fill the family coffers.

John Donne, when he was Secretary to Lord Ellesmere, fell in love with a young gentlewoman, Lady Ellesmere's niece, "that lived in the family", presumably as one of those arrangements whereby such young women were trained in households wealthier and larger than that of their birth. She was a daughter of Sir George More. As soon as he got wind of this sentimental attachment, he

"knowing prevention to be a great part of wisdom, did therefore remove her with much haste, from that to his own house of Lothesley in the county of Surrey; but too late, by reason of some faithful promises which were so interchangeably passed, as never to be violated by either party.

The promises were known to themselves; and the friends of both parties used much diligence, and many arguments, to kill or cool their affections to each other; but in vain. . . ."

The pair were married quietly. She had yearly a child, and when she died after having borne twelve children, seven were still living, a high proportion for that time. Donne, the irreconcilable lover, made himself a voluntary widower for the rest of his life.

Sir William Temple, to whom Dorothy Osborne's famous letters had been addressed, was himself a formidable opponent of the system of arranged marriages, but he was forgetful of the conditions that prevailed in his youth when he wrote in 1685, "I think I remember within less than fifty years, the first noble families that married into the city for downright money, and thereby introduced by degrees this public grievance which has since ruined so many estates by the necessity of giving good portions to daughters."

Many of the aristocracy had much land, often including great acres of unreclaimed waste, heath, mountain, scrub woods and fen. They had comparatively small financial resources, and, if they were to make the best of their property, as they wished to do, they must have money. Marrying a son to the daughter of a wealthy "cit", whose snobbery could be played upon, was one way of getting it. It was a device that was not neglected by the foremost families.

The noble houses of Somerset and Russell did not disdain alliance with the family of Sir Josiah Child, a great clothier, Chairman of the East India Company, and one of the earliest English economists. Wriothesley, aged fourteen and a half years, was married to Elizabeth Howland, aged thirteen, daughter of Sir John Howland, a landowner in Essex and Surrey, but a draper in the city all the same. The girl was a grand-daughter of Sir Josiah Child whose daughter had married Howland. Both these families had made great fortunes by trade. The wedding between these two children was celebrated with great pomp and ceremony in the private chapel of the Streatham manor house in 1695. After the wedding the bride and groom met only at intervals for some years. The bride continued to live with her mother, and the groom was sent abroad with a tutor to make the grand tour.

This was very elaborate and both children were so young that any attempt to disobey the family was unlikely. One young woman, older and possibly less eminent, took matters into her own hands and married an impecunious curate. Her relations thought this a disastrous adventure, but she told them calmly that she had married an honest man with whom, in time, she hoped to settle down comfortably. Whether she achieved this modest ambition or not is to seek.

When a girl had either been successfully married off, or had herself arranged matters in a rather irregular and unfinancial way, her life became one of brisk business. Macaulay put this business at its lowest level when he described the dining-room habits of the country squire and gentry. Their tables were loaded with coarse plenty, and guests were cordially welcomed to partake of it, but drinking to excess was habitual. Imported wine was too expensive for daily use and the usual beverage was home-brewed strong ale. The quantity consumed was enormous, and the ladies of the house whose business it had commonly been to cook and carve the repast, retired as soon as the meal had been devoured and left the gentlemen to their ale and tobacco. The coarse jollity of the afternoon was often prolonged until the revellers were laid down under the table. This places the ladies of the house as cooks and scullions, but, while there is no doubt that they did cook and brew and bake, their position in the household was something more than menial. Contemporary letters, written by husbands and wives alike, show the development of an undeniable affection and desire for each other's company after many years of married life following a bridal arranged in such an apparently unromantic way.

The ideal held by both parties was that the woman should be a "notable housewife". It was only, as Arthur Bryant has said, "when Englishwomen became too grand to look after their own nurseries and kitchens that something of the glory was taken from the profession of housewifery", so that it was reduced to a dull and tedious necessity for the majority whose more lowly position condemned them to it.

A "notable housewife" needed fine qualities of character to manage quite a small house before labour-saving devices were even imagined, and when there was no village shopkeeper nor any number in the local but distant market town. The housewife must take the place of all the tradesmen, providing from the estate or farm,

> "wholesome and cleanly diet for family and dependants, of whom there was usually a good number, comprising men and maids, both indoor and outdoor, all of whom must be fed and possibly clothed from internal resources. So the lady's business in addition to maintaining indoor economy, a complicated matter enough, was to keep cows for the dairy and poultry for the larder, to stock the fish pond and see that the herb garden was not neglected. And there was a constant succession of guests to be looked after."

Some of the noble households were conducted on a scale of princely magnificence, but their number was small. One was the establishment of the Duke of Beaufort at Badminton. Lord Guildford stayed here a week in 1680.

The Duke had then more than 2,000 acres in hand, and this large farm was managed by stewards and bailiffs and worked by servants. There was a good deal of horse breeding. "He bred all his horses which came to the husbandry as first colts, and from thence, as they were fit, they were received into his equipage."

There were no less than two hundred persons in this household. For this company nine tables were laid daily, but not all ate together.

There was an accepted arrangement of precedence and place. Most of them took their meals in a very large banqueting hall with an alcove at one end reserved for persons of distinction. Every guest was conducted to the table proper to his rank. The chief steward, the bailiff and the servants (in husbandry) took their places at a fourth table. The clerk of the kitchen, the bakers and the brewers sat down together at a fifth. Special tables were provided for the inferior servants. This was a stag party; the women were not allowed to eat with the men, with the exception of the Duchess's chief maid. All the rest of the maids ate in a separate room under the strict and watchful eye of the housekeeper.

The Duchess herself inspected every detail of the household in a daily tour of its myriad apartments and departments. Soap and candles were made on the premises. The salt was ground there, after being dried in the sun on the leads of the mansion, and that in sufficient quantity to make all the liquor consumed at the Duke's table.

The day in this vast household began with breakfast in the Duchess's gallery that opened into the gardens. Then a stag was hunted on horses provided by the Duke, or guests walked admiringly round the gardens, or through the parks to look at the various kinds of deer. Twice a day the bell rang for prayers, at half past eleven in the morning and at six o'clock in the evening, when the chaplain officiated in the neighbouring ducal church. The Duchess and her gentlewomen occupied the evening with pastimes in one of the galleries, mainly embroidery and fine needlework for the beds that were made at home.

The meals were served in stately fashion and temperance was strictly enforced, wine being served in single glasses brought to each person on a salver. Protracted health drinking after the meal was frowned upon, as was smoking.

The Duke farmed a large area of his estate. His wife and daughters were employed in many tasks of domestic utility, and necessities of every kind both for the farm and the mansion were made at home, as indeed they had been for centuries in such great establishments, and in very much smaller ones. The number of families that lived in such rural splendour was very limited, but they set a pattern to those on a more restricted scale. The clever housewife made her home a "little commonwealth in variety of resource, utility and self-supporting achievement".

Amongst her other duties it is possible that the Duchess of Beaufort

F

took an active interest in the financial control of her part of the estate business, though whether she did is not certainly known. Many other women, wives of landowners and farmers, played an important part in this side of the management of family affairs. Sarah Fell of Swarthmore Hall, Lancashire, kept very detailed accounts, which illuminate her affairs and methods. This was not an unusual accomplishment. A much greater lady, Francis Stuart, Duchess of Richmond, supervised her husband's building operations at Cobham Hall, Kent, shortly after her elopement with him, an adventure which disgusted and angered the King.

Such whole-time busyness did not leave much leisure for literary pursuits. This may not have been so unfortunate as it sounds. Too much weight can be given to their value. Macaulay, naturally enough, errs in the opposite way. His catalogue of the literary store of the average lady of the manor and her daughter began and ended with a prayer book and recipe book. Even the urban ladies, were, he said, poorly educated. If a damsel had the least smattering of literature she was regarded as a prodigy. This was a half truth, as such flamboyant and picturesque statements usually are.

The general standard of feminine literacy was much lower than it had been in the age of Elizabeth; but in that age learned ladies had sought to emulate their Virgin Queen. In the immediately succeeding age there had been women of accomplishment, but the effect of the Civil Wars and the Puritan outlook had been disastrous.

The returned gentlemen were disappointed to find that there had been a decline in manners during their absence. When there were few of their own class to care for, the ladies had not bothered to maintain the high standard of behaviour that had formerly been essential to the mutual intercourse of the sexes. They had relaxed, as they invariably do, when the men are not present. One went so far as to remark that he found the young girls "extreme clownish" and of "noe breeding". That was not very extraordinary because these girls had grown up in times of stress when they had been obliged to fend for themselves. The financial straits of their families had forced them to undertake a good deal of work of a kind that was normally done by "servants" under their supervision.

With some show of justice, but not very much, the men were annoyed to find these conditions, accustomed as they had been to the straits of poverty in a foreign country. Out of their irritation they took up an attitude which only made it worse. They advised their womenfolk to be content with their domestic and family duties, and to practise the virtue and modesty that were the qualities that were best suited to their sex. If they must read, they could fill up their minds with the beauties of Sidney's *Arcadia*, a book that was still popular, or an odd astrological work like Artemidorus' *Interpretation of Dreams*, a thriller like the compilation *God's Revenge against Murther*, or Taylor's *Holy Living and Dying*.

This sort of literature was acceptable to most women, but the first stirrings of a conscious feminist movement, as apart from practical feminine participation in the affairs of life, are to be found in the writings of ladies of the time.

The plays of the Duchess of Newcastle were performed after the Restoration. They made no great noise in the world, it is true, but they were the work of a female dramatist, a new phenomenon. Mrs. Hutchinson's equal scorn for the domestic trivialities that occupied most women in the previous age has already been remarked upon.

Another lady, Katherine Philips, the "matchless Orinda", died early in the reign of Charles II. For her Jeremy Taylor wrote his treatise on *Friendship*, and she is highly praised as being worthy to be his friend. Although a beloved ornament of the Court, she preferred, like so many other women of this century, a quiet country life with her husband in Wales. She wrote many poems, but published none during her lifetime, which ended tragically when she died of smallpox at the early age of thirty-one. An unauthorized publisher issued a small collection a few months before she died, and five years after a friend edited a full and complete edition of her works. The poems are simple, written to friends, and upon occasions of joy or sorrow in her home circle. Some are full of the praise of the country life she loved so well. All show what Abraham Cowley called "the tender goodness of her mind". One of the last was a lament upon the death of her eldest boy when he was thirteen, only a few months before she herself passed on.

Later in the century many women writers flourished. Aphra Behn, who had an adventurous life as a secret agent in Holland, turned to literature when she found the rewards of this profession disappointingly small and precarious. She was the first English woman novelist, and she wrote plays as well. Mrs. Pix and Susannah Centilivre were two others of a fairly numerous, if not very distinguished company. In the last decade of the seventeenth century Mary Astell published her proposals for a women's college, that would have been the first of its kind; contemporary prejudice was so strong that she was unable to carry the project to fruition. Her spirited attempt to forward the higher education of women was fore-doomed to failure, though it was a voice crying in the wilderness to proclaim the future. If Thomas Shadwell's satiric character of a girl's school is at all just, it was eminently desirable.

"Of a School of young Gentlewomen.
To shew how far they are removed from Court breeding, their Schools most commonly are erected in some Country Village nigh the Town, where to save charges, they have the worst Masters as can be got for Love or Money, learning to *quaver* instead of *singing,* *hop* instead of *dancing,* and *rumble* the *Virginals,* scratch the *Lute,* and *rake* the *Ghitar,* instead of playing neatly and handsomely. As for their Languages, a Magpie in a *moneth* would learn to *chatter* more than they do in a *year.* As for their Behaviour, it is nothing else but a low Courtzie, with a bridling cast of their Chin to fetch it up again."

Between such widely separated ideals there was room for a range of varied attainment and no doubt it existed, even if it was only demonstrated in the activities of those housewives who spent their Sundays listening to sermons and making shorthand records of them for their own greater edification.

Mary Evelyn, daughter of the diarist, was a "notable housewife", and her opinion of the education of women must have been shared by hundreds, if not thousands of her class and kind. She did not think "women were born to read authors or censure the learned. The care of children's education, observing a husband's commands, assisting the sick, relieving the poor or being serviceable to our friends are of sufficient weight to employ the most improved capacities amongst us."

She practised what she preached. In her house morning prayers were usually read at or before 6 a.m. in the summer, and sometimes before sunrise in the winter. On a stone floor and in a perhaps un-heated chapel the winter celebration must have been a chilly business, but our ancestors were a hardy lot. After prayers, the little breakfast was drank, a pint of old ale or a cup of sack, possibly a home-made syrup and a mouthful of bread and then to work.

The dairy was inspected, milk, butter and cheese. The fish ponds were visited and the stock of carp, perch and other coarse fish examined for numbers and well-being since they formed an important part of the regimen. The dove-cote was looked to and its servant exhorted about the need for keeping enough pigeons fat for the table. A dove-cote was a normal accessory to a manor house, and had been for some 500 years. After the Restoration, that great age of building more splendid country houses, some of the most beautiful dove-cotes were built between 1675 and 1725. They were affected by the style of the mansions, designs after Wren and Wycherley. Some were round and others octagonal. Often they were crowned at the roof top by "elegant glazed lanterns or cupolas". Size varied but 365 nest holes, one for each day of the year was not uncommon. Less than 200 was very small, over 1,000 was very large. The poultry yard, too, and its maiden, must be kept up to the mark. Next came the most important duty of the day, the regulation visit to the butteries and kitchen, the conference with the cooks and finally the long-awaited and lengthily eaten mid-day meal. When at last that was disposed of, there was music and embroidery, reading aloud and the pleasures of the still-room. A snack for supper ended the day at what would be for us, an early hour.

Her father, years after her death, in his book, *Mundus Muliebris*, 1690, admonished the young men of that age, that in his youth men courted their wives for just such qualities as Mary possessed. Wives then were chosen:

"for their Modesty, Frugality, keeping at home, Good Housekeeping and other Oeconomical Virtues then in Reputation; and when the young Damsels were taught all these in the Country, and their Parents Houses, the Portion they brought was more in Virtue than in Money. The Presents which were made when all was concluded, were a Ring, a Necklace of Pearl, and perhaps another fair Jewel, the Bona Paraphernalia of her prudent Mother whose Nuptual Kirtle, Gown and Petticoat lasted as many Anniverseries as the happy Couple lived together and were at last bequeathed. . . .

In those happy days Sure Foot, the grave steady Mare, carried the

Good Knight and his Courteous Lady behind him to Church and to visit in the neighbourhood. . . .

Things of Use were Natural, Plain and Wholesome, nothing was superflous, nothing was wanting. . . ."

John Evelyn was not the first and not the last to criticize the present in the light of the golden past he remembered. We all do it today. Sir Matthew Hale, the celebrated Lord Chief Justice wrote much the same sort of thing as Evelyn nearly fifty years before.

"In former times," he said, "the education and employment of young gentlewomen was religious, sober and serious, their carriage modest, and creditable was their habit and dress. When they were young they learned to read and to sew; as they grew up they learned to spin, to knit and to make up their own garments; they learned what belonged to housewifery. . . . And now the world is altered; young gentlewomen learn to be bold, talk loud and more than comes to their share, think it disparagement for them to know what belongs to good house-wifery or to practise it. . . . They know the ready way to consume an estate and to ruin a family quickly, but neither know nor can endure to learn or practise the ways and methods to save and increase it; and it is no wonder that great portions are expected with them for their portions are commonly all their value. . . . If a fit of reading come upon them it is some romance, or play book, or love story, and if they have at any time a fit of using their needle, it is in some such unprofitable or costly work that spends their friends or husbands more than it is worth when it is finished."

These are hard sayings widely separated in time, but most of the young to whom they were addressed probably ignored them, or put them down to the crabbiness of age. Times were changing, and few elderly gentlemen really admire the behaviour of the second generation after themselves. The first was hard enough for them to endure. Though there was the beginning of change, it was not really very marked, and most country living went on in its well-established way.

Personal supervision like that given by Mary Evelyn was not the invariable habit of great ladies. Often these detailed duties were delegated to a "gentlewoman", some spinster of the family, or an employee.

It was mainly to teach gentlewomen of this class, who were in reality only upper servants, that a new literature was developing. One book was *The Accomplisht Lady's Delight in Preserving, Physic, Beautifying and Cookery*, a fourth and enlarged edition of which appeared in 1684. This may, in fact, have aimed at a public composed of all housewives.

Others were definitely intended for the gentlewoman housekeeper or maid, e.g. *The Compleat Servant Maid, or the young maidens' tutor*, fourth edition, 1685. This book laid down in no uncertain manner what she who aspired to be a waiting woman in a wealthy household must be, and do. Her fashion of dress must be suitable, or in other words she must not compete with the mistress and family, but must be properly aware of her situation. She must be skilful in the still-room, write legibly, be good and accurate at figures and able to carve. She was advised to be courteous and modest in her bearing, humble and submissive, sober in mien and conversation, to read good books and to attend well to the Sunday sermons.

Besides being able to vary the family diet from whatever foodstuffs were to hand she must know "how to disjoint a quarter of lamb, to display a crane, unbrace a mallard, wing a partridge, disfigure a peacock, thigh a woodcock and lift a swan", duties that would certainly astonish any modern lady of whatever class were she asked to perform them.

Already this field of enterprise had been attacked by a lady, Mrs. Hannah Woolley, who published her first book on preserving in 1661, and rapidly followed it with her *Cook's Guide* in 1664. *The Ladies' Delight*, 1672, *The Queen Like Closet*, 1670, and *The Gentlewoman's Companion*, 1675. Some of these books went through many editions, and from them can be gleaned something of their author's life and opinions.

She was a strong believer in feminine emancipation and takes a firm stand against the current masculine belief in its own superiority, and the propriety of female subjection. "Vain man," she wrote in *The Gentlewoman's Companion*, "is apt to think we were merely intended for the world's propagation and to keep its humane inhabitants sweet and clean; but by their leaves had we the same literature he would find our brains as fruitful as our bodies."

Strangely enough this opinion was shared by Daniel Defoe. He did not think women ought only to be cooks and slaves, but was prepared to risk educating them, not only in accomplishments such as music and dancing, but in modern languages such as French and Italian. "I would venture the injury of giving women more tongues than one." Uneducated women might be impertinent, talkative, ridiculous, haughty, turbulent, clamorous, noisy, nasty and the devil. Indeed he wondered how it was possible that they were conversable at all since they depended entirely upon their natural parts for their knowledge.

Hannah Woolley must have had some education. At fourteen, then a mature age equal to at least twenty today, she became a schoolmistress. Her own words are, "Before I was fifteen, I was intrusted to keep a little School and was the sole Mistress thereof." Here she made such a mark that at seventeen she was asked to become governess to the only daughter of a noble lady whom she instructed in Italian, singing, dancing and how to play several musical instruments. She could teach writing and arithmetic and most of the housewifely duties as well as pretty things like bugle work on wires, feathers of crewel for the corners of beds, all transparent works, shell-work, moss-work and so on. Some of these occupations were greatly despised only a generation ago as characteristically Victorian; in fact they were nearly two hundred years more ancient, possibly more.

Hannah made such a good impression on her noble employer that she was promoted by stages to be her Woman, her Stewardess and finally her Scribe or Secretary, "By which means," she remarked complacently, "I appeared as a person of no mean authority in the Family." This post, too, assisted her to extend the range of her own acquirements.

At about twenty-four she married Mr. Woolley who was a schoolmaster. Together they conducted boarding schools until his death. A few years later she married again, but again became a widow. It was after her first bereavement that she first embarked upon the hazardous trade of author. The books of recipes and advice that she wrote were very popular and were often plagiarized. They covered the whole range of feminine interests. She said in the preface to *The Gentlewoman's Companion* that it was a "Universal Companion and Guide to the Female Sex in all Relations, Companies, Conditions and States of Life, even from Childhood down to Old Age; from the Lady at the Court, to the Cook-maid in the Country".

Such books as this must have made a welcome change from the

books of sermons that were the staple reading of the literate country woman. Ponderous volumes, in both senses, were laboriously and slowly hauled from London by waggon and carrier's cart, and penetrated to the most remote countryside.

Books of sermons provided food for the spirit; books like that of the redoubtable Hannah and books of recipes recorded how food for the body should be prepared. This was a more immediate preoccupation and as continuous then as now. Food had to be fetched from the market—occasionally now it was obtained direct from London—collected from the garden or the granary or dairy, prepared and consumed, or preserved and stored against future needs. It was then as now a perpetual concern for wives and mothers. Family secrets in the culinary art were valuable heirlooms. An elderly lady's plot for making cowslip wine; a younger one's secret way with candied fruits and smoked ham were confided only to the recipe book that was a family treasury of hints for today and remembrances for tomorrow.

One lady whose excellent puddings caused her guests to believe she had some special secret way of making them, denied the gentle implication quite roundly. "I have no receipe for puddings, nor ever had," she wrote forcefully. "I make them always by guess. Indeed I did teach Mrs. Fountain, but it was with letting her see me mingling them. But I'll tell you everything I use to put in them, and give you the best directions I can, and then you must put them together to your taste." Her cooking must have been an art and not a science. Indeed it often must have been for one recipe for preparing a cod's head that cost 4d. required condiments, etc., that cost 9s.

A quaintly modern touch comes out in one contemporary letter. In it a woman explained that she could not visit a friend because her husband had taken the coach to pieces. How many wives have found the car in the same condition, if their husbands are fond of tinkering!

Naturally all this work made domestic service an important job—almost a profession. A small manor or large farm would employ from seventeen to twenty-five indoor and outdoor maids and men; great noblemen like the Duke of Beaufort had literally hundreds of domestics. The work of the maids, as one Lady Shakerley explained to a friend, who had found her two maids, "is the chambers to look to and pewter to rub, and the washing of my finer linen . . . brewing and baking, and some few swine and poultry, and the scouring of all my pewter once a week, and when I have winnowing the two to winnow it up, which will not be much for you know that I have not much corn to winnow." This was by no means unvaried routine, but obviously a full-time job.

This letter throws out a hint that some of Mrs. Shakerley's laundry was not done at home, a tiny rift in the canopy of self-sufficiency that covered all the needs of the manor house. Some of it was perhaps done by the village woman at home as it was beginning to be elsewhere. When the whole wash was done at home, soap was now sometimes bought, whereas formerly it had invariably been made at home. Hannah Woolley warned laundry maids to be sparing of soap, as well as fire and candles. "Bucking" was a term used to describe a general wash that took place twice a year.

Housemaids were warned by Hannah to keep the chambers cleanly, to turn the beds often and the furniture to be well beaten in the sun, and well brushed. This was ambitious, and was the beginning of a feeling for domestic hygiene that grew slowly more pronounced. Housemaids must also be careful for and diligent to all strangers and see that they lack for nothing in their chambers.

The value of this work was appreciated by employer and employee alike. Those rather harsh-sounding words were hardly yet themselves employed. As Bishop Heber wrote in his *Life of Jeremy Taylor* the interval between the domestics and the members of the family was by no means so great as it was in his own day.

"There was in those days no supposed humiliation in offices which are now accounted menial, but which the peer then received as a matter of course from the gentleman of his household; and which were paid to the knight or gentleman by the domestics chosen in the families of his own most respectable tenants; while in the humbler ranks of middle life it was the uniform and recognized duty of the wife to wait upon her husband, the child on his parents, the youngest of the family on his elder brother or sisters. But while the subordination of service was thus perfect and universal, this very universality softened its rigours. . . . The servants of the manor house were usually the humble friend of the master and mistress whose playmates they had been during childhood, and under whose protection they hoped to grow old."

Women trained in the great houses made excellent wives for the farmers of the village that lived in its shadow. Some of them married the chaplain who had been employed in the same house. While living there the chaplain did a good deal of other work besides his priestly duties, and was often expected "not to be above digging for an hour or two in the kitchen garden, casting up accounts, performing the operations of letting blood and drawing teeth, discharging the offices of a farrier". When he secured a living he had as well to live the life of a yeoman farmer, "labouring by the sweat of his brow in the field and the farmyard, to extract from the benefice the means of subsistence. To drive the plough through the field; to feed the noisy hogs and poultry; to rise early, and late take rest, and to eat the bread of carefulness", was no more and no less the lot of the rural clergy than it was of the yeoman himself. Their wives must have the same ability to share in the partnership, though in a subordinate position. Well-trained domestics brought to the management of such husband's homes just the qualities that he needed. These were, in fact, except in scale, the same as those of the manor house, although when she became mistress of a farmhouse the housewife might find it necessary to help with some of the more arduous and dirty work.

The Office of the Good Housewife of 1672 repeats almost in the words of Barnaby Googe (1612) the catalogue of her duties which had been current time out of mind, though only recorded in the printed word for a century and a half. It was her duty "according to our Custom of *England* (to) look unto the things requisite and necessary about Kine, Calves, Hogs, Pigs, Pigeons, Geese, Ducks, Peacocks, Hens, Feasants, and other sorts of Beasts and Fowls, as well as for the feeding of them, as for the milking and making of Butter and Cheese, and keeping all things neat and clean about the house". She had in addition to the necessary cooking, to look after the hemp and flax, clipping of sheep and keeping of fleeces, spinning and combing of wool to make cloth for the family. The kitchen garden was another sphere of influence; bees another, and silkworms yet another if they were bred, though the silkworm was unusual. To this long list of jobs, fortunately not all concurrent, or they would have been too much even for such energy, were added such heavy labour as spreading muck and holding the plough on the smaller farms, where only family labour was employed except at harvest, when a couple of old women might make a cheap and necessary supplement.

Besides this amazing industry the wife must have what is today called tact. Lady Chudleigh replying to a Parson, who preached against that worst of plagues, those furies called our wives, expressed this need rather differently. The Parson's wife was no doubt cross because he had neglected some farming task when occupied with his books. Lady Chudleigh advises wives:—

> "If you wou'd live as becomes a Wife
> And raise the Honour of a marry'd life,
> You must the useful Art of wheedling try
> And with his various Humours still comply."

The Parson was not alone in his complaint. It was enshrined in some verse that a cheerful milk-woman and her daughter sang to Isaac Walton for the reward of a chub from the angler's basket. The song praises the equability of the country woman—especially those who worked in a dairy. It was:—

> "I married a wife of late,
> The more's my unhappy fate;
> I married her for love,
> As my fancy did me move,
> And not for a wordly estate;
> But oh! the green sickness
> Soon changed her likeness;
> And all her beauty did fail.
> But tis not so
> With those that go
> Thro' frost and snow
> As all men know
> And carry the milking pail."

Whether the wife was tactful, a fury, a weakling, or a robust young woman who carried the milking pail, she was a mother as well as a housewife. In addition to her multifarious other occupations, she very generally bore a child every year. The blessed event was still an annual event, and many a weary woman hoped that her tenth child might be her last.

The art of midwifery was very much a matter for the wisdom of a neighbouring grandmother. Few country housewives had the attention of a trained doctor. None was available, and if there was, he was often imbued more with superstition than science. In the sixteenth century Paré had reintroduced podalic version in cases of difficult position in childbirth, and Chamberlain invented obstetrical forceps early in the seventeenth. This invention was deliberately kept a secret, and handed down from father to son, but even if it had not been, it is very doubtful whether such refinements would have been available in the country at that time. Quacks of all kinds flourished in the towns and great reliance was placed in the apothecary, the white witch, and the housewife herself at the end of the seventeenth century.

In such conditions infant mortality continued high, and, of course, the chances of life were brief, though there are some well-authenticated cases of exceptional longevity. Funerals were consequently frequent. They were celebrated with all possible pomp and ceremony. The death bed was hung with black draperies and these were sent from one house to another as required by the most distant family relations. In well-to-do families mourners who came to pay their respects to the dead and condole with the living were given suits of mourning to wear at the funeral. Rings, gloves and scarves of sable hue were distributed to friends and relations, the total number presented being a measure of the social importance of the heir. Largesse was distributed to the poor, and a funeral feast provided. Everyone wished to have a proper funeral, and, as at weddings, extravagance often led to some financial difficulty, especially amongst the poorer people. Those often incurred expenses at such a time beyond the reach of their purses.

Attendance at funerals was a social necessity if the place was not too far from home. The cottage housewife would go to the next village, if she had relations there, the farm goodwife to neighbouring farms, the gentlewoman would travel across the county or to more distant places. For these journeys there was a special wardrobe. The lady who rode side-saddle or pillion was certainly warmly wrapped up. She wore a safeguard rather like an over shirt outside all—a hood, gloves, a scarf or possibly two or more, perhaps a vizard to protect the face. If she rode pillion she was provided with "Strappins", and a pillion cloth. Tiny babies were carried on a pillow placed before the saddle of an easy-going horse ridden by a servant. Lesser wives travelled on pack horses sitting between the packs, as they did when they went to market.

Farms, hamlets and tiny villages were often a long and lonely ride from the market town. Neighbours would go together for company and mutual protection, as there were dangers on the road for a woman who rode alone. One example will suffice. It could not have been isolated.

Maud, the wife of Thomas Collar, of Woolavington, went to Bridgwater market one day with goods to sell. She had a successful day. A local ruffian, Adrian Towes, of Marke, must have noticed this. He followed her on her way home, assaulted her, and demanded her purse. Another woman, who had been to market, came up and protested. Towes knocked this woman off the saddle into one of her panniers. The outcome was a charge before the Somerset Quarter Sessions in 1659. A close search of the Quarter Sessions records would certainly produce other cases of this kind, as of many other forms of petty and grand larceny.

The housewives who made these venturesome journeys were the wives of the poor husbandmen, the small tenant farmer and many of the class described by Gregory King in 1688 as "Freeholders of the lower sort". He estimated these to be 270,000 heads of families, whose dependants, wives and children, added to them, made a total of 1,410,000 persons out of a total population of about 5½ million. Some other figures from his table may not be irrelevant here. They are:—

	No. of families	No. of persons
Freeholders of the better sort	40,000	280,000
Clergy	10,000	52,000
Lords, temporal and spiritual ..	186	6,920
Baronets, Knights and Esquires ..	4,400	60,600
Gentlemen	12,000	96,000
Labouring people and outservants ..	364,000	1,275,000
Cottagers and paupers	400,000	1,300,000

Simplified still more King's figures show that of the estimated 5,500,000 population, 2,575,000 labourers and cottagers and their families lived in the country. They were employed by some if not all of the freeholders and farmers, whose families comprised another 1,690,000 rural people. Added to the workers they made 4,265,000, or

77$\frac{6}{11}$ per cent of the whole population. A great many of the gentlemen up to the rank of baronet must have lived in the country too, only a few of the more wealthy going to Court, so well over three-quarters of the people in England were country people, and of these at least 2,845,000 were farmers or farm workers' families whose wives lived in the way here described. One note is necessary. The large number of persons King put down as members of families of lords and gentlefolk included servants.

Gregory King estimated that the annual income of the farmers at £42 10s. and the lesser freeholders at £55 so they were in his eyes much on a level, the difference only making for additional comfort and leaving no spare cash for luxuries. A good many of both classes must have had smaller incomes, and the work of their wives in producing goods for market and carrying them to market must have made a very real contribution to the partnership.

The Reverend Richard Baxter, who wrote *The Poor Husbandman's Advocate to Rich Racking Landlords* in 1691 considered King's estimate rather high and suggested £30 downwards, while his modern editor suggests the class was defined by rents from £80 a year down to £5. Some comparison of the value of this range of income with wages is possible. At the Easter Sessions, 1688, the Bucks Justices set the wages of a chief baillif at £6 a year in the Chilterns, £5 10s. in the Vale. An ordinary farm servant got £4 10s. and £4. From the age of sixteen to twenty he was paid £3 and £2 10s., and from twelve to sixteen £1 13s. 4d. and £1. Cook maids and dairymaids were given £2 10s. a year; the other maid servants £2. Another measure of values is that mowers or reapers of corn and grass were paid 1s. 2d. a day, without meat and drink and 6d. if fed, making the value of a day's food 8d. Women haymakers only got 6d. or 3d. a day. Their food was only worth 3d.

All the housewives of these lesser freeholders and farmers, or poor husbandmen, must work both in the house and outdoors. The better off looked after their own dairy, their poultry, their flower and kitchen garden; the rest worked in the fields and meadows beside their husbands and family as another unit of unpaid labour, or for other employers to earn the tiny wages that the Statute ordered for them, less to the farmer than the cost of a man's daily food, and less than half that cost in money when the employer fed the woman.

The life of these housewives was harsh indeed, and they possessed skills beyond those of other women. Some of them were able to plough like their husbands. Sarah Fell of Swarthmore paid several who did this sort of work for her in 1676. Their ability to help in the hay and corn harvest has already been indicated in the statement of wages payable for this work. Housewives sheared sheep in Sussex and Norfolk and possibly elsewhere. Women all over Devon and Cornwall led the horses carrying home on their backs packs of hay that had to be held in place by a man on each side. Celia Fiennes thought these women and men toiled as savagely as their horses. Some housewives had by misfortune, the death of a husband or his absence, temporary or permanent, for any other reason, to take charge of farms and proved themselves capable managers. For example Adam Martindale's wife recovered the family from debt, kept a few cows and so on.

F.B., the writer of *The Office of the Good Housewife* quoted above, evidently expected the housewife to have as good a knowledge of farming as her husband. Every circumstance of her life tended to do this, it had all been lived on farms great and small.

F.B.'s exhortations were superfluous for the majority of farmers' wives. They would hardly need to be told to take care that the cows were provided with a bull, fat, well set together and "well meated", that he should have "a fierce Countenance and terrible to fight". In-calf cows she must not allow to run about too much and immediately before calving they must be kept in the house and fed on "good hay or Turnips, or such other Provender as the Country shall afford, not milking them at all for a good space before their calving". The detailed instructions for the care of new-born calves are much like modern precepts.

The writer had a great distaste for the swine. It was the most ravenous, most filthy and most harmful of all animals, but necessary and useful. They must be kept at open range under the watchful eye of a herd, and a "store of Acorns, Beans, Crabs, wild pears, or some other rotten fruit, or some manner of Pulse, or Coleworts, or boiled Turnips" must be maintained to feed them in wet weather. When they came home at evening they should be fed with a mash made with whey. A very modern note is struck in the advice that sties should be paved with stone or brick, well drained and well ventilated. Hogs must be kept highly fed to prevent cannibalism

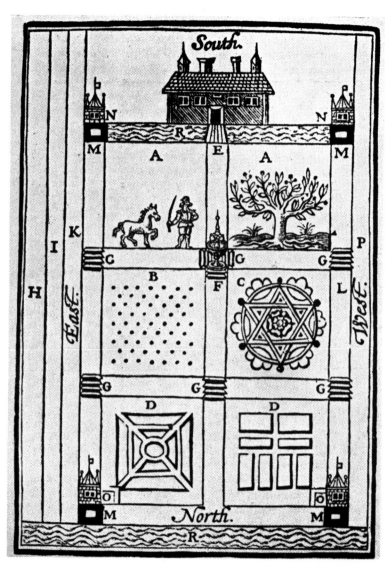

19. GARDEN LAY-OUT from Wm. Lawson's *The Country Housewife's Garden*, 1618. Note the Still Rooms at each corner with the flag flying

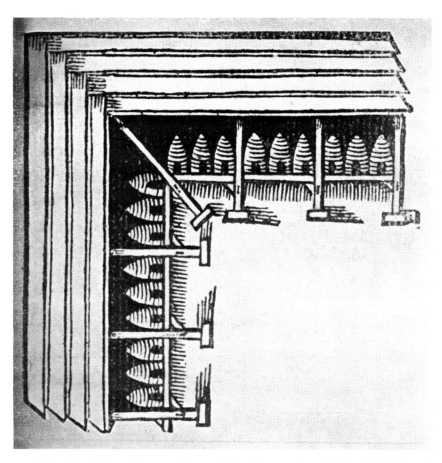

20. THE BEE-HIVE HOUSE. From Wm. Lawson's *A New Orchard and Garden*, 1618

21. A SURFACE DRAINAGE POND at Fressingfield, Suffolk, formerly used for drinking water. The steps were to facilitate dipping the bucket

22. The milkmaids' May Day Dance: from Misson's *Memoirs et observations faites par un voyageur en Angleterre,* 1698

23. FARMHOUSE KITCHEN: note the smoke billowing out into the room: from Knight's *Old England*, c. 1840

24. WOMAN AT WORK IN KITCHEN, seventeenth century: from Sheepshank's Collection, Vol. 10, D. VI

25. SQUIRE'S FAMILY in walled garden: from John Evelyn's
The French Gardiner, 4th ed., 1691

26. "THE WOMAN WORKS; the shepherd snores." From an old print used
for teaching a foreign language

27. WORK IN THE STILL ROOM: from John Evelyn's *The French Gardiner*, 4th ed., 1691

28. "THE WOMAN REAPS; the man sleeps." Another of the old teaching prints

29. AN ENCLOSED PLOT in a garden for growing melons. It is enclosed by a reed fence. From John Evelyn's *The French Gardiner*, 4th ed., 1691

30. BEATING FLAX OR HEMP, combing and spinning. From a set of old prints
designed to teach a foreign language

31. A FORMAL GARDEN just before the change in garden
fashion. From Chas. Evelyn's *The Lady's Recreation*, 1717

32. AN OPEN-AIR MUSICAL PARTY: from a drawing by Philip Mercier

33. THE PLEACHED ALLEY of an early eighteenth-century garden:
from Philip Miller's *Catalogus Plantarum*, 1730

34. Illustration to *Pamela*: from an engraving by L. Truchy after the painting by Joseph Highmore

amongst themselves, or, horrid thought, attacks upon children in cradles. White pigs should be kept for breed and the others killed for food. He did not think pickling was a good method of preservation, and recommended dry salting with bay salt and smoking over a wood fire.

The good wife, he went on, must have a good share in the oversight of the garden, both the vegetable and herb garden, and the garden of pleasure, if any. This was an opinion he shared with most other men, including Sir William Temple, who wrote in his *Garden of Epicurus*, 1685, "I will not enter upon any account of flowers, having only pleased myself with seeing or smelling them, and not troubled myself with the care, which is more the ladies' part than the men's; but success is wholly in the gardener". William Coles in his *The Art of Simpling; and introduction to the Knowledge and gathering of plants*, 1656, went even further, and exhorted even the gentlewoman to do some of the work themselves. His inspiring words were "Gentlewoman if the ground be not too wet, may doe themselves much good by Kneeling upon a cushion and weeding". The hardy housewife in the ordinary farmhouse would have disdained such refinement, if she had ever read the book or thought of it.

Stephen Switzer, a professional gardener who lived a little later, praised lady gardeners like the Duchess Dowager of Beaufort in his book *Iconographia Rustica*, 1718, but it is doubtful if that noble housewife ever went down upon her knees to weed her garden, not even upon a cushion. Her passion was the collection of exotics and foreign plants, and she made the Badminton gardens famous, devoting about two-thirds of her time to superintending them. Another noble lady gardener was "one of the Countesses of Lindsey" who had planted forest trees in proper order. She occupied herself, wrote Switzer, with rule and line and setting out the proper spacing of the young trees. Switzer, too, felt it obligatory to quote some of the verses of the Glorious Orinda, Mrs. Catherine Phillips, in praise of the peace and beauty of country life, to praise the new lay-out of the gardens at Hampton Court ordered by William III, as well as the Dutch garden at Kensington made by Queen Anne.

These great ladies were more concerned with the garden of pleasure, with beautifying their great parks and landscapes with the help of the famous professional gardeners, Mr. Rose, Mr. London and Mr. Wise, than with producing food in the kitchen garden. They, or their

G

gentlewomen, supervised the vegetable and herb garden too, but the actual physical work was done by their gardeners.

The yeoman's wife, often the gentleman's wife, worked herself at cultivating her simples, her flowers and her salad vegetables. The poor husbandman's wife invariably did all this work, and was rightly busier with growing food than flowers, though the old favourite flowers adorned many of the cottage gardens. Peas, beans and turnips, cabbage, parsnip and carrot were of more immediate and practical use to them than the less tangible delight of gazing upon the primrose and the gillyflower. The demand of their families for food was the urgent need that the poor husbandman's wife must help to supply, and one way to satisfy these hungry mouths was to grow vegetables.

Aesthetic pleasure in the garden was very much a secondary consideration. Every country housewife could find that pleasure in her surroundings. The clouds and the blue sky overhead were ever changing. With the passing of the seasons each year brought its expected changes in the appearance of the arable land. The wastes and the woodlands flowered and burgeoned and faded into autumn and winter. Wild flowers glowed in their variety, wild birds in larger numbers and species than those of today glorified the air with their songs. Conscious or self-conscious, appreciation of nature was probably not very widespread, but we can be certain that all these things were noticed and remarked upon as they invariably are in the modern countryside.

Clothes, too, were colourful. The red flannel petticoat and a garment rather like a waistcoat made of the same material was the common wear of country housewives in the eastern counties. On their heads they wore straw hats. "For the poor the outer garments alone sufficed," wrote Arthur Bryant in *The National Character*. "Beneath them and in their beds they wore nothing." Richer people had shirts and bedgowns.

In material ways the little farmer's wife and family were often terribly poor, but the Rev. Richard Baxter did not pity them for their hard work or coarse fare, so long as they had fire and clothes to keep them warm and enough wholesome food to eat. Their diet was limited in range. Baxter thought they could not afford to eat meat more than once a month, at most once a fortnight. A piece of hanged bacon they would gladly eat once a week if they could get it. The few that could kill an old bull, dried the beef in the chimney, and had a piece of beef at similar intervals. It must have been tough. Piglings, chickens, eggs, apples and pears, butter and cheese, must all be sold to obtain money to pay their rent. The family ate the less "vendible" produce, the poorer fruit, skim milk, and skim milk cheese and whey curds. "And," piously ended this reverend cleric, "through God's mercy all this doth them no harm."

The poorer housewife had little meat to cook at any time of the year. The richer was better off for meat, but it was still difficult to keep cattle alive during the winter. Consequently even the upper classes tasted little fresh meat for several months of the year, and were fortunate to be able to eat game and fish. The "hung" beef and mutton and bacon was only smoke dried in the chimney over the wood fire and on the rafters in the smoky kitchen. It had to be disguised with spices obtained by the rich from the world market at Amsterdam. The poor used strong scented and tasted herbs.

Most people used wood for their fires. It could be obtained locally from trees, hedgerow or wasteland. Coal was used in those places not far from the coast or on rivers navigable to the collier's hoys.

The trade in coal—sea cole as it was called because it was transported by sea—was not very large at the end of the seventeenth century, but it was growing. This was an important change, and made it necessary to alter the fireplaces in those houses where it was consumed. These began to take the basket form and finally the hob shape that became more usual in the next century. Most country people continued to use wood and, in places where there were not many trees, were reduced to drying cow dung for use as a fuel to the detriment of the pastures and fields which it ought to have manured. The method of drying was to plaster the stuff on the house wall, and this was remarked upon by astonished travellers in such widely separated places as Northampton and the Isle of Portland. It was probably used more in farmhouses than elsewhere, the great houses getting wood or coal, and the cottagers burning what furze or other wild rubbish they could collect on the grazing common and wastes. Goldsmith, years later, wrote that women went

"To pick her wintry fagot from the thorn,"

and a hundred years before the late seventeenth century, it had been necessary for the authorities at Lyme, Dorset, to order severe punishments for wood stealers, hedge tearers and pullers of trees. Some of these desperadoes were housewives in search of fuel with which to bake their bread. For a first offence they were put in the dark house, for a second in the pillory, for a third were whipped; so there must have been a good deal of fuel stealing in that district, if no other.

An old wife, and most cottage wives were middle aged at twenty-five, old ten years later, and decrepit, if not dead, between forty and fifty, staggering home under a faggot of brushwood was open to worse dangers than being accused of stealing. She it was who fell victim to the superstitious fear of witchcraft that came to a climax in the late Stuart period.

The rise of Puritanism had, as we have said, resulted in a decline in the position of women. The Puritans, like the ascetics of early Christianity, were obsessed with the wickedness of sex. Women, for them, were a temptation, both wittingly and unwittingly, and since Eve first picked the apple, women were more wicked than men, more liable to the assaults of Satan, and more easily drawn into the clutches of evil spirits.

Widows and single women of the poorer classes who lived alone in some tiny cottage away from the village, built perhaps surreptitiously on a bit of the waste and hidden among fern and gorse and bramble, were specially open to suspicion. Their appearance and habits, the result of poverty, and loneliness, made them the object of gibes and mockery by the village children and the hardly more adult grown-ups.

The grown-ups were quick enough to call the old witch in if they wanted help in illness of man or beast, or advice about an unprogressive love affair, help to conceal some petty crime and so on. These old wives took the place of the doctor and the midwife in the isolated villages. The healing art of nursing fell into her despised hands, equally if not more than into the hands of the squire's and yeoman's wife. Herbal lore was handed on from one to another verbally as it was among the higher classes. Perhaps it was more mixed with odd, often disgusting ingredients in the witch's cottage, though even that is doubtful. It was probably mixed with more superstition on the part of the patients, if not on that of their physician.

The possession of unusual knowledge and the power it supplies was envied on the one hand, suspected on the other. It must come from the devil, not from any good source. The wise woman was an emissary from the Prince of Darkness, never mind how often she used her powers to do good.

The belief in witchcraft was age-old, but with the increase of superstition that marked the rise of Puritanism, the antipathy to this supposedly evil art grew more pronounced. The Puritans believed that Satan himself inhabited the persons of witches and that they must be destroyed, but it was not till the second half of the seventeenth century that the persecution blazed forth in its maximum fury.

There had been prosecutions in the reign of James I. There was a great outbreak of persecution in Essex in 1645. Nineteen years later two lonely old women who lived in the tiny fishing village of Lowestoft were prosecuted at Bury St. Edmunds. They were feared and disliked and the children often tormented them. The adults treated them as outcasts and would not even sell them fish. The victims, certainly harmless except for an uncongenial appearance and temper, took refuge in curses and prophecies of evil to come. Some of the naughty children were taken with fits and said they saw the old women coming to punish them, a sure sign of an uneasy conscience. After eight years of accusations and a life of misery these unfortunate women were brought to trial and no less a person than Sir Matthew Hale, who presided at the trial, said he believed the Scriptures proved the reality of witchcraft. The poor women were hanged.

Some three thousand witches are said to have been executed legally during the sittings of the Long Parliament, and many others were murdered by inflamed and ignorant mobs.

After the Restoration scepticism on the one hand and the increase of real scientific knowledge on the other made things easier for such unfortunates, but it was not till 1716 that the last judicial execution for witchcraft took place in England. Even then the superstitious belief in the black art flourished in the villages, and any half-starved, decrepit old woman who lived alone in a retired place might be regarded as a witch, although she might not be overtly persecuted. If she was seen struggling to her home with a faggot she might look even more witch-like in the eyes of anyone who saw her as they hastened from her path.

Wood of the kind that can be taken from a hedge or furze bush was only suitable for heating the bake oven. Thin sticks might at a pinch boil a cauldron of pottage or a pudding. The delights of the tea kettle were as yet unknown in the cottage. Tea drinking was only slowly coming into fashion among the rich; the poor drank a thin kind of home-brewed ale or some other drink concocted by the housewife.

The cottager's roof tree remained much the same as it was a century before, and the housewife laboured under the same difficulties. A single room, without a chimney, was the whole. In it the family lived and slept, sharing some of its limited space with livestock, supposing they had any. Poultry, pigs, the cow, the ass or the pony shared the roof, and were only shut off by a partition, if they were shut off at all. A crowded habitation of this kind made the housewife's many tasks even more arduous than they were in a home where there was more space. Both women and men must have been glad to get out of "the house" to work, either on their own or some employer's land. The housewife must have returned reluctantly to her indoor work where convenience was mainly conspicuous by its absence. Her home "was bare indeed of the least vestige of adornment, and of the rudest furniture there was very little. A few rough deal chairs and a table (perhaps a board on trestles) and an oak chest of rude workmanship, that was all. The bed was a pallet of straw and of woollen covering, which was very expensive, there was none".

Nevertheless the cottage housewife did the same sort of work as all those in whatever grade of the village hierarchy. The lady of the manor, the squire's wife, like her husband, spent her life in the village or visiting relatives and friends in the neighbourhood or neighbouring counties. The Court was not for such as them. The marked separation between rural classes which was to become more clearly delimited as time went on, and the village grandees spent more time following the fashion of the London Season and the round of journeys demanded by the conventions of an increasingly wealthy and mobile class, was not yet. Village life was a routine controlled by the seasons for rich and poor alike, and where all had the same interests, distinctions were not invidious. It was quite possible for all to join in the jovialities which were customary at the religious festivals and upon several agricultural occasions.

CHAPTER FOUR

The Georgian Country Housewife, 1712–1760

JAMES I ORDERED the country gentlemen not to come to Court, and fined them if they did. He sent them home to get on with their country jobs, and the painful penalty of disobedience hit his ungrateful subjects hard where it hurt them most.

George I had no such arbitrary powers. When he arrived in England, the ladies of wealthy families, wives and daughters alike, were more than ever anxious to visit London and spend "the season" there. They wanted to be fashionable at the accepted time and place, and that was only possible in London during the winter months.

When they had succeeded in persuading their men folk, who may not have required a great deal of persuading, to accompany them to the metropolis, they were not anxious to go home. Husbands and fathers, who had tired of the expense and discomfort of lodgings in Town and were satiated with a round of dissipation, wanted to return to their familiar and enjoyable country life and pleasures. They must have had a pretty hard time imposing their wishes upon their reluctant females.

The disappointment of one young lady, who had to leave London after visiting the Coronation, was celebrated by Pope. This malcontent did not like country life, nor that,

"She went to plain work, and to purling brooks,
Old fashioned halls, dull aunts and croaking rooks,
She went from Opera, Park, Assembly, Play,

103

To morning walks and prayers three hours a day;
To part her time 'twixt reading and bohea,
To muse and spill her solitary tea,
Or o'er cold coffee trifle with the spoon,
Count the slow clock and dine exact at noon;
Divert her eyes with pictures in the fire,
Hum half a tune, tell stories to the Squire;
Up to her godly garret after seven,
There starve and pray, for that's the way to Heaven.
Some Squire perhaps you take delight to rack,
Whose game is Whisk, whose treat a toast in sack;
Who visits with a gun, presents you birds,
Then gives a smacking buss, and cries 'no words'."

This young lady aspired to a town life with little or no outdoor exercise, but sweetened with the admiration of poets and wits on whom she was sure she could make a deep impression with her beauty and sensibility, not to speak of her elegant coiffure, bright ribbons and fashionable frills and furbelows. She would have been happy enough if she had been that Stella, the adored of Swift, who could not refrain from repeatedly reproving her sedentary habits and her too great fondness for claret. He bade her exchange her toping and her bottle for a pair of good strong boots suitable for energetic pedestrian excursions. It is doubtful whether she took any heed of these pious exhortations. In general this change had been made before the middle of the eighteenth century.

Stella may have been more fond of claret than the majority, but there was a good deal of rather heavy drinking amongst the women. This was possibly a result of the tippling habits of the late Queen Anne, developed to assuage her many grievous bereavements, amongst which the early deaths of her children were the most poignant. It is certain that the increasing number of well-to-do women hankered after the joys of the metropolis.

These Town pleasures were changing, and were becoming more attractive to the ladies. They were being admitted to social affairs on a basis of equality with superior man. Dancing, that had been an occasional diversion, now became a daily pastime, "while the midday hours, in earlier times free from intrusion, offered entertainments to the pleasure seeker". Besides dancing there were other novel amusements that ladies could attend with or without masculine escort. They could go to the play. The *Spectator* remarked the political partisanship, demonstrated by a special fashion of wearing patches, of some of a female audience. Opera, too, had become a favourite diversion, and there was a constant succession of balls, both private and subscription. Tea and coffee drinking in public, at the coffee houses and in tea gardens, like those set up at Marylebone, were fashionable habits. All these developments led to a pleasant refinement of manners, something that had long been overdue.

The opinion has been expressed, not only in Macaulay's too forceful language, that until Queen Anne's reign a wife had been little more than the best of servants. Upon marriage she lost the power over her own person, her will and her goods, and had to depend for the joys as well as the necessities of life upon the kindness and consideration of her husband, a dependance that was normally fully justified.

Early in the eighteenth century men came to admire and even to demand in women, education, the peculiar ability to act as delightful hostess, the mastery of the art of flirtation, and in general a ready wit and repartee. To meet this demand "private enterprise" schools flourished and produced "finished" young women, the daughters of the rich who visited London—a class of severely limited number—"not unlike the modern flapper", modern, some thirty or more years ago. The more serious result of the education people like Defoe and Mary Astell had proposed in the late Stuart age was the "Blue Stocking" typified by Mrs. Montagu and Mrs. Vesey.

Swift had lamented that "not one gentleman's daughter in a thousand should be brought to read her own natural tongue or be judge of the easiest books that are written in it". *The Spectator* wrote that he was unable to recommend a list of books suitable for female perusal, and one of his correspondents begged him not to think of "nailing Women upon their Knees with Manuals of Devotion nor of scorching their Faces with Books of Housewifery".

Sir George Trevelyan sums up the condition of female education in *The England of Queen Anne*, 1934. "The want of education in the sex was discussed as an admitted fact, one side defending it as necessary in order to keep wives in due subjection, while the other side, led by the chief literary men of the day, ascribed the frivolity and the gambling habits of ladies of fashion to an upbringing which debarred them from more serious interests."

The latter must have had some justice on their side for Mary Astell had written:—

"When a poor young lady is taught to value herself on nothing but her cloaths and to think she's very fine when well accoutred; when she hears say, that 'tis wisdom enough for her to know how to dress herself that she may become amiable in his eyes, to whom it appertains to be knowing and learned; who can blame her if she lay out her money on such accomplishments, and sometimes extends it further than her misinformer intends she should. . . .

If from our infancy we are nurs'd upon ignorance and vanity; are taught to be proud and delicate and fantastick, humorous and inconsistant, 'tis not strange that the ill effects of this conduct appear in all the future actions of our lives. That therefore women are unprofitable to most and a plague and dishonour to some men is not much to be regretted on account of the men, because 'tis the product of their own folly, in denying them the benefits of an ingenious and liberal education; the most effectual means to direct them into, and secure their progress in the ways of vertue."

Far too much weight was placed upon the value of needlework, and it often had a bad effect upon the health. Children bent over such tasks at much too early an age, and extraordinary proficiency in needlework of a decorative rather than a useful kind was rarely the accomplishment of a young woman who did not suffer in her constitution, or so a contemporary writer on domestic medicine complained.

The Female Spectator, a periodical of the 1740s, entered a caveat against producing unwanted and superfluous domestic linen and woollen goods. The writer did not

"by any means approve of compelling young ladies of fortune to make so much use of the needle, as they did in former days, and some few continue to do. In my opinion a lady of condition should learn just as much of cooking and of work as to know when she is imposed upon by those she employs in both these necessary occasions, but no more. To pass too much of her time in them may acquire her the reputation of a notable housewife, but not of a woman of fine taste, or any way qualify her for polite conversation, or of entertaining herself agreeably when alone. It always makes me smile when I hear the mothers of fine daughters say, 'I always keep my girls at their needle'. One is perhaps engaged upon a gown, another a quilt for a bed, and a third engaged to make a whole dozen of shirts for her father. And then when she has carried you into the nursery and shown you them all, add 'It is good to keep them out of idleness; when young people have nothing to do, they naturally wish to do something they ought not'."

Addison had fully agreed. In an early number of *The Spectator* he wrote,

"I have often thought there has not been sufficient pains taken in finding out proper employment and diversions for the Fair Ones. The Toilet is their great scene of Business and the right adjustment of their Hair the Principal Employment of their Lives. . . . Their more serious Occupations are Sowing and Embroidery and their greatest Drudgery the Preparation of Jellies and Sweetmeats. This I say is the State of ordinary Women."

An advertisement of a school that appeared in his periodical on 2nd April, 1711, ran, "Near the Windmill in Hampstead is a good Boarding School, where young Gentlewomen may be boarded and taught English, French, Dancing, Music and all sorts of Needlework." Schools like this may not have been all that could be desired, but they were better than nothing, and probably provided instruction with more emphasis upon literary education than home training would. In the latter domestic duties and sewing and embroidery would be likely to take pride of place simply because they were the mother's main occupations.

There were, as always, exceptions. Elizabeth Elstob, "a Northern Lady of an ancient family and a genteel fortune", spent her life in the study of Anglo-Saxon. She produced a Grammar of that language, and she translated *Aelfric's Homilies,* but she did not make a fortune out of these works. Quite the contrary. Her brother had died, and there was then no women's college or school of a kind to employ a lady of these qualifications. She changed her name, and hid herself in the remote country to avoid imprisonment for debt. This subterfuge was quite successful, but was naturally of no help in adding to her reputation, or winning her a livelihood from her writings. Her refuge may have been in Worcestershire, and her employment that of a higher domestic in some great house. At length she received some royal bounty, and found employment as governess in the house of the Duchess of Portland. These vicissitudes were not a great encouragement for other ladies of the day to undertake works of scholarship as a means of earning a living.

Others did pursue learning as a recreation. A Mrs. Bland, a Yorkshire gentlewoman, studied Anglo-Saxon with Miss Elstob's book, and made herself so skilled in Hebrew that she taught it to her son and daughter. Her husband was an ordinary squire, and became Lord of the Manor at Beeston.

Miss Jane Barker of Wilsthorp, near Stamford, Lincolnshire, was another country lady who indulged in literary pursuits. She had been to Putney School until she was ten years old, and at fifteen had been sent to London to learn Town Politeness. She returned to the country and indulged herself in the composition of literary works, as she would herself have said. In 1723 she published, *A Patch work Screen for the Ladies; or Love and Virtue Recommended; in a collection of instructive novels. Related in a manner entirely new and Interspersed with Rural Poems.* This is not a work of any great merit, nor of much originality, but, like the poems that the lady contributed to *Poetical Recreations,* issued in 1688, the balance of which was written by Several Gentlemen of the Universities, shows that some ladies in the country, and well outside the charmed circle of the Blue Stockings, were interested in other things than housewifery and needlework.

Mrs. Barker was a woman of some strength of character. She had an unfortunate love affair and overcame this emotional disaster by occupying herself with the entire charge of her father's farm. She planned the work, hired the labourers, superintended the daily work that she had planned, paid the wages and kept the accounts. As ever, these wholesome interests of each day left no residue of energy for that indulgence in introspection, that is the frequent resort of a disappointed lover. All that it left was wholesome fatigue at night that was soporific in the evening and gave refreshing slumber.

Elizabeth Blackwell, who was an artist as well as a botanist, engaged in the preparation of a fine book in order to get her husband out of a debtor's prison. It was *A Curious Herbal containing five hundred cuts of the most useful plants which are now used in the practice of physic*. It appeared in 1737, in two volumes. Other than this admirable work, nothing is now known of the lady's life, except that she was the wife of Alexander Blackwell, M.D., an adventurer of the first water.

There were some other learned ladies, most of whom adorned the metropolis. In total number they were not many, and in proportion to the unlearned or those having accomplishments to show for their schooling—if they had any—were very few. Some country housewives had taken their tone from London. Developments there could not fail to have some influence upon the country lady.

The very rich and powerful travelled both to London and more frequently to their county towns, centres for the country aristocracy and for squirearchy activity. These leaders of rural society displayed their interpretation of fashionable behaviour in the Assembly Rooms of cathedral towns like York, Norwich, Worcester, Hereford, Exeter, Salisbury and of plain county towns like Derby, Leamington, Northampton and Warwick. They in turn were copied by the local lesser fry, whose efforts at imitating were all the less successful as they were diluted with the natural and habitual coarseness of bucolic manners in the remote countryside. At the lowest level this attempted assimilation of fashionable ways ceased to be effective, either because of absorption in the heaviness of the daily round, or lack of money or both.

But as Russell M. Garnier put it in his *History of the English Landed Interest*, 1893, the squire's womankind had discovered that embroidery was not the whole of female life. Some of them became fashionable, and took to politics and intrigue; some, on the other hand, remained mere drudges, as it seemed to him, though not to them, and devoted the whole of their existence to the kitchen and the still-room, as they had always done contentedly enough. Most, avoiding both extremes, devoted their time to raising the standard of comfort and intelligence in all those with whom they came in contact.

The *Rambler* remarks that in the days of *The Spectator* young unmarried ladies were content to be employed in the domestic duties, and it is true enough that *The Spectator* had declared that "Female Virtues are of a domestic turn. The Family is the proper Province for the private Woman to shine in." This is not quite the same thing as saying she was content, and elsewhere, as we have said, Addison

was severely critical of contemporary women who were neither housewives nor cultivated.

The *Rambler* continued in a strain that is and always was habitual
to people looking back to a supposedly simpler and therefore happier
life. "Then the routs, drums, balls, assemblies and such like markets for
women were not known. Modesty and diffidence, gentleness and
meekness were looked upon as the appropriate virtues and character-
istics of the sex."

One such lady *The Spectator* disguised under the name of Aurelia.
She was not one who was always talking of clothes and possessions;
she delighted in a country life, and her household was "under so regular
an oeconomy, in its Hours of Devotion and Repast, Employment and
Diversion, that it looks like a little Common-wealth in itself".

The majority of squires continued to look for paragons of this
kind, and acquired wives like her whom the *Vicar of Wakefield* married.
They chose their wives as the wives in turn chose their wedding gowns,
more to wear than to look at. The typical squire's housewife was she
who was hard to beat at pickling, preserving and cookery, capable of
reading any English book without much spelling, but at the same time
a lady, conscious of family and of heraldry and extremely conversant
with the "stud book". She was a living example of the highest breeding,
well aware of her own worth and proud of her exact place and
precedence, one who exercised her duties as well as her rights.

She would not have been embarrassed in the company of a great
lady like Sarah, Duchess of Marlborough, but would certainly have
shared her outlook, particularly towards wasteful amusements such as
the growing rage for horse-racing. The Duchess had heard a gentleman
say that the country was more hurt by the races than by a land tax.

"For the horses make great havoc with the corn wherever they
come, put all people of middling fortune to expenses they can't well
bear and all the young women lay out more than they can well
spare in the hope to get good husbands; which in general ends in
being debauched, or at least in making them not fit for other
matches which otherwise perhaps they could have got."

She would have been able to sympathize with the Duchess who lost
so many of her children in their early years, a son of smallpox at

Cambridge and three daughters, a common enough disaster in those days of child and youth mortality and grave epidemics. Elizabeth, the wife of the Earl of Bridgewater, died of the same fell disease, and her son died of it at Eton. It was no respecter of persons and places. Nearly every family suffered, and faces pitted with the small pox were a common and everyday sight.

All this goes to show that the wealthier countrywoman was changing her outlook in the first half of the eighteenth century. She, or more certainly her daughter, wanted to visit London in order to lead a fashionable life with her peers, especially during the winter months that were coming to be established as the Season. Distance and difficulties and expense of travel did not daunt these determined ladies. They came from Cumberland and Yorkshire, from Cheshire and Wales, and from the wilds of Cornwall and Devon. The call of the town was heard and answered by them all.

To London they would go in spite of all the physical obstacles and dangers of travel, the footpads and highwaymen and other more insidious rascality that frequented the ways. Roads were terrible. The main routes of travel were roughly along the lines of the ancient Roman roads, which had long since fallen into disrepair and in some places been lost track of. The by-roads were narrow lanes or open cartroads across wide acres of wastes or scrubby heath or boggy fen.

Along such roads powerful horses slowly dragged the massive family coach. The running footmen carried stout poles to help ease the coach out of bog holes or over difficult stretches. Overturns were not infrequent, broken linch pins or axles were all in the day's travel. In summer it was often more pleasant to walk beside the coach than to ride inside it; in winter the travellers huddled together wrapped in multitudes of coats and cloaks. It was very different travelling from the easy journeys we take in steam-heated trains or comfortable motor cars. York and Exeter were a week's hard travel from London.

Large sums of money must be carried not only to pay the bills of the innkeepers where the nightly stop was made, but because the family and their servants, coachmen, footmen, maids and often a cook, made up a large party. Often quantities of provisions were carried, and ladies like Sarah Churchill, Duchess of Marlborough, carried her own bed linen, plate and table ware. She could not abide that provided by the innkeepers. Lesser ladies took with them elaborate picnic baskets, examples of which can be seen in some of our museums. They tried their best to make themselves comfortable, but travelling, despite their hardy determination, was no picnic as contemporary fiction amply demonstrates.

Whether their husbands were so eager is another question. Matthew Bramble was not impressed by the pleasures or habits of the Londoner. If a lady could not persuade her husband or father to go to London the less wealthy could probably successfully impress upon the possibly reluctant male the necessity for visiting the local centre of fashion for a week or two. Such countrywomen, the leading lights of their village, the Lady of the Manor, were becoming less the housewife and more the lady of leisure. The duties of housekeeping, which she had shared so pleasantly, were beginning to be regarded as beneath the dignity of the female head of the house, and she was content to supervise in a rather more reserved way, possibly through the medium of her gentlewomen, or housekeeper.

Francis Grose, writing in *The Olio* towards the end of the century, described one of these.

"When I was a young man there existed in the families of most unmarried men or widowers of the rank of gentlemen, residents in the country, a certain antiquated female, either maiden or widow, commonly an aunt or cousin. Her dress I have now before me; it consisted of a stiff-starched cap and hood, a little hoop, a rich silk damask gown with large flowers. She leant on an ivory-headed crutch-cane, and was followed by a fat phtisichy dog of the pug kind, who commonly reposed upon a cushion, and enjoyed the privilege of snarling at the servants, occasionally biting their heels with impunity.

By the side of this good old lady jingled a bunch of keys, securing in different cupboards and corner closets all sorts of cordial waters, cherry and raspberry brandy, washes for the complexion, Daffy's Elixir [a widely used quack medicine], a rich seed cake, a number of pots of currant jelly and raspberry jam, with a range of gallipots and phials containing salves, electuaries, jalaps and purges, for the use of the poor neighbours. The daily business of this good lady was to scold the maids, collect eggs, feed the turkeys, and assist at all lyingins that happened within the parish. Alas! this being is no more seen, and the race is like that of her pug dog and the black rat, totally extinct."

It was not only in the households of bachelors or widowers that a housekeeper was employed and not always was she an old lady. Some ladies took a fancy to a nice young woman, made her a companion and brought her up to dress "above her station". One such was Richardson's *Pamela Andrews*, a fiction so truly drawn that Lady Mary Wortley Montagu recognized her as exactly resembling her own maid Fanny. Pamela must have been very real to be so convincing as that.

She was a young lady whose face and impregnable virtue proved her fortune. Her father was a day labourer and her mother added to the family income by spinning, a very ordinary couple of working villagers. Pamela was their only child. She must have been an engaging child, for when she became maid to Lady B. she made a great hit; became the lady's companion and was trained by her to appear in her company as a gentlewoman. This raising her above her station, though not altogether unusual, was not exactly a real kindness to such maids. It gave them tastes that a humble husband of their own class could hardly hope to satisfy and class was a situation most definitely marked in those times.

Pamela recognized this when she wrote "My lady's goodness had put me to write and to cast accounts and made me a little expert at my needle, and otherwise qualified me above my degree". She even learned to play the spinet.

When the kind lady died, her son made most determined onslaughts upon her virtue, which he hoped to find defenceless. He was sadly disappointed though he tried to suborn the virtuous maid by gifts of rich clothes from his dead mother's wardrobe. Pamela thought these garments of silk too rich and too good for her.

In fear of losing her virtue Pamela at length decided to go home to her parents, but she felt that she could not appear in the village in this silken array. She provided herself with clothing more suited to her station. The outfit consisted of a gown and two petticoats that she made herself from a "good sad coloured stuff" of quilted calico. She had a good camblet quilted coat, and she bought two flannel undercoats for use in case a neighbour should ask her to help with the morning's milking. She made two shifts of a pretty good Scots cloth of which she bought enough to make two more for her mother and two

H

shirts for her father. Two pretty round-eared caps, a little straw hat, a pair of knitted mittens, blue worsted hose with clocks and black leather shoes completed this rustic garb and seemed very proper to Pamela. It was probably more than the average village girl possessed.

Her escape was not to be so easy, but after several more unsuccessful assaults, including an attempted kidnapping on much the lines of *Clarissa's* abductor, this assiduous seducer declared himself defeated. He married the wench, a match that was greatly deplored by the local gentry.

Pamela wanted to live in the country, and her happy swain asked her how she could possibly fill up her time in the absence of town pleasures. She replied in her usual virtuous tenor:

"In the first place, sir, if you will give me leave, I will myself look into all such parts of the family management as may befit the mistress of it to inspect, and this I shall hope to do in such a manner as not to incur the ill-will of any honest servant.

Then Sir, I will ease you of as much of your family accounts as I possibly can.

Then Sir if I must needs be visiting or visited I will visit, if your goodness will allow me to do so, the unhappy poor in the neighbourhood around you, and administer to their wants and necessities.

I will assist your housekeeper as I used to do, in the making of jellies, comfits, sweetmeats, marmalades and cordials, and to pot candy, and preserve, for the use of the family, and to make myself all the fine linen of it, for yourself and me."

Pamela's proposed daily work was what many of the wives of the lesser squirearchy construed as their appointed tasks. They took a share in the actual household work, that of the dairy and the hen roost, just as housewives of their class had always done, and as the current economy of the small estate demanded.

These duties were, of course, the normal duties of the farmer's wife, but if the husband were a rich yeoman she might delegate the actual work to a servant just as the squire's wife did. There was indeed only the technical distinction between the poorer squire and the wealthier yeoman that the squire had the right to bear arms, and was often inordinately proud of it. Defoe in *The Compleat English Tradesman*, 1720, emphasized that ladies of good family, but small fortune, were so stiff upon the point of honour that they would not marry rich merchants.

A superior woman servant who could relieve the more extravagant of these ladies was not an expensive investment. In the early 1700s one who could take charge of brewing, baking, kitching, milkhouse or maulting was worth 40s. by the year and meat and drink if hired by a gentleman or rich yeoman "whose wife doth not take the pains and charge upon her". In spite of these low wages the majority of the wives of the smaller gentry or rich yeomen continued to take the pain and the charge. It would be what their husbands expected of them, and what they expected to do when they married.

Johnson in the *Rambler* described Lady Bustle whose "great business it was to watch the skillet on the fire, to see it simmer with the due degree of heat, and to snatch it off at the moment of projection. . . . She makes an orange pudding which is the envy of all the neighbourhood". She made it in secret having deployed her maids in other parts of the house, and she occupied herself happily in all the traditional jobs of the country housewife. It is a subject to which he returned from time to time, in order to show how dull the modish town lady would find life in the country.

Immediately after her husband's death Lady Bustle took charge of the farm.

"She soon disencumbered herself from her weeds, and put on a riding hood, a coarse apron and short petticoats, and has turned a large manor into a farm of which she takes the management wholly upon herself. She rises before the sun to order the horses to their gears and sees them well rubbed down at their return from work. She attends the dairy morning and evening; she walks among the sheep at noon, counts the lambs and observes the fences and where she finds a gap, stops it with a brush till it can be better mended. In harvest she rides afield in the wagon and is very liberal of her ale from a wooden bottle. At her leisure hours she looks goose eggs, airs the wool room, turns the cheese."

She was, in fact, a competent and painstaking farmer as so many country housewives have been when the like emergency arose.

Lady Bustle may have had justice on her side if her husband treated her like Squire Weston treated his wife.

"The Squire to whom the poor woman had been a faithful upper servant all the time of their marriage, had returned that behaviour by making what the world calls a good husband. He very seldom swore at her, perhaps not above once a week, and never beat her. She had not the least occasion for jealousy, and was perfect mistress of her time, for she was never interrupted by her husband, who was engaged all the morning in his field exercises and all the evening with bottle companions."

Mrs. Weston had accepted her due and proper subordination to her husband. She was one of many thousands who did so, and she received excellent treatment in return. Her husband ignored her and never beat her. Lady Bustle, if she had lived the same married life, and she probably did, though practical, kind and considerate marital partnerships were not unknown, must have rejoiced in her release. She must have found a happy outlet for her energies in the management of the farm.

In spite of Lady Bustle's energy and activity some of the farmers' wives were taking advantage of the times to secure for themselves a release from the more arduous duties their parents and grandparents had performed. Pehr Kalm, a Swedish visitor, who passed through England in 1748, was greatly impressed by the leisure enjoyed by the farmers' wives in Essex, Hertford and Kent. They had not cast off all housewifely duties, but nevertheless had sufficient spare time to be able to pay friendly, gossipy visits to each other.

When going out to call upon a friend they usually wore a red cloak.

"They also wore pattens under their ordinary shoes when they go, to prevent the dirt on the roads and streets from soiling their ordinary shoes. All go laced and use for everyday a sort of Manteau, made commonly of brownish camlot. The same headdress as in London. Here it is not unusual to see a farmer's or other small personage's wife, clad on Sundays like a lady of 'quality' at other places in the world, and her everyday attire in proportion. Paniers are seldom used in the country. When they go out they always wear straw hats which they have made themselves of wheat straw, and are pretty enough. On high days they have on ruffles."

He hardly ever saw a woman about outdoor duties such as tending stock in the arable and meadows.

"The duty of the woman in this district scarcely consists in anything else but preparing food, which they commonly do very well, though roast beef and Pudding forms nearly all an Englishman's eatables.

Besides that they wash and scour dishes and floors, etc., for about cleanliness they are very careful, and especially in these things, to wash clothes and to hem one thing after another minutely."

They did not need to take the trouble to bake because there was a baker in every parish or village from whom new bread could be bought, nor did they get sore fingers by much spinning, or arm ache or back ache from weaving. "It is the part of the manufacturers to make up for this and the men's purses are punished in this matter."

They had bishop'd the care of the cattle on to the men, "even to the extent that the carls commonly milk the cows (Ye Gods Yes)". When he first saw this he rubbed his eyes to make them clear because he could not believe he saw aright. The farmers' houses were full of young women while the men went out morning and evening, milk pail in hand, sat down to milk and afterwards carried the milk home.

"In short when one enters a house and has seen the women cooking, washing floors, plates and dishes, darning a stocking, or sewing a chemise, washing and starching linen clothes, he has, in fact, seen all their household economy and all that they have to do the whole of God's long day, year in and year out, when to these are added some visitors. . . . But they cannot be deprived of the credit of being very handsome and very lively in society. In pleasant conversation, agreeable repartee, polite sallies . . . they are never wanting."

England was indeed a paradise for ladies and women in his eyes as it had then been in the eyes of foreign visitors for some 250 years.

A stranger's observations are, however, likely to be coloured and, though Kalm doubtless saw what he described, there were still many country housewives living the same life as their mothers and grandmothers had, especially in counties more distant from London and less visited by travellers from Europe. Kalm makes one small admission. Though the mistresses and their daughters enjoyed perfect freedom from work "the common servant girls have to have somewhat more work in them".

The beauty, particularly the fine complexions of the Essex women, greatly impressed several other foreign tourists who landed at Harwich and journeyed to London. They did not cross the marshes where the women died like flies, and where men frequently had ten or twelve wives in succession if the story "a merry fellow" told Daniel Defoe is true. The marshmen went to the uplands in search of fresh complexioned wives, but the fogs and damps of their new homes soon finished them off, upon which the undaunted but heartless widowers bent upon the same quest, would pay a renewed visit to the uplands. Marrying of wives was "a kind of good farm" to them.

Kalm's comment upon the industrious wives' washing of clothes is an indication of a change of fashion causing a change of habit. The growth of overseas trade in the late seventeenth and early eighteenth century had brought many novel goods to the market. The use of tea and coffee has already been mentioned. Now the East Indiamen brought home increasing quantities of cotton fabrics, calico and so on, and these were rapidly adopted for dress materials. These were much lighter and easier to wash than the heavy woollen garments previously worn, and encouraged habits of cleanliness formerly unknown. This must not be exaggerated. Most people were still lousy. If one person was not, she ran the risk of being infected on a visit to a bosom friend, like the people who visited in James I's time.

This is difficult to believe, but we commend scoffers to the contemplation of the back scratchers preserved in many museums. A shrewd commentary on personal habits was made by Thomas Turner, the Sussex diarist, who declared that it was good for the health to take a bath, a purge and a blood letting in the spring. This treatment got rid of all the "humours" piled up by poorly balanced diet in the bad weather.

Baths were not, in fact, to be found in most houses and facilities for washing in the bedrooms were conspicuous by their absence. Rich men did no more to provide a basin and ewer in every bedroom than they had ever done. Lord Dorset, it will be remembered, had only one in his great home at Knole a hundred years before this time. The passing of this century had made little difference. None at all was owned by a rich squire, a baronet and a very wealthy commoner in 1727. If these people washed they did so under the pump in the yard as Alderman John Boydell did in London town. Boydell was the famous publisher of mezzotints, and lived in Ironmonger Lane throughout the major part of the eighteenth century.

Whether they washed themselves frequently or infrequently, the change in the material used for women's clothes made them more washable. Besides that a printed calico would look much more bedraggled than a more substantial woollen dress if worn crumpled and dirty. The woollen material would hold its shape better even if it was dirty. Perhaps the camlet made of wool and silk would do so as well. Calico was therefore washed.

There was another factor that helped to decide how much washing should be done. Soap was necessary, and though there were some soap-boilers it had always been the custom to make soap at home.

In a time when most country houses were warmed by a wood fire and the heat for cooking was obtained from the same material a lye could be made from the ash. Unfortunately the lye had to be mixed with tallow (mutton fat), or some other similar grease, to solidify it and help to make it scour. But mutton fat was wanted for making rushlights and candles as well as soap. Supplies were not very plentiful because mutton was not eaten too freely, and the housewife was faced with the problem whether to make rushlights and candles for use in the early morning and winter evening, or soap to wash herself and her clothes. The balance must nearly always have been in favour of light at the expense of soap.

The choice was not, of course, so restricted in great houses where wax candles, either bought or made from the produce of the hive, were used, particularly on special occasions. In these houses, too, more meat was eaten and so there was more tallow.

Soap making with wood ash and tallow was a simple though tedious task. It was of two kinds, hard soap and ordinary soap. Though the former could be made at home it was more commonly bought. It was known as India, Venice, Marseilles, Castile and London soap, doubtless from its place of origin. It was made with a lye of pot-ashes so thick as to float an egg. Twenty pounds of this were mixed with two pounds of goat's or sheep's fat and boiled for an hour, "or so long till it come to a due consistency". Next it was strained while hot through a linen cloth into a "Broad" earthen or pewter vessel where it was left to get cold. When it was quite cold it could be cut into blocks or bricks and then the soap was ready for use.

The ordinary soap that was made in the farmhouse and cottage was a little more complicated. It was made by mixing three parts of oak or beech ashes with one part of quicklime. The ashes were moistened a little and then the quicklime was mixed "layer on layer" with them. This mixture was put in a large vat and left while the lime slaked. When it ceased to "make a noise" it was moistened a little more. Then "with a sufficient quantity of boiling water, extract the fiery Lixivitous Lye, commonly called by the Workmen, the *Magical* or *Capital* Lye". This must be strong enough for an egg to swim in, a very usual method of testing the density of a solution. This must be drawn off. Another lye, not quite so strong, was then made of the same materials and the oil, fat, lard or tallow mixed in. This was boiled over a slow fire till it grew white. At this point *Capital* lye was added at the rate of three times the quantity of fat used. The whole was boiled till it coagulated.

If it tasted sweet more *Capital* lye was required; if "biting" it had not been boiled enough; if "more than ordinary pungent" more oil should be slowly added. When it had been boiled until it began "to roap and run clear and transparent from the ladle", the job was nearly done. Just go on boiling for another three hours.

Making a batch of soap must have taken nearly, if not quite, a whole day. It was more complicated than making the rushlights and candles that competed for the available tallow and the time occupied in making must have been something of a discouragement. Industrious housewives made it when supplies of fat permitted and were stimulated to do so by the needs of their new calico gowns. Many must have wished to buy soap as they could so many other things.

If they could have done so they would have been spared the pain of making it, and they would have had more tallow for rushlights, thin candles whose wicks were peeled rushes. Lights of this kind were of immemorable antiquity, and were always made at home.

Aubrey, writing in 1673, makes the manufacture of rushlights sound a very simple matter. He said that at Ockley in Surrey, "the people drew peeled rushes through melted grease, which yields a sufficient light for ordinary use, is very cheap and useful and burns long". This economical practice continued until the middle of the nineteenth century amongst the smaller farmers.

Making rushlights needed care and patience as well as practice. We should not try to improve upon Gilbert White's description of the process in the *Natural History of Selborne*.

"The proper species is the common soft rush, found in most pastures by the sides of streams and under hedges. Decayed labourers, women and children gather these rushes late in summer; as soon as they are cut, they must be flung into water and kept there, otherwise they will dry and shrink, and the peel will not run. When peeled they must lie on the grass to be bleached and to take the dew for some nights, after which they are dried in the sun. Some address is required in dipping these rushes into the scalding fat or grease. The careful wife of a Hampshire labourer obtains all her fat for nothing; for she saves the scummings of her bacon pot for this use . . . where hogs are not much in use, and especially by the seaside, the coarse animal oils will come very cheap. A pound of common grease may be procured for fourpence; and about six pounds of grease will dip a pound of rushes, which cost one shilling, so that a pound of rushes ready for burning will cost three shillings. If men that keep bees will mix a little wax with the grease it will give it a consistency, render it more cleanly and make the rushes burn longer; mutton suet will have the same effect."

It was calculated that there were 1,600 rushes to a pound and that each burned for half an hour, or 800 hours in all.

Special holders were used with the rushlights just as various types of candlestick were used with the more substantial tallow candle that was moulded round a cotton wick suspended in a hollow cylinder. These were used by the richer folk or for festivities when a brighter light than usual was wanted.

Though it was possible in some places to buy the grease used for making candles or for soap, the majority of farm and cottage housewives confined themselves to supplies produced in the household. Necessarily, as we have said, supplies of tallow made in the farmhouse were small, and in the cottage negligible, and the housewife had to decide between the virtue of light in winter mornings and evenings and cleanliness of person and clothing. Probably she decided on a compromise and made some candles and some soap. If she had the money she could buy soap from the grocer in the market town, but economy was a necessity in most farmhouses, especially the smaller ones, and it was decidedly better to make the things at home in spite of the extra work. Unpaid labour of the housewife and her daughters cost nothing but fatigue.

It is quite certain, too, that the large majority of farm and cottage housewives still made the family clothes from the spinning of the wool or flax to the completed garments. This work was not, however, still necessary everywhere. Manufactured materials could be bought from the pedlar who called at the door, or from the store set up at the annual fair in the neighbouring market town. The complete self-reliance of the rural household was being subtly undermined by the commercial production of clothing and other things for sale.

Itinerant merchants would be ready to sell Spitalfields silk for the richer woman's gown and petticoat, chequered stuff made at Bristol or Norwich for her bodice, black calamanco from Norwich for an under petticoat, and a material made of flannel and swanskin in Wales and at Salisbury from which the inner and final petticoat was made. Stockings were made at Leicester and Tewkesbury, lace at Stoney Stratford, edgings at Great Marlow, and muslin was imported. Gloves were made in Somerset; shoes at Northampton. All these things were to be found in the country town; all that was necessary was to have the money to pay for them. Most of the rural housewives were constrained to rule out the purchased manufactured material for the sake of the pennies they must save at the expense of their own tired fingers.

They did their daily work clothed in a petticoat or two, and a bodice, a pair of worsted stockings and low shoes. If they went out into the surrounding mud they wore a cloak and bonnet and fitted pattens over their shoes to keep them out of the mud. Clogs were in general use in the dairy and kitchens in the north, whereas in Wales and other districts remote from London, the homely habits of an earlier date prevailed until well into the nineteenth century. Purchases were often limited to hats and shoes.

Farmhouse and cottage furniture was made by the village carpenter, or the simpler pieces fudged up by the man of the house, who was the same clever handyman as so many of our country dwellers are today. It was none too plentiful and was quite simple in design.

Housewives in these homes did not require the art of carving in its varied and eclectic complexity as did the ladies in the manor houses. Better for them that they should know how to send to the table a boiled artificial pheasant, a dainty dish made of rabbit disguised in trussing it. It had been invented by a Mrs. Johnson who kept an eating house in Devonshire Court near the Temple in London. A boiled cabbage pudding of the kind made in Suffolk was another dish that deserved to be more widely known amongst country housewives. It was made with raw or underdone salt beef, chopped small. An equal quantity of boiled cabbage, also chopped small, was added to the beef and the whole seasoned with pepper and salt. Two or three eggs were beaten up into it to mix it in the manner of forced meat. Any other seasoning handy might be added, and when all was beaten into a thin paste it was tied up in a linen cloth and boiled. The pudding was supposed to be about the size of half a quartern loaf, and if made with partly cooked meat, must be boiled an hour, if with raw meat an hour and a half. It was served with butter and gravy and lemon juice.

Cakes and biscuits of great variety were made by these clever housewives. Biscuits from potatoes, then only in the infancy of popularity, were one dish now forgotten, though the quantity of sugar required would prevent us from making them. The potatoes were boiled in their skins till tender, peeled and the pulp mixed with its own weight of fine sugar. A little butter, some mace or cloves finely sifted, was added "and a little Gum Dragon steeped in Orange Flower Water, or Rose Water". The whole was beaten up together in a stone mortar till it became a paste and then dried in a gentle oven. Parsnip cakes were made by drying thin slices of parsnip in the oven and beating them to powder. An equal quantity of flour was added to this powder and mixed to a paste with cream and spices. The cakes were baked in a gentle oven. "The sweetness of the parsnip," it was advised, "answers the want of sugar."

Examples of simple recipes of this kind could be almost indefinitely multiplied. Many of them might serve today, though some ingredients might have to be changed slightly or reduced in quantity. Doubtless the economical housewife used her judgement in precisely that way two hundred years ago. She must often have been short of the more unusual condiments and of the luxuries. The number of eggs used in a dish was limited by her stock of preserved eggs or the number of fruitful hens she kept; the quantity of cream she could use was restricted by the demand upon that article for making butter for sale and for domestic use.

Many things had two or more uses in the home, and careful judgement had to be exercised in deciding how much of the raw material should be used for each purpose. If the article was one that could equally well be sent to market as used in the home, the imperious need for a little cash in hand often weighed down the balance in favour of sale. The household could go without.

The lot of the small farmer was hard; that of his wife almost harder. Work was day-long and wearing despite the variety of tasks that had to be crowded into a waking period of eighteen hours. There was little respite, though there might be a few minutes here and there to gossip or to stand. The lesser farm housewives were little different from the wives of the labourers. The distinction was, in fact, often almost impossible to draw so imperceptibly did the one merge into the other class.

For the husbandman or cottager it was impossible to live unless the women and children worked. Political wisdom of that time assumed that it was a benefit to the nation if the women and children were obliged to work. It was naturally beneficial to the family at a time when the man's wages were regulated at a level that would not maintain himself and his family without their supplementary earnings.

Before marriage these housewives had usually been the "common servant girls", to whom the more well-to-do farm housewives were beginning to depute their proper work, and for whom Pehr Kalm had a word of praise. This was not too enthusiastic. He only went so far as to say that these young women had "somewhat more work in them" than their mistresses.

Both the girl and her prospective husband had lived-in while single, and although wages were small expenses except for an annual fairing or so, were almost nil. If thrifty (and such people were almost excessive in their thrift), there were good prospects of marriage, renting a cottage and working for themselves. Often enough marriage was heedlessly entered into because the couple had little or no foresight, or the connubial bond was more or less forced upon them by the impending birth of a child.

If there was no cottage to be had in the village, or the young couple had insufficient capital to take over an existing holding of the smaller size, they could build themselves a hut on the village waste for a few pounds' worth of timber. With the help of the man's friends four walls were built, a roof of thatch put on and a chimney to one side. Should all this be accomplished in the dark of the night the young couple believed that they could not be disturbed by the village authorities. Such a building was known as a "one night house", and many were built all over the country, usually in the counties more distant from London.

Once established in a cottage on the waste the man could enclose a bit of land for cultivation either with or without the consent of the manorial or parish authorities. On such a holding, and their number had increased and multiplied through the centuries, the man worked for wages when he could get day work. He left the care of any stock and the cultivation of the little enclosure almost entirely to the women and children. They were the happy maids remarked by Dorothy Osborne and Isaac Walton a century before. Even if the husband succeeded in obtaining the tenancy of an acre or two the same conditions prevailed in his household.

While the man was working either on his own piece of land in the village arable fields or elsewhere, if he had any, or for wages if he had none, his wife and family had to seize every opportunity of helping to get the family living. How much they could add from the husband's privileges, if any, on the commons and wastes of the manor, depended, first on the livestock they owned, and second on their care and industry in looking after it. The value of the grazing and other privileges on the wastes was a subject of great controversy both then and later. And truly watching a cow or two, a few goats, a donkey or some poultry, as they wandered at will through the furze and brambles trying to pick up a living, was not a very arduous employment.

Most of the contribution the housewife and the children made in this way was to the cooking pot, although anything beyond home needs was sold in the local market in order to secure a little money. For example, if the family owned a cow, the wife had cream for butter, milk for cheese and skim milk for porridge. Goat's milk could be used for the same purposes, and ewes were milked as well by the peasantry, for drink and cheese making. If there was a pig or two, the occasional slaughter yielded offal in all its manifold forms as well as pork and bacon, both of which were very sparingly used. At long intervals an old hen beyond laying or an ancient cockerel might be spared for the pot, and if there were poultry there were eggs. Bee-keepers, and they were many, could make mead or eat honey. The produce of the little plot of arable or garden, supplemented by gleaning in other people's cornfields after harvest, provided bread corn, which was milled locally and baked in the cottage oven heated by furze gathered on the common.

This description makes it sound a halcyon life, but there were many hardships and shortages that would bear heavily on modern people. Addison had seen how misguided some of the town-bred enthusiasts for life in a country cottage were. "People who live in cities," he wrote, "are wonderfully struck with every little Country Abode they see when they take the Air and 'tis natural to fancy that they could live in every neat Cottage (by which they pass) much happier than in their present Circumstances." Many modern people have been bitten by the same phantasy. They see the cottage embowered in pretty flowers and shining in the summer sun. They do not realize its dampness in the winter, the chill of its brick, stone or tile floor, the inconvenience of the sloping roof of the bedroom on which the outside thatch looks so romantic. The lack of running water, of any attempt at sanitation, were things to which our ancestors were all accustomed, and which they accepted as of use and wont; but even they would have probably felt differently if they had deserted the town for a humble country cot.

The cottages were scantily furnished. Most families had only one table, or at most two, two or three chairs and possibly a bench or settle, perhaps only a stool or piece of thick tree trunk for each child. For cooking, a pot, a kettle and a frying pan was all. A few pewter or wooden plates, a porringer or so, formed the table ware. A spinning wheel was to be found in most living rooms. Above stairs, if there were any stairs and not a ladder, was a bed with a flock and a feather mattress, a bolster and pillows, a sheet or two and some blankets with a coverlet for all. The children would not have beds, but slept upon a flock upon the floor. A cofer and a pair of bellows often figured in the miscellanea of inventories. It was not much; but perhaps this did not matter when all the family were out all day employed upon their different tasks.

One of the tasks, to which the children were often set to work, was gathering wild fruit and nuts in their season. Nothing possible was neglected. Blackberries are still gathered "from hedgerow and common bramble". Then elderberry was gathered for wine and puddings. Wild strawberries grew in profusion in some places. Crab apples and bullaces could be found by the wary. Sloes made wine or were used to disguise the rawness of gin that itself could be made from juniper berries. Many flowers were gathered for wine-making and many now neglected leaves like dandelion were collected for salad. Some species of nettles were used as a vegetable. The children could wander at large and collect these things and were set a specific quantity as employment of a definite time. For instance an old gipsy whose family was squatting on a Surrey common some twenty-five years ago and who was himself at least seventy years old then, has told us that when he was a child he was sent out to gather whortleberries (locally hurts). He dared not return until he had gathered a quart under penalty of thrashing—a big job for a little boy and heavy discipline. This can only be an example of a long-established habit, and there is every reason to suppose that the children of cottagers were made to work in the same way as those of the gipsies.

The daughters of the cottagers could obtain employment as dairy-maids in many parts of the country, even in the Home Counties like Essex, where Kalm, the Swedish traveller, believed the women had "bishopped" all this work upon the men. The system that he observed in Essex was for the cows to be milked in the pastures where they were grazing by the men both morning and evening. The men carried the milk home, and handed it over to the girls. The latter put it into wooden vessels in winter, but in large square leaden boxes, four to six inches deep, in summer. Some milk was sold to people who did not keep cows, the surplus being treated in this way. The cream was skimmed and made into butter in tub-shaped churns that the maids turned round by a handle. The skim milk was sold to the poor or used to fatten swine. In other counties the young women milked the cows and brought home the milk as well as carrying it round for sale. Of such parentage doubtless came the Marion praised by Gay:—

> "Marion that soft could stroke the udder'd cow,
> Or lessen with her sieve the barley mow,
> Marbled with sage; the hard'ning cheese she press'd."

In Yorkshire and other woollen districts, the Eastern Counties, Gloucester and the South West and Wales, nearly all the husbandman's, cottager's, and squatter's housewives added to the minute money income of the family by spinning, or some similar home employment. Kalm only saw Essex, Hertford and Kent, and if the women did nothing but housework and cooking in those counties they were quite exceptionally favoured. Lace-making was a by-employment in Bedfordshire. Here as in Buckingham, Hertford and the adjoining counties, a good deal of straw plait was woven in the homes of the cottagers; perhaps for the hats of wheaten straw that Kalm saw on the heads of well-dressed women. Again there was some spinning of linen and woollen thread. This was sent to the local weaver, of whom *Silas Marner* was a slightly later example, and came back as material ready to be made up into all sorts of clothing and articles for household use.

At busy seasons of the year the housewife and the children could get work in the fields. At hay and corn harvest their strength was indispensable; at other times of the year they could earn a little at stone-picking, weeding and spreading manure. The actual monetary reward for all this industry was very small. At harvest 6d. a day was paid to a grown woman; the children got even less. Two shillings for a full week was probably the maximum a woman could earn, though she might get a meal each day and drink in addition. Her husband got a shilling a day when employed. But little money was necessary for people, most of whose scanty needs were provided by themselves, and who lacked the modern inducements to spending. A little was wanted to provide against illness, mishap, bad seasons, the death of a beast, but such families could normally rub along contentedly enough with none. If they did fall into destitution, they were in some meagre sort taken care of by the parish. Meanwhile they lived, contented with very little.

35. Busy DAIRYMAIDS, milking, churning, fetching water, etc.: from Richard Bradley's *The Country Housewife*, 1736

36. MILK DELIVERY IN THE EIGHTEENTH CENTURY. The pails here are covered, but many were just open buckets. The measures hang round the bucket. The whole must have been very heavy. Drawn from a contemporary picture

37. DUCKING CHAIR at a village well: from an old print

38. PROPER DRESS for an industrious working-class
woman. From *The Hymns*, etc., used in the Magdalen
College, c. 1730

39. THE FARMER'S DOOR: after George Morland, 1790

40. THE SQUIRE'S DOOR: after George Morland, 1790

41. A PARLOUR FIRE: basket grate in an open fireplace. Tongs, poker, etc., resting in dogs. In use about a century ago

42. AN EIGHTEENTH-CENTURY KITCHEN: from a contemporary cookery book

43. "A matron old, whom we Schoolmistress name,
Who boasts unruly brats with birch to tame"
Frontispiece to Shenstone's *Poems,* 1812 ed.

44. An eighteenth century Mop Fair: from a contemporary drawing

45. THE FARMYARD: after Henry Singleton, 1790

46. THE TITHE PIG: after Henry Singleton, 1793

47. PUMP once standing at Hammersmith (London), apparently used by the academic fraternity. From an early nineteenth-century print

48. THE VILLAGE PUMP at Fressingfield, Suffolk: still used

49. DR. SYNTAX AND THE DAIRYMAID: from Dr. Syntax's *Tours in Search of the Picturesque*, 1812. Showing cheese-press, butter-churn and creaming dishes. Drawing by Rowlandson

50. MAKING OATCAKE in a farmhouse kitchen: from Walker's *Costume of Yorkshire*, 1814

51. SPINNING in a cottage kitchen: from Walker's *Costume of Yorkshire*, 1814

Our pastoral poets like Gay were only too prone to praise the countrywoman. He wrote:—

"What happiness the rural maid attends
. . . And rich in poverty; enjoys content—
. . . She never feels the spleen's imagined pains,
Nor melancholy stagnates in her veins;
She never loses life in thoughtless ease,
Nor on the velvet couch invites disease;
Her home spun dress in simple neatness lies . . .
And health, not paint, the fading bloom repairs."

He was right enough in saying that she did not lose her life in thoughtless ease. She had too much to do for that, or to become diseased through laziness. All the members of the family, father, mother and children, did a long day's work compared with their descendants in an industrial world, but there were plenty of intervals between one job and another, and the work could be done at their own pace.

Some of the squatters, who carved out little holdings on the wastes or in the forests, led their lives in the most ghastly isolation and loneliness very little different from that of settlers in a new country. Sometimes they suffered from neighbours just like the homesteaders of the Wild West a century later.

A traveller lost and benighted in Charnwood Forest in the year 1750 wandered desperately on through five miles of uncultivated waste without a road. At last he found a building which unfortunately he did not describe. In it lived a family. The man was tall and strong, his wife young, handsome, ragged and good natured. They had a family of three children and maintained "a hideous aunt". They were desperately poor, partly because a mob of freeholders, jealous of their rights of grazing in the forest, had destroyed his outbuildings and so prevented him from keeping beasts to graze upon the commons. They had no candle in the house, and a fire that would hardly have roasted a potato. There was nothing to eat in the house, except some pease pottage that they were ashamed to offer the wanderer, though he was glad enough to accept it. For bedclothes he was given the housewife's petticoat. She robbed her bed to supply his. Their condition was no

I

better than many another in that poverty-ridden age, but was perhaps the worse from the kindly action of their better-off neighbours.

Gay satirizes the difference between the landlord's diet and the workers' in the passionate declaration of his lovesick shepherd.

> "In good roast beef my landlord sticks his knife,
> The capon fat delights his dainty wife,
> Pudding our Parson eats, the Squire loves hare
> But white-pot thick is my *Buxoma's* fare;
> Whilst she loves white-pot, capon ne'er shall be,
> Nor hare, nor beef, nor pudding, food for me."

Whitepot could hardly have been Buxoma's sole nourishment because it was made partly of purchased goods. It was a dish made of cream, sugar, rice, currants, cinnamon, etc., and was a great favourite with Devonshire people. If made with barley or whole wheat it would have been more readily to the hand of the average cottager, whose diet varied in different parts of the country.

Whatever their diet it was always simple and often exiguous, and they worked long and hard to win it. And though the richer ladies, wives in the castle, manor houses and great farms were beginning to set aside any actual participation in the daily task, self-sufficiency was still, to a very large extent, the controlling factor in the life of the country house, farm and cottage.

It was only in the degree that the great lady and her more well-to-do imitators had withdrawn already that the future was to be discerned, when the rich would frequently, and finally almost always, be absent from the village. Then there would cease to be the same community of interest between all who lived in the village and shared its life, and the stratification of rural society would become even more marked than it had been.

CHAPTER FIVE

The Country Housewife under George III

NEW THINGS, crops and machines, rotations, even, in a very elementary way, new methods of breeding livestock, were gradually introduced to farmers from the date of the return of Charles II to his father's throne. Most of them were more talked about and written about than practised by the farmer; but the talking and writing had its effect.

And more and more new things were coming into the country from overseas. Tea and coffee, cotton goods and mahogany, tobacco and sugar were becoming everyday necessities in a growing number of households. They must be bought, and the landowners, who were the wealthy and the rulers, found heavier demands upon their pockets. They must increase their rent rolls, but before they could do so the farmers must earn more money in order to pay higher rents. This they could only do in better conditions upon enclosed farms, and by adopting improved methods to give them bigger harvests of grain, better milking cows and beef cattle, larger sheep with heavier fleeces and monstrous fat pigs.

As farming conditions got better and more profitable, agriculture aroused more and more enthusiasm, both as an agreeable life and a way to get wealthy. Farming, indeed, became all the rage when George III, himself proud of his nickname, Farmer George, was King. A new era had opened when landlord and tenant alike were making money and were consequently ardent in pursuing it; so how could the ladies escape it.

It was the age of Arthur Young, the first of whose two hundred and

131

fifty volumes on farming appeared in 1767; of Sir John Sinclair, who organized *The Statistical Account of Scotland*, and wrote many other works, including *The Code of Agriculture*; of Coke of Norfolk, the rental of whose estate rose from £2,000 to £20,000 a year because he "improved" it. Everywhere there was experiment, a trying of this and that, many failures, but enough success to stimulate a continued enthusiasm.

The wives of the great landowners were still nominally responsible for the management of their great establishments, but had, in fact, now deputed most of their duties to hirelings, housekeeper, steward and what not. Many of them played a purely decorative part in life like Lady Elizabeth Craven, who as a new-born baby was so nearly sat upon by Lady Albermarle. She had been laid casually on her mother's bedside chair. Lady Albermarle took the bundle on the chair for a piece of flannel, and was just going to sit on it. Only the terrified screams of the nurse prevented a catastrophe. They might very well have precipitated one.

The infant was rescued from complete neglect by the lady who had nearly flattened her. She had been told of the parent's disappointment at the birth of another girl, one so puny that she was not likely to live and not worth making any fuss about. Lady Berkeley had already had female triplets before the birth of Elizabeth, and only wished for a son and heir. Lady Albermarle took up the cudgels for Elizabeth, declared that she would live if properly looked after, sent for a wet nurse and saved the life of the infant she had so nearly destroyed. The miserable-looking baby, whose nurse and mother had almost left her to die, lived, and developed a quite precocious passion for reciting and dancing, perhaps because she was too delicate to be tossed in the air and jolted about on the nurse's knee. A French critic of English habits declared roundly that this tossing and jolting was an infamous custom that caused water on the brain.

Though a daughter of Lady Berkeley she was more sensibly educated than the ordinary young lady of that time. Her Swiss governess made her dress herself and make her own bed. When the weather was too bad for outdoor exercise she had to sweep the rooms and arrange the furniture. When at Berkeley Castle this aristocratic young woman and her sisters received regular instruction in housewifery, visiting in turn the kitchen, the laundry and the cheese farms. Her brother, the wished-for heir, taught her to ride, shoot and row, and she loved music and private theatricals. She was married at seventeen and went to live at Ashdown Park in Berkshire, later dabbling in authorship, and meeting such celebrities of the day as Horace Walpole, Samuel Johnson, David Garrick, Joshua Reynolds, Mrs. Montagu, Fox, Lord Thurlow and Wilkes. She became a permanent Londoner towards the end of her life.

London was indeed becoming more and more the Mecca of the ladies from the larger country houses. They travelled to London for the season, and they sent to London for all sorts of things that had now become indispensable to their comfort, things which had formerly been unknown, or had been made at home.

Christiana Spencer of Cannon Hall, Yorkshire, wrote to her father, who was in London, asking him to send a bottle of salad oil, "a Band of Sweet Soap", anchovies, capers, pickles and tea and coffee. All these things were required in the house, and were to be labelled "Near Barnsley, by Pheasant's Waggon". Amongst other things ordered from London by members of this family were a bookcase and a dozen mahogany chairs. Materials for clothes were ordered, and a hat was sent as a present by one of the family to a relation.

The men were more mobile than the women and children, and some member of the family was often left behind when the rest went to London. Servant troubles were not unknown. On other occasions it was necessary for a lady to take a hand in the management of her brother's affairs. When John Spencer inherited Cannon Hall his sister Anne Stanhope wrote to him at London about the difficulties his new domestics were making. The new cook expected to dine in the housekeeper's room, at a second table set up there. Both cook and housekeeper objected to sleeping in the same room as the rest of the maids. They thought they each ought to have a room to themselves. The housekeeper, too, objected to the cook eating with her—a pretty kettle of fish.

John Spencer made short work of all this. Employers were able to then. "With respect to my *Grand Servants*," he replied, "I shall insist upon the Housekeeper sleeping in the same Chamber with the other Servants and by that means she will have a proper Awe and Command over them."

A little farther north lived the Millbanks of Seaham House, Durham, the parents of Lady Byron. They lived the characteristic life of country gentry, went to London for the season and spent the autumn and winter at home, occupying their time in the common social activities of their class. Hunting and shooting were the business of the day; gambling, drinking and theatrical performances the evening employments. Balls in the Assembly Rooms of the different market towns were attended by the *élite*, and those who wished to be considered so, from a wide radius around them.

Mrs. Millbank, a true Diana, rode to hounds with great regularity, and walked with the guns. She was like the lady of an earlier epoch who could gallop after the hounds all day and after a fiddle all night, or so she professed. The only thing that young woman could not do as well as her brothers was shoot flying. Mrs. Millbank had not quite all these accomplishments, but she could and did accompany her husband's voice and fiddle on the harpsicord, a pleasant and harmless evening diversion. She, like Lady Craven, knew several London celebrities, her *salon* there being graced by the presence of Sarah Siddons, Joanna Baillie and Maria Edgeworth.

Ladies like these could no longer be described as country housewives, though there were still some country ladies who were interested in all domestic matters. One of them, "free from the disease of gentility", said that she was as real a country Joan as ever frequented a hen house or dairy and ended a letter rather abruptly because she had to go to see to her cheese chamber and apple loft. The number of landowner's wives who resembled her was growing less, as the fashion of living was modified by the economic and social changes that were taking place. But of those who did, there is a good example in Smollett's *Humphrey Clinker*. Miss Tabitha Bramble of Brambleton Hall in Wales accompanied her brother on a journey to Bath, thence to London and on to Scotland, arriving back in Wales at last by a circuitous if not circular route. All the time she was travelling her housewifely cares travelled with her, and her letters to her housekeeper are full of painstaking instructions. She was quite sure that nothing would be done properly if she was not there to see it done, but she did her best by exhortation and precept though at what was somewhat long range in those days.

In the early stages of the journey her letters are emphatic on the necessity for keeping the bedrooms aired by constantly having fires lighted. The maids, who had nothing else to do, must be kept busy spinning. The wine cellar must be kept locked so that the men servants could not get at the strong ale. The house was to be protected by having the gardener and a farm worker to sleep in the laundry. They were to be armed with the blunderbuss, and in turn protected by a mastiff.

The reports she received justified her fears that things would go wrong in her absence. The thunder turned two barrels of beer sour in the cellar, a phenomenon that Miss Bramble could not understand. She ordered it to be kept for use as vinegar in the servants' hall, thus diminishing the loss. She may have suspected this beer had been drunk, or would be, and took this precaution against what she thought a device to save the drinkers from being discovered. When she was getting near home again she ordered the housekeeper to have her accounts ready for inspection, and the house to be warmed, the beds to be properly "tousled", and the carpets laid.

Miss Bramble was a portrait of many careful housewives in the homes of the lesser gentry. Mrs. Anne Coke was a real example of a housewife and helpmeet in one of the more stately homes, Holkham in Norfolk. She was a quaint mixture of timidity and social self-possession.

Ladies' hair was then dressed piled up round a soft padding to the height of a foot or more. It was a work of art that took time and patience to erect. Pomatum was used to fix it, and a dressing of powder made it white. Little curls were arranged to hang at the sides. It must have been very troublesome, and was impossible to arrange daily; so at night the whole thing was covered with a bag tied tightly to keep it in position.

The houses were infested with mice and the pomatum and powder was an attractive meal for these pests. Occasionally one of them was able to find a way into the bag while the beauty slept. Then there was a pretty how d'you do. Screams and hysterics, frantic maids and desperate husbands fluttered about and at last the victim was rescued. This happened to Mrs. Coke when she was with child and the consequences were so horrible that she had a miscarriage. A possible son and heir was delivered prematurely, dead. To have a mouse entangled in a mass of hair inside a bag tied to one's head must have been a shocking experience, and there is every excuse for Mrs. Coke's misfortune.

In other ways she was as self-possessed and as athletic as many of her contemporaries. She was never at a loss in a social difficulty. Two well-known farmers, Mr. J. Boys of Betshanger, Kent, and Mr. J. Ellman of Glynde, Sussex, arrived unexpectedly one day to look over her husband's farms and house as anyone was welcome to do. Coke himself showed the visitors round part of the estate on the day of their arrival, but the next day was his rent audit, and he could only spare a few hours of the early morning with them. Mrs. Coke took over after breakfast, something she was well able to do, because she was just as enthusiastic and knowledgeable as her husband about his numerous enterprises. She rode no less than thirty miles with these visitors before dinner, then an afternoon meal, and roused their most hearty admiration by her fluent descriptions of each improvement she showed them. They must surely have been equally impressed by her hardihood as a horsewoman, a somewhat contradictory character when considered with the mouse.

Mrs. Coke was able to act as her husband's deputy because she knew her subject, but she did not play a prominent part as a farmer herself like some other ladies of her day, who did become practical farmers on their own responsibility and not as partners with a husband or brother or other male supporter. These eminent country housewives studied the new methods, and described their experiences and experiments in the new farming journals, like Young's *Annals of Agriculture*. Names are infrequent, many articles only being initialled (a bad habit), but a Mrs. Clarke discussed the relative merits of broadcast sowing by hand or drilling wheat by machine. Another lady asked the question whether whole potatoes or only the eyes should be planted. Others praise the new crops, and another Mrs. Coke, who lived at Fishponds, near Bristol, declared that she had found chicory a good feed for pigs.

Aristocratic ladies started experimental farms and became the leading improvers in their districts. Amongst them, Lady Coventry and Mrs. Bouverie hoped to become leaders in the newly fashionable occupation. The Marchioness of Salisbury and Lady Melbourne managed farms in Hertfordshire. Less high-born ladies were awarded prizes by their local agricultural societies. Mrs. Boxer and Miss Hayes helped in improving the Southdown sheep, and in Cardigan women farmers won prizes for such varied endeavours as reclaiming five acres, making a water meadow, a crop of buckwheat, rye grass seed, and a wheat crop. Still others earned the premiums of this society for breeding the best horses and bulls in the district.

The exact social status of these less eminent countrywomen is not defined, but they were probably tenants or owner-occupiers of smaller farms. On the other side of the country in East Anglia and elsewhere there were large farms. Across the limestone escarpment from Lincoln to Wiltshire on all the new "sheep and barley farms" where the new systems were being adopted, and the money coming in fast as a result of the investment of increasing capital, the standard of comfort was rising. The tenants were getting rich, and their wives became more and more reluctant to take a personal active part in the farm work, or indeed in the house itself. They wanted to be ladies like the female aristocrats who in turn wanted to be leading farmers.

Various economic factors helped this class of countrywoman to achieve her ambition of freedom from work, and the display of "accomplishment". In some parts of the country new farms were being carved out of the waste, and these were larger than the ordinary farms of an earlier time. At the same time there was a tendency in some districts, particularly in the light land districts where the new methods were most successful, to lay farm to farm in order to make large holdings. Much larger capital than had been commonly necessary was required to run these big enterprises, and the returns were correspondingly great. They were corn and cattle farms; the petty business of the dairy was not for them, except for a few milch kine to supply household needs. And the possibility and preference which Peter Kalm had remarked in 1748, for such people to buy clothes rather than to make them at home developed rapidly as the century drew towards its close. The richer farmer's wives were relieved at a stroke from the farm work that had been their mother's province, from the weekly visit to market to sell the produce of that work, and from the domestic tasks of spinning and clothes making that had employed her mother's and grandmother's indoor hours.

Idle hands must find some occupation, so in girlhood these women began to be sent to expensive boarding-schools, to acquire the art of employing this new-found leisure. Part and parcel was to adopt, or at least imitate as passably as may be, the manners and tastes that had been the exclusive privilege of the landowner class a generation or so before. The majority of that class indeed had only themselves begun to aspire to such heights about half a century earlier.

The minor boarding-schools were more largely concerned with producing apes of gentility than with real education, and many a farmer and his wife regretted sending their daughters to a boarding-school when the child was "finished". The curriculum at such schools was the same as that described in the last chapter. The subjects taught were polite letter writing, and a smattering of French, history, geography, needlework, music and dancing. A great deal of emphasis was placed upon the importance of deportment. Towards the end of the century a smattering of botany was thought desirable. It impressed upon the adolescent mind the wonders of nature, and its practical study involved a good deal of salutary walking exercise in the fresh air at all seasons of the year.

A good many women authors produced textbooks for use in these new schools. Among them several wrote on botany. The great standby for teachers was *Mangnall's Historical or Miscellaneous Questions for the use of Young People*, first issued in 1800. It was used until the 1880s. Its method was that of question and answer; the answer being learned and repeated by rote, automatically, was deemed to indicate the possession of knowledge. Mrs. Barbould believed that this was the best way of learning, and her opinion was shared by the leading female educationists of the time, Mrs. Chapone, Hannah More, Mrs. Sherwood, Mrs. Trimmer and Maria Edgeworth.

Maria Elizabeth Jackson wrote *Botanical Dialogues for the use of Schools and adapted to the use of persons of all ages*, in 1797. Later she wrote other books on the subject.

Priscilla Wakefield, a great writer of books for the young of that date, adopted another method. She adopted the alternative of a series of letters. Among other things she wrote *The Introduction to Botany in a series of Familiar Letters*, the second edition of which appeared in 1798. It was an illustrated work. The Right Honourable Lady Charlotte Murray was another lady who wrote on botany. Her book, *The British Garden*, was a descriptive catalogue of plants indigenous to the British Isles. It came out in 1799. Sarah and Mary Fitton produced *Conversations on Botany* at about this time, and besides these botanical textbooks there appeared "Conversations" and "Familiar Letters" on a wide diversity of subjects, ranging from Political Economy to Chemistry and Vegetable Physiology. Whether the boarding-schools for young ladies of all classes made much use of them or not is altogether another question, though they must have used some textbooks, and almost certainly would choose those written by ladies.

Unfortunately many of these schools, as ever, sent home unconscionable young snobs, who were inclined to despise their almost unlettered parents, and more especially their employment. Hannah More said that they came home with a large portion of vanity grafted on their native ignorance, laughed at their parents' rustic manners and vulgar language, and despised and ridiculed every home-bred girl in their native village. This is not, of course, an unusual result and both novelists and dramatists have made great play with this situation.

There were some good boarding-schools like that of Mrs. Latournelle in Hans Place, London. Both Jane Austen and Miss Mitford attended it. Indeed Elizabeth Montagu revived the idea of a college for the higher education of women that Mary Astell and Defoe had mooted nearly a hundred years before. She even went so far as to undertake to found it, and endow it out of her own fortune, and offered the post of principal to Mrs. Barbould. But it was not to be. Mrs. Barbould, though herself very highly educated by her schoolmaster father, was quite timid and retrograde in her outlook. She actually believed that the safest way for a woman to acquire knowledge was in conversation with one of her parents, or possibly a friend, "in the way of family intercourse".

This opinion was derived from her own experience, but she was perfectly willing to accept the subjection of women that was an accepted canon of her time. Young ladies ought to have a general tincture of knowledge, just enough to enable them to make themselves agreeable to men, and to entertain themselves rationally in a solitary hour. Any deeper knowledge should be disguised. A contemporary doctor advised his daughters that if they happened to have any learning to keep it a profound secret, so even if a young woman acquired any real education at her boarding-school, or in any other way, she could not display it. Society combined to produce a cheerful rattle, a rather vacuous and vain type that might well return to the farmhouse a good deal spoiled for the simple living that had always prevailed there.

One important result of all this was to separate the farmer and farm worker more definitely into distinct social classes and to provoke a distaste for the rich farmer and his wife aping gentry on the one hand, and for the vulgarity of the farm worker on the other. As always the

women were more conscious of these social differences than the men,
and this led, especially in southern England, to the farmers' wives
raising objections to the ancient custom of unmarried farm servants
of both sexes living in. Boarding men and women was not only hard
work, but it had involved what had come to be thought undesirable
social intimacy; so on many farms the old system of all eating together
in the great farmhouse kitchen changed. At first the change was to a
separate table for the master and his wife. Next the family took their
meals in a separate dining-room, the men and the maids in the kitchen.
Finally when it proved cheaper to pay small wages than to provide
houseroom and food in part payment for services, the men and maids
lived at home, or in lodgings, instead of in the farmhouse.

By this means more money was put into the farmer's pocket, the
cost of labour being less, and the housewife found life easier. She had
more leisure to take part in the social whirl, competing with the wives
of the manufacturers, shopkeepers, tradesmen in the local town (who
were also getting richer), and with the wives of the squirearchy who
displayed their fashionable modes and manners to the perhaps astonished villagers. The change has been summed up in a sentence, "the
farmer's wife now drove, not indeed to market, but to an Assembly
in a post-chaise". Did they go so far as to take snuff like some great
ladies. Perhaps snuff-taking was as general among ladies as cigarette
smoking is today.

Some of them were certainly oddities, but in the remote countryside
even today individuality is often so marked as to be almost eccentricity.
It was then to be found everywhere. On the outskirts of London two
odd maiden sisters, whose name was Capper, managed a farm in the
1770s. It was at the north-west end of Great Russell Street. They made
themselves conspicuous to all who passed by, because they invariably
wore riding habits and men's hats. Besides their farming they had each
her favourite recreation. One sister rode an old grey mare armed with
a pair of shears. She chased any boys who were flying their kites in the
neighbouring fields in order to cut the strings. There were evidently
large ponds or lakes on the farm for the other sister used to amuse herself by lying in wait for the lads who came to bathe. When they did, and
she could manage it, she carried off their clothes. Perhaps she was
justified in dealing thus with a pest of trespassers, but the lads must
have found themselves in an extremely awkward predicament. On

1st January, 1773, Godfrey Bosville wrote to John Spencer of Cannon Hall telling him that the weather had been so fine that he had seen Mrs. Capper's forty cows dancing fandangoes. If Spencer could have had them at Cannon Hall they would turn the tables and set his dumb Orpheus a fiddling, remarks that show how amusing the beaux found both sisters and their cows.

These two women farmers did not belong to the class who acquired a modest literacy and were anxious to be mistaken for gentry, but the increasing number of that type attracted the attention of Grub Street. About 1780 a special cookery book was published with the title *The Farmer's Wife; or Complete Country Housewife*. The author is not known. It was an ambitious effort, and had the professed intention:—

> "Instructions, full and plain, we give,
>   To teach the Farmer's Wife,
>   With Satisfaction how to live,
>   The happy country life."

These instructions deal with poultry, pigs, curing bacon and pickling pork, how to make sausages and other things from offal, wines from English fruit, cider, perry and mead, dairy work, butter and cheese making, pickling fruit and vegetables, brewing beer and ale and keeping bees. All this indicates that a great many farm housewives were still living as their ancestors did. Not by any means all of them had become rich enough to shed all these household duties. Equally these useful instructions could be used by a housewife who confined her activities to the superintendence of her maids or even to giving orders only.

The recipes for cooking were "for dressing such dishes as are commonly made use of in the farmhouse". Methods of cooking all kinds of meat, poultry and game, are set out, and the usual galaxy of still-room work.

Several other cookery books were published at about this time, but none was directed specifically to the attention of the farmer's wife. One of the most famous, that was often reprinted, was written by Elizabeth Raffald. It was *The Experienced English Housekeeper, For the use and ease of Ladies, Housekeepers, Cooks, etc.* It was published in 1769, and was dedicated to the Hon. Lady Elizabeth Warburton, whom the author had served as housekeeper. She had later set up as a confectioner in London. By one of those curious accidents of arithmetic eight hundred subscribers were secured before publication to a book that contained eight hundred recipes. Miss Raffald left out all the physical recipes that had formed such a substantial part of earlier housekeeping books. She thought, quite properly in the advancing state of medicine, that physical recipes should be left to the physician. In this book again the cod's head crops up. It must have been a favourite fish dish, but the sauce for it that Miss Raffald advised was to be made from a whole lobster. That seems rather extravagant. The sauce must have cost more than the dish.

This book was intended for gentry like Lady Warburton. The only farm housewives likely to have used it were those who were getting rich and were ambitious to become or be taken for gentry. They must have been a comparatively small proportion of the whole number of farm housewives.

As always in a time of rapid change (or any other time for the matter of that) when some farmers were getting richer quickly, others were losing a pleasant competence, and becoming poorer just as quickly. Many small farmers, both owner-occupiers and tenants, lost their holdings and sank to the level of day labourers, or went to work in the new industries in the new towns. There is now no possible measure of either of these changes so they must not be exaggerated. Many people were undoubtedly affected in both ways. Possibly those owner-occupiers whose resources were failing hung on a little longer than the tenants, and felt the fiercer blasts of adversity in the slump of 1816–36 more acutely as a reward of their endurance. For all that, the small farm survived in many parts of the country, and still does today.

All the farm housewives of the lesser sort did the same old round of household jobs. Meat might upon occasion be bought from the butcher but these occasions were few and far between. What meat was eaten was usually pig meat, and the housewife saw to its preservation and use. When a pig was killed she cured the hams and smoked the bacon, melted the lard, made the tripe, sausages and chitterlings. She made the pickles and preserves, the fruit and flower wines. She was just as busy as her mother and her grandmother had been, and she did her work over an open fire of wood, just as they had done. Not for her the new stoves of Count Rumford that were being installed in town houses. She must strive in the smoke and heat with sooty pots and pans, though her roasting might be done on a spit, either turned by clockwork or the efforts of an unfortunate dog on a treadmill.

The work increased and multiplied at special seasons of the year and we can imagine that the more food there was to prepare the greater would be the hardship and discomfort of the cook; but the old customary feasts must be provided at haymaking, harvest, sheep shearing and apple gathering, or the work would never have been done. On a fine summer day trestle tables would be set up in the yard or an adjacent meadow, but in less propitious weather the festive boards were dressed in a barn that had been specially cleared. Any number of persons might sit down. One haymaking picture of the time shows nearly a hundred and fifty people at work.

Hannah More in her *Tales for the Common People* described a Somerset sheep-shearing feast.

"Mrs. White," the housewife, "dressed a very plentiful supper of meat and pudding and spread out two tables. The farmer sat at the head of one, consisting of some of his neighbours and all of his workpeople. At the other sat his wife, with two large benches on each side of her. On these benches sat the old and infirm poor, especially those who lived in the workhouse, and had no day of festivity to look foreward to in the whole year but this. On the grass in the court, sat the children of his labourers and of the other poor, whose employment it had been to gather flowers and dress and adorn the horns of the ram. His own children stood by the table, and he gave them plenty of pudding which they carried to the children of the poor, with a little draught of cider to every one. The farmer, who never sat down without begging a blessing on the meal, did it with suitable solemnity on the present joyful occasion."

This is a halcyon scene, but allowance must be made for Hannah More's personality. It is rather doubtful whether most farmers would have invited the workhouse inmates to share in a feast that was provided mainly as a reward for work done. It may have been usual in North Somerset, of course. The farmers here had shown their quality in 1789 when Hannah More decided to open a Sunday school in the village where she lived. This novel idea filled the local farmers with dismay. They declared that teaching the children "religion would be the ruin of agriculture". It had done nothing but mischief ever since it was brought in by the monks of Glastonbury. They did all they could to prevent this shocking innovation. None would allow Miss More the use of a room in which to hold her school. She was a woman of resource, and began to teach the children in the shade of an apple tree. This was forbidden by the owner of the tree because hymn singing had already blighted one apple tree belonging to his mother. Some landowners and clergy assisted in this opposition. These rather unenlightened people could hardly have feared the recreative effects of the school in creating a taste for pleasure amongst the children. Hannah More did not wish the poor to be taught to write, and did not encourage gaiety amongst them. Her Sunday School was conducted on the severest and most colourless of Puritanical lines. Her school treats were not occasions for a frolic, but for solemn and decorous behaviour. The children played no game, they did not romp and they sang no secular song.

Whether they lived in farmhouse, or erstwhile manor house, the farm housewives were often extremely "houseproud", though those who lived in the depths of the most terrible poverty must be excepted. A very modest home was the pride of Rebecca Wilmot's heart, according to another of Hannah More's *Tales for the Common People*.

"A spot on her hearth, or a bit of rust on a brass candlestick would throw her into a violent passion. Her oak table was so bright you could almost see to put your cap on in it. She would keep poor Hester (her daughter) from Church to stone the space under the chairs in fine patterns and flowers. She was sulky and disappointed if any ladies happened to call and did not seem delighted with the flowers she used to draw with a burnt stick on the whitewash of the chimney corners."

This housewife had a peculiar idea of interior decoration to modern notions. Hearthstone drawn in patterns on a stone floor and sooted drawings on whitewashed walls would not be likely to appeal to a professional interior decorator of today (though on second thoughts they might to some), but they show that the essence of the idea was present in that humble housewife's bosom.

Rebecca Wilmot was a pattern of the small farmer's wife in the more remote districts about 1800. She was almost indistinguishable from the wife of a labourer. It did not take very many or heavy onslaughts, slings and arrows of outrageous fortune, to reduce that kind of farmer to wage earning.

The wives of those small farmers whom adversity reduced to the condition of day labourers found that they, too, like the more fortunate wives of the increasingly wealthy men, had more leisure. Such women had been fully employed, but when the home was a tinier cottage she had not so much housework to do. When, too, the livestock, cows, pigs and poultry had been sold up on vacating the farm, or the absorption of cottage rights in some enclosure, she could no longer make her substantial contribution to the sustenance of the family, and to the annual or half-yearly payment of rent. She had leisure thrust upon her, unwanted and unappreciated, because it was to the general disadvantage of her family. Worse off still was the widow or single woman whose use of the common (she may have had no legal rights there, but was suffered) had enabled her to keep herself alive, if no more, especially if she did a little poorly paid spinning, lace making, straw plaiting or other domestic manufacture as well, or perchance kept a tiny dame's school. When the common was enclosed part of her livelihood vanished, and as factory production developed, the other part followed it. Her only chance of earning was by casual day labour in the fields, or by doing odd jobs for other people in the village. There was little enough work of this kind, and the scarcity of employment for women was regarded as one of the great evils of the day.

The effects of the change-over to factory production were most severe in areas like that round Halifax in Yorkshire, reputed the most populous parish in England. The farms were small, and nearly all had a weaving shed attached to them. The wives and children of these men, and of the farm hands, if any were employed, spun and prepared the thread either at home or in the farmer's workshop, though this job was mainly a spare-time occupation. From 6d. to 2s. a week was commonly earned by a wife, the children added a few coppers each. Some housewives' incomes were increased by as much as 2s. or 3s. a week by the industrious family. As this work was absorbed into the new factories, these earnings vanished, because the wife could not leave her home and younger children, though the elder ones from six

K

or seven years old were obliged to accept work in them. East Anglia, Wiltshire, and the Cotswolds must have been affected in the same way, as their woollen manufacture was transferred to the North. Indeed, it has been suggested that this change, even more than the enclosures, was the cause of many families undoing, and collapse on to parish relief.

For the cottage housewife, either if she had the help and comfort of a husband, or if she struggled along without that, it was quite impossible to make ends meet. Their existence and that of their families was drawn out on the barest minimum of food. This was because the men's wages were, as we should say, uneconomic from the point of view of the receiver, though very economical for the payer. The scales of pay, if such they could be called, were calculated upon the supposition that the money wage was to supplement other resources, free fuel, free feed for a little livestock, perhaps an acre of corn, and were not intended to provide the purchasing power necessary to sustain the worker's family. The loss of these resources in some places, coupled with the loss of the housewife's and children's minute earnings, reduced the farm worker to begging and dependence upon the grudging charity of the poor law authorities. During the forty years from the outbreak of the French Wars to the passing of the New Poor Law in 1834 they came to regard poor relief as a right. They called it their "lowance".

The depression of the worker and his family was accentuated because prices had been steadily rising during the eighteenth century, and wages did not rise in anything like the same proportion. This made the loss of the supplementary sources of income even more serious. When a man had his own cow, a pig, or a few poultry running on the village waste, he always had something to eat even if his other resources were tiny; but whatever small quantities of this wholesome food his family had been able to consume disappeared from his table when he was no longer able to use the common. They had been able to drink a little milk, make a little butter and cheese, perhaps eat an egg or two and an occasional old hen, but the milk disappeared when the cow had to be sold. Tea, the leaves used over and over again till the last tinge of colour and taste had been extracted, was the substitute. Bacon was very dear to buy for a man whose wages were so small, and who may have once been able to keep a pig. Beef or mutton had always been unusual dishes on the cottage table. The cost of bread rose to heights outside any living person's experience, especially in bad seasons. These people were frugal with a desperate frugality; though Arthur Young thought it admirable and virtuous when exercised by the small farmer and the cottager. He would not have cared for it himself. Indeed when he, like these unfortunates, was forced to exercise some much smaller measure of self-denial to further his many projects, he complained with a voluble bitterness that could not have been expressed by the workers' inarticulate tongues. They endured in a less complaining way a life that is almost inconceivable today, and it grew steadily worse.

Increasing poverty leads to increasing indifference, but it was not altogether the lowered morale of the poorer country housewives that made them give up the tasks by which their mothers and grandmothers had helped to sustain the comfort of their families. Part of this work they could no longer do because resort to the common and waste was becoming impossible. The housewife came to depend upon the village baker for bread, and his oven for the baking of the Sunday dinner, if any. Contemporary observers saw this as laziness and degeneration; but that was not accurate observation. Free fuel had been collected by the women and children, turves, furze, heath and brushwood. When it could no longer be picked up, the housewife could not cook at home, because she could not afford to buy fuel, and so in the South of England the cottagers were reduced to a diet of bread and tea. In the North, except the manufacturing areas, the old habits continued longer, because conditions did not change so completely. Dishes unknown in the South were cooked, more vegetables were eaten and milk was used on pottage and potatoes. This was so in Wales, some parts of the Marcher Counties, and the more remote parts of Devon and Cornwall.

The tea drinking of all classes had been condemned by Joseph Hanway in the beginning of the eighteenth century. Arthur Young condemned the farm workers for drinking tea at its end, though poor souls, they would probably have preferred beer. Young said tea drinking was the cause of their poverty. Tea certainly was expensive, costing 16s. a pound, and Young thought that what the cottage housewife spent on it would have been better applied to other uses. He made one of his famous arithmetical examples. It was as profoundly illuminating as some of the vague figures about production and so on that were dispensed over the wireless during the war. He calculated that two people drinking tea once a day all the year amounted to one-fourth of the price of the wheat consumed by a family of five persons. Twice a day is half, if wheat was 6s. a bushel. What this proves is not quite clear. But one thing Young was convinced of; the women injured their health by drinking so bad a beverage, a prejudice which has only died out very recently. He did not, or would not, realize that the cottage housewife had no choice as she had little choice in the other unfortunate expedients she was forced by economic circumstances to adopt.

Prices grew so prohibitive once or twice that there were housewives' riots. They had no more effect than the East End housewives who upset a profiteering barrow boy's stall a few years ago. In 1795, and again in 1816, the country housewives at different places held up waggons of corn, etc., on its way to market or to the quayside to be shipped for the Navy. They compelled the owners to sell the goods at lower rates for local consumption. Once or twice their shocking action was helped and protected by troops escorting the goods. No real or permanent result could come from such desultory action though these outbreaks of the hungry were regarded by the ruling class as a symptom of the inbred lawlessness of the lower classes, a fearful indication of the possibility of an English revolution as bloody and class conscious as the French. It was nothing of the kind, of course, only the last resort of the hungry and desperate.

The diet of the farm worker's family, especially in the South of England, always restricted, degenerated into an unimaginable sameness and monotony. Bread was its staple; potatoes a second string. What little else was added to these might be a trifle of skim-milk cheese as hard as rock, a morsel of bacon in the pot at the week-end, and that was about all. It was a poorer diet than had been enjoyed by the lazy squatters on the heath. A contemporary inquiry disclosed that many of the labourers in the Midlands and South were mainly living on rye or barley bread or potatoes, strong tea instead of beer, and whey and water in the place of the milk they had been able to drink.

Home-made clothes, too, went out of use from compulsion rather than choice. They were generally believed to be warmer and harder to wear out, having a long life that justified the work absorbed in making them, but the minute wages of the head of the family, even when combined with his "lowance", were insufficient to permit his wife to buy the raw material. Clothing, apart from the men's boots, was cadged from the better off, cast-offs being very acceptable. The only purchases were of second-hand goods bought for a few pence in a neighbouring town.

If the small farmer's wife or the cottage housewife could find the money to buy her clothes the prices were not high except in relation to the husband's earnings—the all-important point. Men's wages when in full employment, a rare occurrence, were from 1s. to 1s. 6d. a day, and overtime payments were unheard of. At harvest a special payment for the period was annually arranged, or the work of mowing grass might be done by the acre. This special fund was consumed by the rent and boots for the man, or other tradesmen's debts that had accumulated during the year.

In proportion to these wages the cost of new clothes was almost prohibitive. A common stuff gown cost 6s. 6d. at a shop near London. Other articles that could be bought there were:—

	s.	d.
Linsey-woolsey petticoat	4	6
A shift (chemise)	3	8
A pair of shoes	3	9
Coarse apron	1	0
Check apron	2	0
Pair stockings	1	6
A cheap hat that would last 2 years	1	8
Coloured neckerchief	1	0
A common cap		10
Cheapest cloak (to last 2 years)	4	6
Pair stays (to last 6 years)	6	0

This outfit, which comprised the usual clothing of a working woman of the time, would have cost her £1 16s. 11d., a sum almost impossible to save, though doubtless replacement of the whole was never necessary at one particular time, each item, if bought, being purchased at irregular intervals, and only when the garment in use was worn to shreds and rags.

In the most northern counties, where the change was not so great, the housewives had not abandoned, or been forced by circumstances, to give up spinning. They bought wool and flax, if necessary, and sent the yarn to a dyer or weaver, like Silas Marner, to be made up into cloth. Consequently the housewife's clothes cost a little less. Her usual dress was a black stuff hat that cost 1s. 8d. She wore a linen bed gown, stamped with blue, usually made at home. In the shops it would cost her about 5s. 6d. Round her throat was a cotton or linen neckcloth, price about 1s. 5d. She wore two flannel petticoats, the outer dyed blue, that together cost 11s. 6d. Home-made woollen stockings worth 1s. 8d. A linen shift was made by her own busy hands out of 2½ yards of material at 1s. 3d. a yard. Her stays or bodice could be had at different prices. She made her own gown of woollen material, using 6 yards at 1s. 6d. a yard. On Sundays she was splendid in a black silk hat and a cotton gown.

This class of country housewife was quite inarticulate. She had neither the leisure nor ability to write autobiography, or to keep a diary. She would not consider the humble incidents of her daily life of sufficient importance for her to spend time in recording them in the improbable event of her possessing the art of doing so. Few other people were interested in that subject either, with the exception of a few of the ruling class who were becoming gravely concerned at the miseries of the poor, and the burden their shocking state placed upon the poor rates. One of these, Sir Frederick Eden, related the succinct biography of Anne Hurst, the daughter of a day labourer, in his great work *The State of the Poor*, 1797.

Anne was born at a cottage in Surrey. As soon as she was old enough she went out to domestic service. At work she met James Strudwicke. She married him before she was twenty, and they began housekeeping in a cottage. James's wage was a shilling a day, and he deserved a long-service premium because he worked on the same farm for sixty years. Seven children, one boy and six girls, blessed this happy union. All the daughters lived to marry, and they married day labourers, as was natural, almost inevitable.

Until 1787 Anne provided for the family on her husband's meagre seven shillings a week. Then the husband died, and for seven years Anne lived alone until her death at over seventy years of age. The only money she earned during the last seven years of her life was what she got for weeding a gentleman's garden, probably not more than 6d.

a day. A friend supplemented this tiny income with an allowance of 20s. a year. By extraordinary self-denial and fortitude, this strong-minded woman was able to exist without parish help. She was always frugal to the point of desperation as indeed she was forced to be. Her husband, Eden was told, had not spent so much as five shillings on ale-house beer during the whole of his life. Anne's character was formed by a life of scraping and saving and semi-starvation, and before her death she had become proud, bitter, peevish and miserly. What else could she have been? Pride and bitterness must have been the natural outcome of such stoicism. How she could have been miserly is impossible to understand.

Only in her teens could Anne Hurst have resembled Clare's happy milkmaid, who was as merry as youth can be in whatever conditions it lives. Clare wrote:—

> "The milkmaid singing leaves her bed,
> As glad as happy thoughts can be,
> While magpies chatter o'er her head,
> As jocund in the change as she;
> Her cows around the closes stray,
> Nor ling'ring wait the foddering boy,
> Tossing the molehills in their play
> And staring round with frolic joy."

Care-free youth disappeared when these young women married, if it was any more real than most poet's dreams. Many people are cheerful enough who work hard and live on short commons. The peasant peoples of the world are examples, or so they seem on the superficial acquaintance of a traveller. This cheerful milkmaid of the late eighteenth century worked long hours, and if in a cheese dairy at arduous and heavy labour.

Milking began at 3 a.m. or 4 a.m. according to the season. The farmer's wife, whose maids were not below stairs by 3 a.m., bustled into their bedroom crying "Come! Dunderheads, Dunderheads, will you let the sun burn your eyes out?" Each maid was expected to milk ten or twelve cows, work that occupied an hour and a half or two hours twice a day, according to the number of animals. Milking was usually done in the fields where the cows were grazing, often at some distance from the house, though wise planning put the pastures close to the farmhouse, and chose the more distant fields for growing crops. The milk was either carried home by the maids in pails hung to a yoke upon their shoulders, or in wooden tubs carried like panniers upon a pack saddle on a horse's back in charge of a male labourer. Cheese was made twice a day on a large dairy farm, and the work was very heavy. William Marshall thought it too severe for a woman. He described the whole process in great detail in his *Rural Economy of Gloucestershire*, 1788. The ostensible manager, even in the largest dairies, did all the work of making cheese, except the last breaking, and the vatting process in which she had an assistant. In a dairy of 80–100 cows he thought this was too much for any woman. It was painful to him to see it. Some cheeses weighed over a hundredweight and turning them, rubbing and cleaning was no job for a housewife, but it was almost invariably done by them in Cheshire, the most famous of cheese-making counties. The milkmaid in a butter dairy was not so severely taxed. The hours were shorter and the work not so heavy. Churning was done only twice, or at most three times a week, and the butter was made in the forenoon. The maids were then free to do household work, and we may be sure that they were not allowed to be idle, especially as it was thought that spinning would return their wages, which were from £2 10s. to £5 a year plus board and lodging. When she married she might give some time to this work until her family cares increased or she might if fortunate have a cow of her own to take care of. The chances of that became more and more remote as the enclosures swallowed up more and more waste and common land.

A milkmaid employed by a gentleman sometimes had quite exceptional treatment, not of course in the size of her wage but in accommodation. Capability Brown laid out the grounds of Weston Hall in the Clee Hills during 1766–8, and James Paine designed a temple within a Temple Wood and beside a Temple Pool. In the temple there were all sorts of refinements, an orangery, a circular tearoom, an octagonal music room. Besides all these there was a room for a dairywoman, and a bedroom for her to sleep in, situated below the dome that was over the north front. She was more fortunate than many of her sisters.

Poor food, overcrowded cottages and wretched clothing do not make for happiness and energy; quite the contrary. Housewives who were economically unable to provide a good home, warm, comfortable, with a pleasant meal at regular intervals, fell into despair and lost all interest so that many neglected homes fell from bad to worse. While the husbands and sons resorted to the ale-house, the wives spent their time in tea drinking and gossip with neighbours, as so many of Morland's pictures intimate. Other painters and engravers of the rustic scenes that were so popular often chose similar subjects.

All these changes did not take place in a day; but the pace was growing faster all through the eighteenth century, and was more rapid in the second half, quickest as always, during the wars from 1792 to 1815. Besides annual wages for "servants", the Justices at the assize over large parts of the country had always laid down day rates of wages to be paid to women for particular jobs, so casual labour by the wives and daughters of cottagers and small holders had not been uncommon. It became essential as the eighteenth century developments progressed, and this need for continuous earnings by the housewives and children of the family began to create a class of women day labourers in a sense that they had not existed before. They must now work for wages whenever work was to be had.

Women had always helped at harvest because all hands were needed at that season. In the northern counties they did nearly all the reaping with the men binding the sheaves and stooking them. The Bath and West of England Society gave prizes to two women, Philadelphia Bateman and Sarah Cook, for good reaping in the south-west. Marshall did not approve of women reaping corn in the southern counties where he once had a farm at Addiscombe, near Croydon.

"If ever I employ women in harvest," he wrote, "it must be from a scarcity of men; and it must be from real necessity, if I employ more than two. Two women after the first or the second day will do as much work as half a dozen. By this time their stories of scandal being reciprocally communicated, they begin to work for amusement." He advised, too, that men and women should be kept separate otherwise they would waste their time. One old man, in whom the fires of life were banked down, could be put in charge of the women, or one handsome wench put to work with a gang of men would "animate it more than a gallon of ale".

It is not very clear why he did not approve the employment of women at harvest in the south, because he was sufficiently enthusiastic about the part they played in winning it up north. "The number of hands is increased, the poor man's income is raised; the parish rates are in consequence lessened; the community at large are benefitted by an increase in industry and an acquisition of health. And the work of Harvest, so far from being thought a hardship, is, by the women who have been bred to it, considered as a relaxation of domestic confinement and less agreeable employments." Indeed the harvest, though hard work, was a time of fun and merrymaking, accompanied by plenteous food and drink, and doubtless some frolicking between the sexes; so it had other compensations besides the comparatively high wages paid.

When the paid harvest was done then the women and children were allowed by ancient custom to go gleaning, and part of their cheerful work at that season must have been in anticipation of this valuable privilege. If the family was industrious and lucky they might pick up enough of the sheaf binder's and raker's leavings to make their bread for a whole year, and on the beanfield enough beans to feed a pig. To glean sufficient grain to provide the family with bread for a year was rather above the average, but in the ordinary way a woman could obtain five or six bushels of free grain in this way. This was by no means enough for one person for a year, since a man is believed to have eaten that amount or rather more by himself. It was a substantial and valuable addition to the larder at a time when a bushel of wheat cost nearly two weeks of a man's wages.

Women, both unmarried girls and housewives, were also employed at haysel for the same reasons. Besides these two seasons of extra work on the farms when all possible labour was collected, when not only the women, but the artisans and tradesmen of the neighbouring towns dropped the tools of their normal trade and went to work on the harvest, the number of women servants in husbandry, who were willing to do the actual hard physical work of ploughing, hoeing, carting and spreading manure, driving the harrow and so on, were increasing. In Northumberland, for example, a "hind" was only engaged if he agreed to supply the labour of at least one woman, wife, daughter or hireling, in addition to his own.

The women servants in husbandry like the men secured their jobs at the annual "Mop" or Statute Fair which was held at most places all over the country. Men and women attended decorated with the badge of their calling. In the north the women wore a large posy or bouquet of flowers, but in the south they wore distinctive indications of the job they wanted. The dairymaid, like the cowman, showed her inclination by wearing a lock of cowhair in her bosom, a less fragrant bouquet than flowers, but more definite in its sign language.

Women day labourers, doubtless cottage wives as well as single women, were employed in the south-west at 8d. a day on spreading muck and in weeding. William George Maton, a tourist, saw women ploughing in Devonshire in 1794. At Dunster 3d. or 4d. a day was paid to children for picking up stones. All over this part of the country, but especially in Devonshire, pauper children of both sexes were apprenticed to farming. Girls were expected by their hard-hearted employers to do every kind of farm work and work exactly like a boy, or it might almost be said, like a man. One girl child apprentice, when she was nine years old, had to drive the bullocks out to the field and fetch them home again. She had to clean out their houses and bed them up. She washed and boiled the potatoes for the pigs. She milked; she led the horses at plough; she mixed lime for spreading; she dug potatoes and turnips. She did anything that came to hand like a boy.

The child rose from her bed on five mornings a week between five and six o'clock. On the other two mornings she got up at three, because the waggon went to market on those days. She went to bed at half past nine.

Her life was not abnormal, but some contemporaries thought it was too arduous. Andrew Pringle, writing about Westmorland, felt it was painful to a man of any sensibility to see young women toiling in the severe labour of the field leading the plough or harrow team. He felt that it was much worse, though uncommon, "to see sweating at the dung cart, a girl, whose elegant features, and delicate nicely proportioned limbs, seemingly but ill accord with such rough employment". Pringle was evidently a romantic. He did not realize the strength of those nicely proportioned limbs, nor that the girl was accustomed from childhood to the necessity of the commonplace task she was doing when he saw her.

Such employments were usual all over the north. At Thornborough, near Leyburn, in the North Riding, where women were not only employed during the hay and corn harvest, but also for spreading manure, weeding, stoning and working in the lime kilns the wages rose slightly during this period. The rise was from 6d. a day to 8d., a very large percentage although not equal to the rise in what we should call the cost of living.

Though the enclosures had been a hardship in some ways by absorbing the land upon which the cottage housewives and young women had watched their husbands' or fathers' livestock or poultry, had cut furze for the bake oven, or turves for the hearth and had collected other things that could be used in their homes, in one way the new farming provided more paid work for them. The new root crops required a good deal of hoeing, some of which was done by horse-drawn hoes, but some of which must have been done by human beings who were selective. The first hoeing was known as bunching. It was cutting out the surplus plants in the rows and required judgement. Next came singling, when all but the plant chosen for survival were hoed out. Neither of these jobs could be done by horse power and women's labour was used because it was cheap, and the men's labour must be supplemented in some way if this additional work were to be done.

Sometimes there was not enough women to be found or they secured a more comfortable job. Charles Vancouver, writing about Devon in 1808, said that growing carrots had to be given up by the farmers about Ottery St. Mary because the women formerly employed to hoe this crop had found more suitable employment in the woollen manufacture.

The fact is that the tendencies which had already appeared in the first half of the eighteenth century developed faster in the second half. The well-to-do, landowner and farmer alike, grew richer and changed their way of living, because they were able to make it more comfortable and to their taste; the less well-to-do became poorer and changed their way of living because they had to. The stratification of society according to a new system went on apace, and the several income grades of women in rural society, like their husbands, drew steadily away from one another because the disparity of their incomes caused such wide divergences in behaviour, outlook and environment.

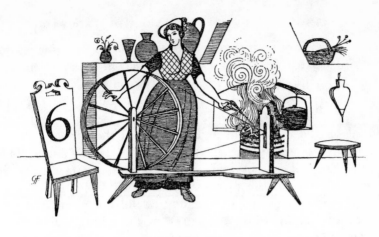

CHAPTER SIX

Regency and Early Victorian Countrywomen

ALREADY BY THE accession of Queen Victoria one of the chief features of the life of the nobility and gentry of England was their annual visit to the metropolis. This was said to have a most essential influence upon the general character of rural life. Those who made this yearly migration relieved their minds of the circumscribed and rustic colour, inseparable from living in the secluded countryside as the lord of great estates, amidst the adulation and flattery of farm tenants and labourers, whose very living depended upon the favour of the owner of the land they worked.

The culture of the metropolis was, it is true, diffused throughout the countryside in that way; but this culture was largely limited to the families who made the annual journey, then about to be facilitated by the building of the railway network. And the landowners whose annual visit to Town made them so much the less bucolic were by just that proportion removed still further from the lesser squirearchy, the farmers and the labourers, than they had ever been. There were longer and longer periods of the year when the family "was not in residence".

Among the lesser gentry the old life persisted. So late as 1860, perhaps later, there were old squires in remote parts, like the Yorkshire Dales, who led the life of their fathers, a life of coarse and jolly plenty, with the long customary hours, drinking, and amusements of old. Necessarily in such men's houses their wives and daughters continued to live in the same way as their mothers had.

The housewives of the larger country houses and estates had, however, delegated their domestic and household duties a century or more before. Various functionaries presided over the departments of a service establishment, including a home farm and extensive gardens, that was often as large as a small village. The meat and poultry were produced on the home farm and slaughtered there, vegetables and fruit and flowers were grown in the gardens and glass houses, butter was churned, beer was brewed, wines, cordials and medicines were concocted, eggs preserved, soap and candles made, laundry worked in vast quantities, and each job had its prideful master or mistress to whom appertained a status of dignity in the servant's hall. In the carpenter's shop furniture was repaired and even made, and gates and fencing produced, while the blacksmith in the adjacent forge could make and repair farm implements.

Vast quantities of coal were used in these houses, often a ton a day or more. This alone required the strength of men to handle it from the coal house into the halls, rooms and galleries where large fires burned during the winter, though these luxurious fires were quite unable to combat the piercing cold and draughts. In these great houses, the curtained four-poster beds, the wearing of nightcaps and bed socks, the temporary warmth of the copper warming pan, all testify to the freezing temperature that prevailed a few feet from the immediate neighbourhood of the fireplace. Wintry backs and scorching faces were the commonplace experience of a fireside group.

None of the work of such a household devolved upon the lady housewife. The women of the family really had very little to do were it not for pastimes. They have been described as almost torpid in the absence of modern country sports, although ladies had always ridden and some of them hunted. An occasional oddity vied with the eccentricities of the men. One, a Mrs. Thornton, competed in a horse race against a professional jockey, Mr. Flint. The jockey met with some opprobrium because he was ungallant enough to win.

Besides riding, the ladies could and did go in for archery, a graceful but useless revival, croquet, boating and walking. Going out on a wet day was dangerous and forbidden. It certainly would have been no good thing to get the mass of clothing these ladies wore sodden by rain and filthy from dragging in the mud.

The delegation of household management and domestic manufacturing did not leave the ladies of the household without indoor occupation. Quite the contrary. Women of their class were generally well educated, read serious books, often in several languages. And besides the pursuit of literary knowledge, which provided material for discursive "intellectual" conversation, these ladies could display accomplishments like drawing and painting, music and fancy needlework with a trifle of botanizing and natural history. William Hazlitt believed that there was no class of people who led so laborious a life, or took more pains to cultivate their minds as well as their persons, than people of fashion, a category in which ladies of the great country houses must certainly be included. "A young lady of fashion who has to devote so many hours of the day to music, so many to dancing, so many to drawing, so many to French, Italian, etc., does not pass her time in idleness . . . nor does a reviewer by profession read half the same number of productions as a modern fine lady is obliged to labour through. . . ." As well as being interesting to do and talk about, these things were fitting subject matter for the copious letters that were an admired amusement of a day when the ability to write elegant and entertaining letters was a necessary part of a young lady's equipment for society.

Mr. Willis, an American, has left a description of country-house life at Gordon Castle. There the ladies, visitors and family alike, were generally invisible between breakfast and lunch. The morning was no doubt occupied in some one or other of their accomplished pastimes, reading, letter writing, embroidery, music. In the afternoon various riding and driving parties were formed of ladies and gentlemen together. On their return there was an interval mostly spent on the toilet, then dinner, followed by the men's ritual drinking, a visit to the drawing-room for music or cards or conversation. The ladies retired to bed about midnight, and the men refreshed themselves with another meal and more drinking.

Some of the ladies' afternoon excursions may have taken them into the village to look in upon the school, if any, or to do a little of what Florence Nightingale called "poor peopling". This became a popular amusement for the wealthy. Possibly it was not so popular with the patronized, who may, having had their "station" made abundantly clear to them, not have felt the resentment at such intrusions their descendants would undoubtedly display. They would have concealed such emotion, if they felt it, for politic reasons.

These visits were not always condescending. One eminent lady recognized that the tenure of property implied being at the service of those in need, a patriarchal opinion then not at all uncommon, which often had strange results. Presents of the finest claret in the cellar were made to a sick tenant on this estate. The best horse in her stables was used to send many miles to fetch a better doctor than the village apothecary to attend a sick villager.

On the other hand Jean Ingelow in a contemporary novel told a story of two young women who were staying at a country house in the south-west. The only useful thing they did was to go into the neighbouring town twice a week to a coal and clothing club, setting down the savings of the poor and keeping the books. The rest of their time they spent with the young people of the family huddled in an old tub of a punt eating cakes and curds for lunch, or having a picnic in the woods. On wet days they played at "Parliament" in the long loft.

Young women like these, daughters of the middle class that was a new phenomenon of importance in society, were conscious and proud of their position. Jane Austen described in *Pride and Prejudice* how Mrs. Bennett set the Rev. Mr. Collins right when he supposed he was making his cousins a compliment on the excellence of the dinner he was eating in their home. He inquired which of the young women was responsible for cooking it. Mrs. Bennett assured him with some asperity that they were very well able to keep a good cook and that her daughters had nothing to do in the kitchen.

In spite of this snobbish example, many of the lesser gentry's wives still lived in the old way. *Tom Brown's* mother looked after the house, children and servants, and dealt out stockings and calico, shirts and smock frocks and comforting drinks to the old folks. Madamr Grym of Grymstone, Devon (one of Baring Gould's fictitious names foe a real person), attended the parish vestries where she made her will felt, and pursued with implacable animosity such farmers and landowners as did not submit to her dictation. In a Herefordshire vicarage of 1847 poultry, but not cows, were kept as a help to the family subsistence. Another of Baring Gould's incognito ladies was a widow and alone when her rascally son died. She took over each farm in the parish as it fell vacant, farmed it herself, and succeeded so well that, when the rival gentle family in the village fell into difficulties, she bought their estates. She was a humble prototype of "the Little Duchess", Elizabeth, the wife of John Henry, fifth Duke of Rutland, who, three days before her death, rode out on horseback over her extensive farms and plantations to visit some fat stock intended for exhibition at Smithfield. Her management had "embellished" the villages, and "while her general views were enlarged and magnificent she did not disdain to interest herself in the most minute details that could improve the habits and increase the comforts of the poorest cottager".

Ladies like these had often strong political prejudices but, of course, no political status. Indeed a married woman ceased to have any legal existence. She lived only in the shadow of her husband. The early Victorian male had no doubts of his superiority. Economically women were dependent upon men; fathers, husbands, brothers. Socially she was his inferior. She had no vote. It was considered as unnatural for a young woman of the middle and upper classes to wish to be independent of her father, as for a married woman to wish to dispose of her own income. That woman should be dependent upon men was the Divine Will, an arrangement "which woman's inferior capabilities rendered necessary to the progress of civilization". Elderly spinsters who possessed their own money were the only exception. They were figures of fun anyhow. Their eccentricities were of no account, and could be regarded with a pitying smile.

The incongruities of the position of women were realized by Disraeli, who described them to the House of Commons in 1845.

"In a country governed by a woman," he said, "where you allow women to form part of the estate of the realm—peeresses in their own right for example—where you allow women not only to hold land but to be ladies of the manor, and to hold legal courts, where a woman may by law be a churchwarden, and an overseer of the poor—I do not see, when she has so much to do with the Church and the State, on what reasons, if you come to right, she has not the right to vote."

Women farmers of all degree had done so well that their competence could not fail to be recognized. A great lady farming a great estate, or rather managing it, and a lady running all the farms in a parish were bound to be respected, if only for the power they exercised in their neighbourhood, a power little short of life and death. An ordinary woman farming alone was not protected by the ramparts of a great

L

fortune, and sometimes at least provoked jocund and fleering nick-names. Elizabeth Ham called a Miss Hood, whose paternal acres were her care, Captain Sally, and noted that she looked after the cultivation and stock and regularly attended the markets and fairs with the other farmers. She was something of an Amazon too, having horse-whipped with her own strong hands a man who had jilted her. A less vigorous woman farmer is exemplified in Hardy's Bathsheba Everdene.

Elizabeth Ham herself received such education as the local schools provided for a yeoman's daughter. A very skimpy diet was supplied in the boarding school she was sent to. The rule of the day there was to rise and get fully dressed. When this had been achieved the face and hands were rinsed in cold water in a pewter bowl. Then breakfast, one ½d. hot roll and some tea. At dinner boiled mutton, squab pie, potato pie and suet pudding were the staple dishes, but were insufficient in quantity. Tea was literally tea only, but the pupils could buy from an old woman, who called daily, little biscuits garnished with carroway seeds at three for ½d., if they had any money. For supper they had "a little bit of bread and a little bit of cheese".

Education, indeed, had become one of the things the yeoman wanted for his daughters. That she might not be successful in assimilating the limited education provided by the curriculum of the available schools did not occur to him. One schoolmarm informed a father that his daughter had not the capacity to learn all he wished, only to be told to buy one for her. Others assimilated the learning all too well, and became genteel. Dorothy Stuart in *Regency Roundabout* quotes a con-temporary novel, *Oakwood Hill,* in which a gentleman's housekeeper comments upon the young daughter of a neighbouring yeoman: "She's too high flown for me. She's too fond of reading to be good for anything. But it's her mother's fault and so I told her. Here, Mrs. Free-man, said I, you keep slave, slave, slave, and let your daughter sit reading the *Pope* and the *Four Seasons* and the *Young Night Thoughts* when she ought to be making a pudding or sweeping up the house." Miss Freeman had, however, the practical ability to do some things. In her bedroom the blue and white linen curtains of the window and the bed were the joint manufacture of her mother and her aunt. Everything else showed some touches from her own hands. The walls she herself had painted light blue, but no more of this was seen above the chairs than served for groundwork for the display of her accomplishment in drawings and landscapes in cut paper, surely a weird and wonderful decoration. She had embroidered the counterpane and cushions and even a "carpet of canvas" with knots of flowers. These were not such menial tasks as sweeping the floors and making puddings, but allowable accomplishments.

Naturally a limited range of interests led to a limited outlook. Though they had no political status the yeoman housewives shared their husband's political prejudices. There was hardly a woman of this class, who really and intelligently concerned herself about politics, but they were all "blues" or "pinks", though they would have been at a loss to say why. They demonstrated their correctness in the neighbouring market town where the "pinks" all went to the "pink" shops and the "blues" would have thought it wrong not to give their custom to the tradesmen who voted "blue". The great families could send to London for goods, but even they would have found it embarrassing to buy in a local shop of the wrong colour.

These limitations were perhaps natural to women whose sphere was the home and who were not expected to desire any other part in life. The example of the Queen herself, though she was sufficiently despotic upon occasion, was upon the whole one of domestic felicity, and her example determined the behaviour of the Court and of the various grades of the middle class, each of which with somewhat sickening sycophancy imitated in whatever degree it could the behaviour of its slightly richer contemporaries. The home played a most important part in the social system and it was amongst the womenfolk, in spite of their silly snobbery, that the amenities of life were preserved in the nineteenth century "cockpit of Mammon that constituted the English middle class". But the housewives were slaves to domesticity. Housework was much more arduous than it is today. There were no carpet sweepers, Kilner jars, or other modern labour-saving devices. Home was "its own laundry, jam and preserve factory, and child bearing was exacted (as it always had been) with a pious and pitiless rigour". The housewives became narrow and conventional, but many of them maintained a high standard of decorously conducted homes and pleasant behaviour, though their ideas were formal and imperfect. "Prunes and prisms" the phrase runs.

The economic struggle was so fierce that the shadow of disaster was never very far away from these middle-class families, and, once a financial reverse had reduced a parent's circumstances, carefully brought-up and protected young women might have to seek amongst a formidable crowd of competitors for a genteel place as governess. Should she be fortunate enough to secure one her lot might well be one of brutal and shameless exploitation.

Agnes Grey, from the book of that name by Anne Brontë, became governess to three children for the large sum of twenty-five pounds a year. She might not punish them in any way. They might torment her, refuse to learn their lessons, dress or eat, but in the eyes of their fond parents the fault was entirely hers. When life seemed unbearable, she looked in the direction of home and said within herself:—

> "They may crush, but they shall not subdue me!
> 'Tis of thee that I think, not of them."

Old-fashioned people complained of the change in the behaviour of the refined yeoman housewives and daughters. More than fifty years ago Roger Luxton of Haleval in North Devon, then aged seventy-six, could remember the time when singing men used to be welcome at every farmhouse to enliven all shearing, haymaking and harvest feasts. He complained that all the farmer's daughters learned the piano and sang naught but twittery sort of pieces that had neither music nor sense to them. Worse there were then no more shearing and haysel and harvest feasts. All these had been given up by the 1870s. "Taint the same world as used to be—tain't so cheerful," said the old man unconsciously repeating the centuries old complaint of the aged. "Folks don't zing over their work and laugh after it. There be no dances for the youngsters as there used to was. The farmers be too grand to care to talk to us old chaps and for certain don't care to hear us zing. . . . 'Tis all 'Pop goes the Weasel' and 'Ehren on the Rhine' now."

Roger Luxton was looking back on the good old times of the early nineteenth century and observing the changes that had come to the life and way of living of some of the farmers. He lived in a county far from London, and changes were taking place even there. In those districts where the new ideas were rampant the change was more noticeable, but in Devon, as in other counties where physical conditions of elevation, soil and climate did not permit the new farming to be so rapidly adopted, plenty of old-fashioned farmers survived. They lived almost in the same way as their Elizabethan ancestors.

In their homes the man and wife were up at five o'clock in the morning, the wife hurrying the servant wenches from their beds, crying "Up, up, boulder heads", having them up to light fires, sweep the hearth and get to milking, cheese-making, churning and what not. The wife herself was ready to take a turn at the churn, or to turn up her gown sleeves to the shoulder, and kneeling down upon a straw cushion, to press the sweet curd to the bottom of the cheese pan, and conduct all the other numerous processes of cheese-making, to see the calves properly fed, to feed the poultry and collect the eggs, manage the dairy and make the butter, just as Tusser had advised nearly three hundred years before. These homely wives took the produce of their labours to market, on horseback perhaps, "as fresh, hale and independent as their grandmothers were".

They were of the sisterhood that Tom Pinch saw when he went to Salisbury to meet Martin Chuzzlewit. These farmers' wives, dressed in beaver bonnets and red cloaks, were riding shaggy ponies, purged of all earthly passions, who went soberly into all manner of places without desiring to know why, and who, if required, would have stood stock still in a china shop, with a complete dinner service at each hoof.

One farm housewife, mistress of the household on a large farm, Three Mile Cross, near Reading, was full of merriment and good humour, combining a happy ease and serenity of behaviour with an astonishing capacity for getting through both business and pleasure. She did not suffer from the besetting sins of her station, a dread of the vulgar or an aspiration of the genteel. She, like her husband, was hospitable to a fault.

Her pets were her cows, her poultry, her bees and her flowers, chiefly her poultry, but next she loved her flower garden. She was a real genuine florist and adored the oddities that importation and crossing had produced rather than the simple beauty of natural flowers. This was the only flaw in an otherwise perfect character.

One of the most popular forms of recreation for country housewives and their daughters, not to speak of husbands and sons, was visiting each other in the dead season of the year, especially at seasons like Christmas and the New Year. The more numerous the family the larger was the number of relatives that gathered at one farmhouse or another. Brothers, sisters, aunts and uncles, cousins to the third and fourth degree, and all of several generations made a crowd.

Squire Cass, who was really no squire but a largish farmer, a character in George Eliot's *Silas Marner*, gave such a Christmas party followed by a dance at New Year's Eve.

"This was the occasion when all the society of Raveloe and Tarley, whether old acquaintances separated by long rutty distances, or cooled acquaintances . . . concerning runaway calves, or acquaintances founded on intermittent condescension, counted on meeting . . . fair damsels who came on pillions sent their bandboxes before them, supplied with more than their evening costume; for the feast was not to end with a single evening. . . . The Red House was provisioned as if for a siege; and as for the spare feather beds ready to be laid on floors, they were as plentiful as might naturally be expected in a family that had killed its own geese for so many generations."

Ladies riding pillion to attend such a function wore a garment known as a "joseph" and a drab beaver bonnet with a crown resembling a small stew pan. The "joseph" was cut like a coachman's greatcoat, but the capes were on a lesser scale. After their arrival they had to share a bedroom with a dozen others of their own sex, often of varying degrees of social importance, especially each in her own eyes. One young woman told her fellow guests that she and her sisters had been obliged to pack their boxes the day before because they must bake that day and prepare a large batch of meat pies for kitchen consumption during their absence.

This sort of private entertainment was less frequent, at least in the early years of the nineteenth century, than the meetings for dancing, music, etc., at the Assembly Hall in the local centre. Here precedence and place were more marked than on the less formal occasions in the farmhouse. At the County Ball the gentry danced at one end of the room; their humble admirers and imitators occupied the rest of it. The gentry, noble or not, were satisfied with this haughty exclusiveness and their tenants, the professional families of the town and the tradesmen would have been the last to resent it. Social condition was inevitable, an accepted and everyday thing.

The Vicar of East Dereham, Norfolk, took his wife to the Assembly on 1st December, 1853. It was a very brilliant affair though somewhat thinned by deaths in Lord Sondes' and Lord Paget's families. Nothing in the vicar's opinion, could exceed the taste of many of the dresses. This was one of several occasions when this couple disported themselves at Assembly dances and they also attended concerts and lectures. This real vicar's wife was a good deal more fortunate than Mrs. Barton, the wife of the Rev. Amos Barton in George Eliot's *Scenes of Clerical Life,* or indeed the spinsters in Mrs. Gaskell's *Cranford.*

Mrs. Barton struggled continually to keep the family respectable on too small a stipend. She practised "make and mend" long before the phrase was invented. Whatever leisure she had, and that was all too scanty, her fingers were busy with some piece of sewing, making a garment for one of her numerous family. Her life was not remarkable for pleasant interludes, though it was often relieved by gifts of food and drink from the more prosperous farmers of the parish.

These ladies had not much in common with Mrs. Transome, one of George Eliot's characters, this one from *Felix Holt.* This lady was a real farmeress. She was "used to be chief baillif" on the estate and to sit in the saddle two or three hours each day, because she had two farms on her hands besides the Home Farm. She was an ill-fated woman who had a paralysed husband and an idiot for an eldest son. She had filled life with the trivial round, the common task as an anaesthetic. "She had begun to live merely in small immediate cares and occupations . . . had contracted small rigid habits of thinking and acting . . . and had learned to fill up the great void of her life with giving small orders to tenants, insisting on medicines for infirm cottagers, winning small triumphs in bargains and small personal economies." And she bolstered her ego with the servile attitudes of her tenants. She liked to see one stand before her bareheaded while she sat on horseback, to be bowed and curtseyed to by all the congregation as she walked up the little barn of a church. She was an example of the pride and arrogance of the squirearchy.

George Eliot has provided a sketch of a tenant farmer's wife that fits well with Miss Mitford's real person. Mrs. Poyser, friend of Adam Bede, whose house-place or living-room kitchen shone with the application of elbow grease and polish, where the oak clock case and oak table had both been so long treated by this application that they gleamed more brightly than varnish.

When she was working there Mrs. Poyser was dressed in an ample checkered linen apron that almost covered her skirt. Her cap and gown were plain, because her practical mind despised frivolous adornment.

It was not for such practical country housewives that an anonymous writer produced a little handbook *Farming for Ladies* in 1844. The book was intended for the instruction of the growing number of housewives of middle-class husbands who were employed in the professions, or as what would now be called "executives" in the industries. This class were the first suburbans. They lived in villas, cottages and what not, on the outskirts of the towns, and usually had a piece of ground attached. Later they were swamped by the advancing streets. Meanwhile the anonymous writer of *Farming for Ladies* exhorts the wives to fill up their time and help to provide the larder by keeping poultry, a cow and a pig. This would ensure fresh eggs and butter, something that was worth the not inconsiderable trouble involved. His exhortation to these housewives is exactly similar to that given by earlier writers to the manorial farmhouse and cottage housewife. "In order to be supplied with the delicacies of fresh eggs from your poultry yard along with pure cream and butter from your dairy, without intrusting the care of them wholly to domestics, the mistress must rise early to superintend the feeding of her chickens, the milking of her cow, the churning in her dairy." . . . By this means she would be so full of employment as never to be idle and uninterested—as Nancy Cass was advised by her sister— again in *Silas Marner*.

Villa housewives would be likely to employ a dairymaid or at least one domestic servant whose lot would be extremely varied and very exacting. The arduous work and miscellaneous duties of such a female domestic servant, who was an unpaid relative, niece of a small-scale farmer, included all that was necessary at Coombe Cellars. She helped with the household washing, worked in the garden, fed the poultry, worked in the kitchen, in all household work; and when people came to eat cockles and drink tea (the farm was on the Devonshire coast) Kate was employed as a waitress. There was no time for pretty accomplishments in such a life, nor in the life of a labourer's wife which was its natural sequel. It was, however, the only life that the majority of such young women could look forward to.

Few of them were so fortunate as Hannah Bint, who lived at Three Mile Cross, near Reading. Her list of domestic virtues was almost unending.

"Besides being an excellent laundress, she was accomplished in all the arts of the needle, millinery, dress-making and plain work; a capital cutter out and incomparable mender and endowed with the gift of altering, which made old things better than new. As a dairy-woman and a rearer of pigs and poultry she was equally successful. . . . She was also a famous scholar; kept accounts; wrote bills, read letters and answered them; was a trusty accomptant and a safe confidante."

She was strictly a home girl too. She never went to dances. Her only recreation was to stand at her garden gate on Sunday evening—yet somehow she managed to meet and get married to the son of a wealthy hatter in the neighbouring town.

Where Hannah obtained her learning is not stated. Perhaps she was like Margaret Catchpole, who got a place with Mrs. Cobbold. At that time Margaret was ignorant of letters and of many of her domestic duties but she was willing and eager to learn. So satisfactory was she and so apt that she was allowed to share in the lessons the children took under a governess. The opportunities enjoyed by these two young persons were exceptional.

The average cottage child did not enjoy such chances. The girls helped their mothers, the labourers' wives, almost as soon as they could toddle. Scarcely more than infants themselves, they were given the care of yet younger children, and lugged them about though they were almost as heavy as themselves. As they grew older they became useful at home in addition to getting themselves and their younger brothers and sisters out of the restricted space in the cottage so that the work could be done. They soon learned to mop and brush, to feed the pig if any, and to run errands to the village shop. As soon as they achieved the mature age of ten or twelve years old they were dispatched to some farmhouse as nursemaid. The next step was full domestic service, dairymaid and housemaid, scrubbing and scouring and lending a hand in the harvest field till they married, very likely at what we should consider a shockingly early age, some young fellow who had probably been born in a cottage only a stone's throw away from their own home.

Their employment as young girls was probably the easiest time in the cottage housewife's life. The work was hard and the hours long, but the girl was well fed and passably clothed. She may have slept in an attic, but that was possibly more spacious than the cottage bedroom she knew at home. Some of her work, too, was done in pleasant surroundings, picturesque in the eyes of town visitors.

An Essex dairy was described by one of these town visitors. It was at the back of the house and sheltered by it from the midday and afternoon sun, and from the morning's sun by a plantation, so that it was cool. It had a stone floor and plaster walls and was ventilated by two windows protected by gauze shutters. The roof was slate with two feet of thatch over it, and the churn was turned by a wheel outside, which was rotated by donkey power. It was of the most exceptional cleanliness. All the sycamore wood utensils were washed in hot water with soda and carefully dried. Friday's milk was made into cheese, a change from the old days when it was made into butter for sale at the Saturday market. No doubt the life of the dairymaid in this cool atmosphere of cleanliness seemed very attractive to these city visitors. It was probably better than the married life for which the dairymaids were so ready to leave it.

Cobbett stated that a labourer who earned 10s. a week and lived a spartan life, avoiding tea and the beerhouse, who had a garden and a wife who could bake, need not see his children crying for bread, but few labourers were in such comfortable circumstances. They were not expected to be. Their situation was, in theory, rightfully one in which both husband and wife earned some money, minute though the wife's earnings were. The *Gentleman's Magazine* of 1834 pointed out that formerly the female poor had earned their living at home while their husbands were earning theirs abroad, the latter's wages never having been at a rate high enough to support the family. Indeed women who did not work for wages were regarded as having "become a burthen on the father of the family and in many cases upon the parish". When the father was already likely to be upon the parish this is hardly surprising, but we believe that the authorities were more concerned when the weight fell upon the parish than when it fell upon the father.

The condition of the women field workers was miserable in the extreme. With all the fiery indignation he was so capable of Cobbett described it in the most convincing detail. In places so far apart as Leicestershire and Wiltshire the country labourer's wife was striving against an environment that it was impossible to combat effectively. The cottages were dilapidated to the worst degree in Knighton, a

Leicestershire village, only "hovels, made of mud and straw, bits of glass or of old cast-off windows, without frames or hinges frequently, but merely stuck in the mud wall". The furniture was "bits of chairs and stools, a few wretched boards tacked together to form a table, a miserable make-shift for a bed", and the denizens' clothes were rags. At Marlborough in Wiltshire he saw a group of women labourers "who were attending the measurers to measure their reaping work". They presented such an assembly of rags as he had never seen before, and though some of them were pretty girls they were as ragged as colts and as pale as ashes. The day was cold and frosty and their blue arms and legs were so pitiful that they would have made any heart ache.

It was little wonder that local agricultural societies had long thought it necessary to encourage them by rewarding industrious women farm workers with money premiums. The Sussex Society in 1798 gave premiums in a descending scale from four guineas to Mary Blunt, widow, for working 185 days in a year, three to Mary Carver, wife, for working 124 days, two to Mary Taylor, wife, for 112 days, and finally one whole guinea to Mary May, wife, aged seventy-five, for eighty-six days. The Essex Society also paid the same sort of premiums, but for a higher average number of days worked.

These women were day labourers working for wages. In former times women had done farm work and been dairymaids, but except at harvest this work was usually to help on the husband's small holding, or to look after the beasts and poultry owned by husband or father, grazing at open range on the manorial wastes. By the end of the eighteenth century the woman day labourer had become a commonplace on the farms, so much so indeed that her exceptional industry was rewarded by a premium from the local agricultural society. As in modern times a great deal of this work was done in the nursery and market gardens which were cultivated on the then outskirts of London, in Kensington, Hammersmith, Chiswick, Brentford and Twickenham, and in the parts of Essex bordering on the east end of the city.

During the first half of the nineteenth century the employment of the labourers' wives as day workers became widespread. By 1843 the special Assistant Poor Law Commissioners were able to report upon this work in Somerset, Devon, Dorset and Surrey, in Suffolk, Norfolk and Lincoln and in Yorkshire and Northumberland. Though some of the conditions varied the average daily wage was 8d.; in the most favoured districts it might be 10d.; and during harvest could rise to a shilling, but harvest work had always been paid for at higher rates than that of the rest of the year. In some parts of the country, too, the farmers had taken up the attitude that they had a prescriptive and prior right to call upon the labour of the local women, and particularly upon that of the wives and daughters of their own employees. The lace-making and straw-plaiting of Buckinghamshire and the neighbouring counties was complained of, the shirt-button making of Dorset was a nuisance; but the women could earn more at these jobs and naturally preferred them.

The actual work that cottage housewives did on the land was much the same all over the country. Stone picking was one job. Weeding corn and hoeing roots was another, dibbling wheat, i.e. dropping the seeds by hand into holes made by a dibber another. Lifting roots was one of the most arduous and was destructive to the hands. Feeding and tending cattle was another job, though by the middle of the century the women in many counties objected to milking. Tacitly it had been agreed that leading the plough horses or driving the plough was too hard for a woman, involving as it did walking ten or twelve miles a day up and down the field. It was no longer possible to see a woman holding a double furrow plough in 1843. Capt. Williamson had seen one on the Mendips in 1810, but with the exception of the more remote parts of Devon this job was always done by men elsewhere. Helping to feed and to tend the threshing machine was another job that women did.

When she was so fully occupied in outdoor employment, the domestic work of the cottage housewife was bound to suffer. A woman who had been working in the fields all day was tired. She had not only worked all day, but had probably walked several miles to and from her work as well. She did not possess the energy to plunge into a mass of housework after she reached her home in the evening. The restricted accommodation and overcrowding in many of the cottages too, must have been discouraging, nay disheartening, to any housewife who had managed to retain sufficient energy to want to do housework.

The famous and picturesque village of Milton Abbas, Dorset, that had been built in the late eighteenth century, and has been written about with great admiration since, was the scene of overcrowding.

Mary Cox, who first went out to work in the fields when she was sixteen or seventeen, was thirty-five when she told the Assistant Poor Law Commissioner about her early life there.

"When I was about seventeen I lived with my father and mother, two sisters older than I was and a brother fourteen years old in a cottage at Milton Abbas. Robert Vacher and his wife with three children, about one, two and three years old, lived in the same cottage. We had the two rooms downstairs, and the Vachers the two rooms upstairs. There were only four rooms in the cottage. There were two cottages in the building. My father and mother, two sisters and young brother slept in the back room downstairs. There were two beds. My father and mother had one; my sisters and brother the other. I slept out at my grandmother's. The Vachers and their children slept in the back room upstairs. The Vachers still live in the same two rooms, and they have six or seven children living with them. My brother and his wife live in the two rooms downstairs, and they have five children. The cottages in Milton Abbas are very crowded; there are many families that live together in one room; they sometimes put up a curtain between the beds! I believe there are a great many bastards in Milton Abbas."

Another family of eleven, mother, father, three daughters and six sons had a two-roomed cottage, one down and one up. They all slept in the bedroom. Examples could be multiplied from places all over the country. Indeed some two-room cottages are still occupied in Dorset, or were about fifteen years ago.

The moralists of the day were inclined to believe that working in the fields made for coarseness in behaviour, for the use of uncouth, often scandalous language, and for sexual delinquency; but the men the women worked with in the fields were the men they married, and it is doubtful whether they modified their behaviour in any way because they were out of doors. The real reason for the all too frequent bad sexual behaviour was the animal nature of the natural man combined with overcrowding and complete lack of any privacy in the cottage, despite all the pitiful attempts of the right-minded inhabitants to secure it by hanging curtains between the beds, and other devices.

The Rev. B. J. Armstrong, Vicar of East Dereham, Norfolk, made a glowing tribute to the character of the cottage housewife when he wrote in his diary: "I find cleanliness on the increase in the parish but no diminution of illegitimacy. The girls see nothing sinful in it, and their mothers, apparently, connive at it."

This clergyman, too, was one of the few people who thought that field work was harmful to the health of the women employed. Once he walked from Dereham to Etling Green to visit a young woman who was dying, "a victim of *field work*, a disgrace to the country". He was singular in his opinion. Most other people, including the women themselves, thought that open-air work was healthy, though some things like thistle picking and root pulling often blistered the hands very badly, and made it difficult to continue with the task.

If any injury was suffered as the result of field work it was partly the result of inadequate food. The evidence of the women themselves, of their employers and such eminent persons as the agent to the Marquis of Lansdowne, all agreed upon cottage diet. The cottagers lived upon bread, potatoes and a very small quantity of bacon. Some had cabbages from their allotments. A little beer and tea was drunk, but more water. They very rarely had butcher's meat.

One Wiltshire woman, who was a widow, with one son aged eight, was prosperous by her own criterion when her husband was alive. They lived very comfortable. They had four gallons of bread a week, 1 lb. or 1½ lb. of cheese, bacon, salt beef, butter, tea, sugar, candles and soap, with beer on Saturday night. The man had small beer at his work given by his employer. Since her husband's death the face of things had altered. The Guardians allowed 1s. 6d. a week for the child and the widow was able to earn 4s. 6d. Her outgoings were:—

	s.	d.
Rent 1s. 6d...	1	6
1½ gallons of bread.. ..	1	6
½ lb. candles, ½ lb. soap ..		4½
¼ lb. butter		2¾
Tea		1½
½ lb. sugar		2
Rent of allotment		5¼
	4	4

This left a balance of 1s. 8d. a week for firing, shoes, etc. On her allotment this indefatigable woman grew three bushels of wheat and enough potatoes to keep herself and the boy all the year.

Other cottage housewives throughout the south and south-west confirmed that bread and potatoes formed the mainstay of their diet. In some parts there were local traditional dishes. The Cornish pasty is famous and saffron pies were made there. Nevertheless, a great deal of barley bread was eaten, eased down perhaps with the pilchards or other fish. Conger eels were much appreciated, and were dried in the sun. A. K. Hamilton Jenkin quotes an old rhyme that jeers at the monotony of the ordinary fare, fish and potatoes:—

> "Scads and 'tates, and scads and 'tates
> Scads and 'tates and conger,
> And those who can't eat scads and 'tates
> Oh! they must die of hunger."

After a good catch the more prosperous Cornish farm housewives would lay in hundreds of these fish for a winter provision, and would dry them in the smoke of the wood fire or salt them down. The bread the housewives baked was raised with a bit of sourdough. The original pasty was by no means so appetizing as its modern successor. Potatoes or leeks, or turnips or pepper grass were rolled up in a barley crust and baked under the ashes of the open fire. A broth made of a scrap of meat and vegetables was their Sunday dinner. Breakfast was an economical and unappetizing (or would be to us) dish known as sky blue and sinkers. It was made by boiling a pot of water and adding to it a thin mixture of barley flour and skim milk. After simmering a while this concoction was poured into basins containing a few small bits of barley bread. The bread stayed at the bottom covered by the sky blue liquid from which the dish took its name. If the cottager could keep a pig his family were fortunate.

From Cornwall eastwards to Kent the cottage housewives made do with an even more restricted diet than those of Cornwall. A Wiltshire woman of forty-eight who had worked in the fields since her early teens, and had borne nine children, eight of whom lived, had to send her three youngest boys out to work with about one pound of bread for their midday meal. Only in prosperous times did they get a bit of cheese with it. They had to walk five miles to work and to start at five o'clock in the morning after a breakfast of potatoes and a little tea. They had some more potatoes and tea when they reached home in the evening a little after seven at night. These boys of fourteen, sixteen and eighteen earned respectively 2s. 6d., 3s. and 3s. 6d. a week.

Many philanthropists thought allotments would be a great help because the cottagers could then provide some of their own subsistence. In Sussex for example allotments had proved of great use in teaching the children of both sexes to work, to understand planting and clearing crops. The provisions obtained from them enabled the housewife to improve her cooking, an art she had lost and forgotten in all the years she had been feeding her family on little else but bread and butter and cheese from the village shop. There were, of course, exceptional opportunities for women's work in the hop fields that ranged from Farnham across Surrey into Kent.

In East Anglia and Lincolnshire, where the enclosures had created large new farms and where no provision had been made for cottages, or, as in some parts of Norfolk, cottages had been let fall down, or been deliberately destroyed, the gang system of employing women and children had developed.

It originated at Castle Acre, Norfolk, where it was operated from 1826, if not before. Castle Acre was what was known as an "open" parish. The cottage property there was owned by a large number of different people. The neighbouring parishes were owned by one or two or very few proprietors, and were known as "closed" parishes, because the few owners of the large farms were unwilling to invest money in cottage property. They did not wish to increase the working-class population in case they became unemployed, and fell upon the poor rates. Consequently they refused to build new cottages or to repair the old ones. This forced the workers to find homes elsewhere, and the only place they could do so was at Castle Acre.

Since there were so many workers at Castle Acre and so few in the other parishes the farmers began to apply to someone at Castle Acre to provide labour for seasonal work, and this originated the gang system. One Mr. Fuller was the chief gang master in 1843. Another was a Mr. Moulton.

The gang masters contracted to do a piece of work, turnip hoeing and other work on this crop, wheat hoeing and other farm work that

52. THE COTTAGE FIRESIDE: from an engraving, c. 1810, in the author's collection

53. A COTTAGE INTERIOR: from Leigh Richmond's *Annals of the Poor,* c. 1805

54. THE DAIRY: from an engraving, c. 1810, in the author's
collection

55. AN OUTING—father, mother, daughter: from an illustration by
Leech to Geoffrey Gambado's *An Academy for Grown Horsemen*, 1825

56. RIDING PILLION to market: from Thos. Miller's *Rural Sketches*, 1822

57. To market by boat: from Thos. Miller's *Rural Sketches* 1822

58. DAIRYMAID using a barrel churn: from R. O. Pringle's *Practical Farming*, c. 1860

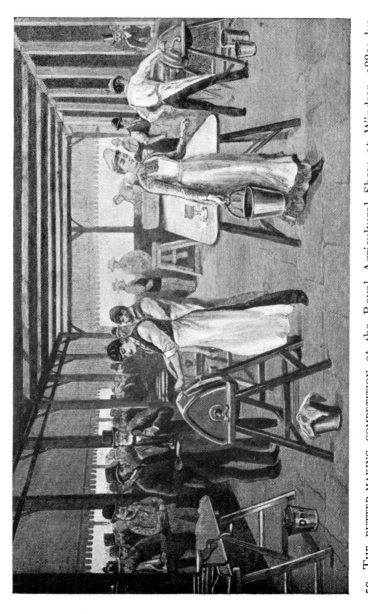

59. THE BUTTER-MAKING COMPETITION at the Royal Agricultural Show at Windsor, 1889: by permission from J. A. Scott Watson's *History of the Royal Agricultural Society of England*, 1939

60. WOMEN HOEING: from Clifton Johnston's *Among English Hedgerows*, 1899

61. WASHING CLOTHES in stream: from an old photograph

62. SWEET HAYMAKERS: frontispiece to S. Baring-Gould's *A Book of the West*, Vol. I, 1899, Methuen

63. MAKING STRAW ROPES: from L. G. Seguin's *Rural England*, 1885

64. THE CORN HARVEST: from L. G. Seguin's *Rural England*, 1885

65. THE GLEANERS: from L. G. Seguin's *Rural England*, 1885

66. "Mrs. Pyecroft makes a pudding": from E. C. Hayden's *Travels Round Our Village*, 1905

67. A NINETEENTH CENTURY MOP FAIR: from an old water-colour

could be done in this way. The gang masters paid 8d. or so a day, and some of them, Mr. Fuller, for example, had flour shops and so on at which they forced their employees to deal. This was not the only disadvantage.

The gangs were of mixed sexes and all ages from little children to adult men and women. Often quite young children were obliged to walk seven miles or more to the job, and if the weather proved wet had their walk for nothing. Parents complained of the language used in the gangs, and of the opportunities for immorality that such work provided when done under inadequate supervision. Fuller himself was accused by one woman of having ruined a great many young girls before he became a Methodist and a Rechabite. When the work was too distant for the workers to return the same day they slept in barns or outhouses with no proper accommodation and no provision for washing or cooking.

In spite of all its disadvantages from the worker's point of view this system had so many advantages from the employer's that it spread over a large area of the Eastern Counties. During the first half of the nineteenth century immense amounts of reclamation were done in Lincolnshire. Lincoln Heath was made into farms, and other parts of the county as well. Cobbett commented upon the miles of turnips he saw without a weed anywhere, and he was greatly pleased by the other crops. Much of the cultivation here was done by gangs largely composed of women and children because much of it was on land newly taken in from areas of waste in places where there was no accommodation for the workers.

After the Parliamentary inquiry of 1867 an Act was passed that forbade the employment of children under eight years old in a gang, or to employ any woman or child in a gang where men were employed. In 1873 it was made illegal to employ a child under eight at all, either in a gang or as an individual employee. Indeed no child of eight might be employed unless it had been to school for a prescribed minimum number of days in the previous year. The child was exempt from these conditions when it had passed the fourth standard. In 1876 the age below which children might not be employed was raised to ten.

This legislation led to many complaints by farmers who felt that they were deprived of a pool of cheap labour. Many of them declared to a later Royal Commission in 1880 that the loss of the school children's

M

labour had forced them to neglect some details of good farming because they could not afford to pay men's and women's wages for children's work.

The cottage housewife, too, must have felt the loss of the few pence a week the children earned. Though these infant's wages were so minute, their few pence were a notable addition to the family income. When the child had to go to school, these few pence were lost and greater economies had to be forced upon an income already insufficient to meet everyday necessities.

Where there were no gangs, the women were employed individually by the farmers, and the account of a family with five children who lived at Lavenham in Suffolk is instructive. It was a family industrious and frugal to a degree. Only the two youngest children, a girl of six and a boy of four, did not work. They had the reputation of always being neat and clean and their lives must have been an example of how to do the impossible. The actual figures are:—

Name	Age	Earnings		Expenditure			
		s.	d.			s.	d.
Robert Crick	42	9	0	Bread ..	..	9	0
Wife	40		9	Potatoes	..	1	0
Boy	12	2	0	Rent ..	..	1	2
Boy	11	1	0	Tea ..	..		2
Boy	8	1	0	Sugar ..	..		$3\frac{1}{2}$
				Soap ..	..		2
				Blue ..	..		$\frac{1}{2}$
				Candles	..		3
				Salt ..	..		$\frac{1}{2}$
				Coal and wood			9
				Butter ..	..		$4\frac{1}{2}$
				Cheese	..		3
		13	9			13	6

Mr. Scott, who handed in this account, said that it was given to show that, even with industry and frugality, their diet consisted principally of bread and potatoes. Only when the family was grown up and earning full wages could they hope to get a bit of meat at the week-end, and perhaps at supper time. Scott did not remark that this family could make no provision whatever for the renewal of clothing or soft furnishings. Whatever was done in that way must be done out of the harvest money.

Harvest was a time of joy for that reason—a little more money than usual—and because it was one of the times of the year when there was a seasonal celebration to break the drab monotony of such an appalling way of life. The horkey or harvest home of the Eastern Counties has been described in detail by Richard Cobbold in *Margaret Catchpole*, 1845.

Margaret was at that time a domestic servant at Priory Farm, and at the end of September had a great deal of work to do in helping to prepare the harvest supper for the farm men and their women and children.

"Once a year," wrote Cobbold, "the good farmer invited the married men, with their wives and families, to supper; and this supper was always the Harvest Home. This is the day on which the last load of corn was conveyed into the barn or stackyard, covered with green boughs, with shouting and blowing of the merry harvest horn."

The merriment was justified. It was one of the few days in the year when the men and their families were certain of a full meal. They gorged themselves to repletion with all the gluttony of continuous semi-starvation. Fifty years ago at such a celebration men ate in a gargantuan fashion, first a plate of beef and vegetables, then another of mutton and vegetables and if they could get it from the servers, poultry and vegetables on top of which they crowded several helpings of puddings. Their bellies bulged. This we can vouch for. We saw it.

At Priory Farm a hundred years ago all the men, the nine married with their wives and children, and the five batchelors, gathered at the farm at six o'clock in the evening. The women helped Margaret with her work.

"One pair of hands could not, indeed, have prepared sufficient eatables for such a party—smoking puddings, plain and plum; piles of hot potatoes, cabbages, turnips, carrots, and every species of vegetable which the farmer's lands could produce—beef, roast and boiled, mutton, veal and pork, everything good and substantial

(the food that normally graced the farmer's own bounteous table);
a rich custard and apple pies to which the children did ample justice,
for all were seated round this well-furnished table in the old kitchen,
celebrated for its curious roof and antique chimney piece.

The lord of the feast, or head man in the harvest field, took
his station at the head of the table, whilst the master of the house,
his sister and even his daughter, were the servants of the feast and
took every pains to satisfy and gratify the party.

After the feast, and a flowing jug or two of brown ale had been
emptied, the wives and children were invited into the best parlour
to tea and cakes, whilst the merry reapers were left to themselves to
enjoy in their own way the stronger harvest ale, which was just
broached by the hand of their master."

It is to be hoped that this joyful evening was not spoiled by the
appearance of ghosts and apparitions on the way home. Sober, these
rural people were full of tales of hauntings, of fairies and of witches.
Every falling star was a portent; every cloud that passed over the moon
had its significance. Merry from the harvest feast it was easier than ever
to see such things.

A tale is told of two young men who had to pass a monumental
stone put up to commemorate a murder in a lonely lane. As they
approached with trembling nerves they saw a monster ghost, about
three feet high with erect horns and large eyes glaring at them from
the foot of the monument. They were no less terrified than the harmless
heifer which had been lying down beside that murderer's monument.
Belief in such things was not difficult for people, most of whom could
not read or write, and who would have had little time to indulge in
such occupations, had they possessed the ability.

Coming home from a hard day's work in the fields, exhausted and
hungry, it was easy for them to see the will-o'-the-wisp gleaming on the
surface of some stagnant pool on a lonely heath. It was a fearful thing
to meet an old woman stumbling towards her lonely hut along the rough
uneven track. She might well cast upon the timid passer the spell of her
evil eye, unless he was careful to walk in the middle of the road and
keep his footsteps to the roughened track made by the horse's feet, the
only safe place from that evil eye. Nobody would admit perhaps that
they believed in witchcraft, but everybody would pay humble pie to

serve it. A cottage wife would not dread her confinement if a shilling, out of what scanty resources, had been paid to the local witch. Another 6d. would be handed over when the sow was due to pig.

The poor old woman who picked up pence in this way and for love charms, charms to heal a sick animal, and the like, probably lived in some shoddy-built hut set up on a piece of waste land remote from the village. In spite of the enclosures there was still infrequent opportunity for building these squatter's huts a century ago.

They grew by trifling stages, and with all the slow pertinacity that rustic character shows. An example of the kind of thing was the quiet encroachment made by a hurdle maker. He began by stacking his faggots near a spring on the common. The wind was cold in winter, so he built a shed to keep the wind off, and as a stable for his donkey. Later he built a wattle fence round his stock of wood to keep out the cattle that grazed on the common. Nobody questioned his right to do so; he had always been there. The wattles were the beginning of a hawthorn hedge which grew up round them. The son went courting, and another hut was built for young John and his family. A brick chimney was built, and then the timber framework for a wattle and daub building was added. So by slow stages the hurdle maker became the owner of a house and a piece of ground. Many another must have done likewise. The housewives and daughters of such a family would either go out to work or be very busy with their own animals and gardens. None of them were unaccustomed to the tasks they would be expected to carry out. We have seen the slow progression from a railway carriage dwelling to a brick walled and slated house built round it in a lonely spot within the past decade.

In Yorkshire, where William Marshall had been enthusiastic about the housewives' harvest work, married women worked in the fields at very much the same tasks as they did in the southern counties. Here it was said that the unmarried went into indoor service or maintained themselves by home industries like weaving or knitting sailors caps and jackets, or glove making. There was little or no education, and what little had been acquired in babyhood was speedily forgotten. Cottage accommodation was of the same dimensions as in the south. There were many two-roomed cottages, but others of four rooms, and some few with three bedrooms. Food was little different.

There was a bad mode of payment in the East Riding which

cancelled out the benefit of comparatively high wages. The men were fed in the farmhouses, and the farmers deducted a shilling a day for the food and drink. Though wages were 13s. a week in January, 1843, only 7s. were left to take home after 6s. for meals had been subtracted. It was all that the housewife had with which to confront the rest of life. Out of this she had to provide food for herself and the children, rent, fuel, and all the other necessities. No labourer's wife could spend a shilling a day on food for herself and the children. If she did there was nothing over, so once again it was the women that suffered. The farmers liked the system because they thought the men worked better when well fed. The men liked it because they got better meals than they would have done at home; but the women and children suffered. "Poor things," said one man, "they cannot live well; I defy them." The best that can be said is that they were better off than the Dorset labourer's wife who had to provide food for the man as well as the family out of a total wage of 7s. or 8s. a week.

The peculiar conditions governing the employment of male farm workers in Northumberland and the Lowlands were mentioned in the previous chapter. In these parts the man was hired by the year at a small money wage and a variety of "truck goods, mainly food in an unprepared state". Each man was required to have a female worker to hand who could do farm work at any and all times of the year when required. She was known as a bondager. This system has been variously described as a remnant of feudal days, and both Cobbett and William Howitt were sufficiently indignant about it. The more probable explanation was that of the Assistant Poor Law Commissioner who reported that in the absence of villagers, each farm, and everybody is agreed that the new farms in Northumberland were very large, must depend upon its own resources for labour. It was essential that there should be a supply of women and boys "always at command". The result was the bondager system.

The head of the family was paid from £3 10s. to £5 a year in cash, and was supplied with a quantity of grain, mainly oats, barley and peas, a little wheat and occasionally some rye. He was supplied with potatoes, or potato ground was ploughed and planted for him. He got a cow's keep for a year, had his cottage and garden free and his coals carried home from the pit. The adult members of his family were paid by the year, and probably got more money than he did.

One such man's half-yearly account with his master was:—

	£	s.	d.
Jane Thompson, the bondager, 121½ days at 10d. ..	5	1	3
Catherine Thompson, a child, 24 harvest days at 1s. ..	1	4	0
„ „ 73½ days at 5d.	1	10	7½
Elizabeth Thompson, a younger child, 7¼ days ..		1	9¼
Isabella Thompson, a dressmaker at other times, 35¾			
days at 1s.	1	15	9
Isabella Thompson, 20 harvest days at 2s. 3d.	2	5	0
Wife, 9 harvest days	1	0	3
His old father, 52 days	3	18	0
His own half year's cash .-	2	10	0
	19	6	8

The bondager handled about twice the money that went into the hind's pocket, and he was apparently responsible for all these people. This account does not disclose whether they paid him for their food, but that is doubtful. Presumably he gave them their provender out of the grain supplied to him, as he must find them all houseroom in the single room about 17 feet by 15 feet that comprised the whole of the normal Northumberland cottage.

On one end was a fireplace with an oven at one side, and a boiler at the other. At the other end of the room there was a partition for the beds, usually two, provided with sliding doors or curtains. The ceiling was roughly made of poles nailed across from one side of the roof to the other and covered with matting. Since the poles were rather above the place where the roof sloped upwards there was a space for decoration. This was covered with a piece of chintz or showy calico print or with ordinary wallpaper. The floor was the naked earth. It is easy to believe Howitt's remark that many of these places were very naked, dirty and squalid, in spite of all that the devoted housewife could do.

Cobbett regarded the diet of these people as exactly what he was accustomed to feed to the pigs upon his Hampshire farm. Dr. Johnson it will be remembered held something of the same opinion. The oatmeal was eaten in porridge. The barley meal and the pea meal were mixed together as they were two centuries before on Henry Best's farm at Elmswell in Yorkshire. The mixture was baked in cakes upon an iron plate put over the fire. These griddle cakes were about eight inches in diameter and half an inch or more thick. One of the Commissioners agreed that this pea and barley bread would not be liked in the south, but said it was wholesome and nutritious, "and really by no means disagreeable" though the taste of pea could be clearly discerned. Potatoes were also largely eaten. Milk was obtained from the family cow kept by the farmer and many of the hinds had a pig. So in spite of the contemptuous remarks of southern visitors there is little doubt that the hind of Northumberland and Durham and his family lived upon a more varied diet than his brother in the south. The housewives in their one-roomed houses had an even more difficult task than the southern housewife in her cottage of two or more rooms, but most of them must at least upon occasion desert their housewifely duties for work in the fields.

From Waterloo to the accession of Queen Victoria was a time of depression in farming; from 1837 to rather beyond 1860 the famous era of high farming prevailed in some parts of England and upon some farms. This made the farmers of this class prosperous again. It also provided a great deal of field work for women and children. There were large changes based upon fluctuating fortunes that made upon the whole for improvement.

With increased rents and with industrial development the landowning class as a whole were steadily withdrawing from the rest of the rural community. They were indeed more and more frequently absent from their great country houses, and for this reason alone were forced to depute more and more of their duties to agents, stewards and solicitors. The great lady was no longer the leading example of a country housewife. That part was left to the farmer's wife, and many of the richer farmers' wives were as good at aping the gentry as the wives of the rich manufacturers, professional men and wholesale tradesmen of the new towns. All these were astonishingly genteel. The lesser farmers' wives all over the country continued to live the life of their foremothers. They were excellent housekeepers, renowned locally for their special dishes, their dairy skill, their skill as nurse and midwife and with animals. In the lowest rank of all the wives and daughters of the labourers were forced to leave their housework, as indeed they had always done at some seasons of the year, but now had to do more frequently, in an effort to help their underpaid menfolk to get together a meagre livelihood for their families.

CHAPTER SEVEN

The Late Victorian Countrywoman, 1860–1900

BY THE MIDDLE of the nineteenth century the network of railways that was to cover England was well in hand. Communications had been made easier both by land and sea. The steam age was the new age of progress.

Those changes which had been coming into the lives of the great ladies of the countryside during the two previous centuries were accelerated by their increased mobility by train and steamship. The journeys to London that had occupied days or even weeks were now accomplished in a matter of hours. No longer was the countryside isolated and inaccessible. The wives of the ruling class, and the new wealthy manufacturers and traders who aspired to that class, must go to London for the season. They must, too, live in the country at the accepted times.

The great lady had abandoned her interest in housekeeping almost completely by that date. She took only a nominal interest in the direction of her household. Doing the housekeeping became little more than a daily interview with the housekeeper and the cook. These ladies had not been brought up in the still-room, and they were accustomed to a plenitude of servants.

This nominal duty completed, there might be shopping in the neighbouring town to be done, perhaps more as an amusement than for serious buying. The main supply of clothing and what not was obtained

185

in London during the season. Even the largest of provincial towns would hardly have provided fashionable enough goods in those days. The remainder of the day might be spent in study by the more serious-minded ladies of whom there were a good many like *Four Victorian Ladies of Wiltshire*, Anne Moberley, Mrs. Alfred Morrison, Barbara Townsend, and Mrs. Percy Wyndham.

All enjoyed ample leisure. It was the warp and woof of their lives, and on it they could "an they would" trace a pattern of individuality. Many did, but the great majority were sadly lacking in that quality, as were the stereotyped forms of needlework that was one of the unending occupations of their class. Most of the young ladies undoubtedly preferred to spend most of their time in pleasure. They had ample scope for entertainment even when living in the country for the greater part of the year. Garden parties, river parties where possible, picnics, balls, tea parties, informal routs, musicales, bazaars, archery, croquet and the new lawn tennis, each was part of what the more formal of her elders condemned as "the perpetual round of amusement". The evening family party, if not cumbered with guests, played whist, consequences, twenty questions and the piano, and in the larger gatherings, charades and private theatricals.

Clouds House, East Knoyle, where Mrs. Percy Wyndham lived, was built between 1875 and 1885, one of "the last great batch of English country houses". Life there has been described by Miss Edith Oliver. As she said, some people were rich in those days and families were large, so building was fashionable. Clouds House was "an emblem of some of the more outstanding aspects of Victorian aristocracy; its opulent, assured presentation of a dignified home life; its patronage of the arts; its large hospitality; and its natural assumption of the leadership of rural life". Life at Clouds House was typical of its time and caste. Miss Olivier's sketch from life is confirmed by George Meredith's fictional sketches in *The Egoist* and other books, and in the memoirs and diaries of the day. It was a magnificent display while it lasted, and its serene self-confidence was based upon a certainty of the system continuing for ever.

Week-end parties developed with the railways. Much greater distances could be travelled, and distance was being annihilated. At first the invitations were confined to relations. Always the great landowners had been great travellers, making interminable month-long visits to one another, and including the most distant relatives in the charmed circle of their families. As the train services developed and were improved it became possible and worth while to undertake journeys in order to spend a couple of days at a place. In the days of horse transport such lengthy travel would only have been justified if the visit was intended to be prolonged. The younger people began to bring their friends for a week-end, and the party became quite clastic in its inclusive exclusiveness.

One of the most obvious of country pleasures is walking, although the motor vehicle has rather disguised it nowadays. The younger women of the great houses spent long afternoons in this way, despite the handicap of long skirts and those buttoned kid walking boots that never looked very suitable for the occasion. This outdoor costume was topped by an odd, but rather neat pork-pie hat. Often enough an objective was supplied by the pedestrian paying a charitable visit to some aged or incapacitated dependant or villager, or to teach some child. Though they may not have competed with the performance of some strenuous young modern "hiker", these young women often covered a good many miles in their ample skirts and high-heeled, long-legged boots.

And, of course, there was riding. Henri Taine, a Frenchman, who visited England at that time, greatly admired the English young ladies. "On horseback especially and at full gallop they are amazons," he wrote. Many of them hunted at the end of the century. By that time almost as many women as men followed the hounds. Earlier sportsmen, Mad Jack Mytton, Nimrod, Squire Osbaldiston, would certainly have been astonished at the sight if they could have seen it, particularly as these Dianas were the wives and daughters of the men, and rode just as hard as their husbands and fathers. Individuals had always done so, but had been regarded as peculiar. Hunting the fox was the popular sport of both sexes in the rural districts at the end of Queen Victoria's reign.

Taine, in vein characteristic perhaps of his country, did not admire the matrons so much as he did their daughters. He thought them broad, stiff, and destitute of ideas. To his surprise, however, he found it possible to discuss serious subjects with "those athletes", their daughters, to obtain correct information from them, and to reason with them as with a man. Their constant concern was, he said, to find an employment for their faculties, or to acquire a talent to serve as a remedy for weariness. He names several of the great female novelists of his day. Such women learned French, German or Italian, might learn Latin, studied botany, natural history, geology and so on, and that in spite of the lack of formal education available to them.

Few of these achieved fame and few desired it, but a glowing example was Miss Eleanor Ormerod, whose work was of the greatest value to farming. Born in 1828 and bred on her father's estate at Sedbury Park, Chepstow, Monmouthshire, she shared in the management of the farm and the estate in her father's declining years. He had been fascinated by insect life, and one of Miss Ormerod's earliest recollections was of being sat in a chair to watch some large water grubs in a glass. To her amazement one of these creatures that had somehow been injured was devoured by its companions. This appalled her, but aroused an interest that never waned in creatures that could do such dreadful things. Throughout her life it spread from insects to plant and bird life, and her farm management of her father's estate attracted her attention to the benefits and ravages insects and birds might inflict upon crops.

About 1868 the Royal Horticultural Society and the Science and Art Department at South Kensington co-operated in the collection of specimens of insects useful or injurious to cultivated crops. To this Miss Ormerod contributed many species of insects at various stages of development, and examples of the injury done to timber, corn, roots and other crops. This Society recognized the value of her work by the award of the Flora Medal, and later she received silver and gold medals from the University of Moscow for her models of insect injury to plants. In much of this work she was enthusiastically assisted by the farm labourers at Sedbury because she consulted the large stores of knowledge they and their employers had acquired in the course of their practical work. She herself acknowledged her large debt to both local farmers and local farm workers for help in collecting insects and examples of the mischief they did.

When her father died Miss Ormerod made the study of entomology her life work, and was encouraged in this decision by Dr. Maxwell Masters, editor of the *Gardener's Chronicle,* and by J. Chalmers Morton, a famous agricultural writer of that time. In 1877 Miss Ormerod issued a small pamphlet, *Notes for Observations on Injurious Insects.* This was widely circulated to persons who would, it was hoped, become observers

in a co-operative effort to study the subject exhaust
successful that the author was able in the autumn of
report upon the information obtained, and to do so an.
many years.

When there was a particularly bad outbreak of turn.
the large number of observations her collaborators colle
her to publish her first special report. This publication   .ier
appointment as Honorary Consulting Entomologist to t.e Royal
Agricultural Society of England in May 1882, a position she held for
many years. Many of her reports on insect pests were published in its
journal. She only gave up this work in 1891 because of poor health.

Besides her published work, this busy woman was able to find time
to lecture on Economic Entomology at the Royal Agricultural College,
Cirencester, and to act as examiner in Agricultural Entomology for
the Royal Agricultural Society. She became a Fellow of the Meteoro-
logical Society, and received many honours from both British and
foreign institutions and societies. The University of Edinburgh made
her a Honorary Doctor of Laws, an honour she was the first woman to
hold.

Though she made many special investigations, her work on warble
fly, which made ruinous attacks upon cattle, was perhaps the most
valuable in aiding farmers in their efforts to fight this pest. An admirer
declared that no one of her sex ever rendered such valuable service to
agriculture as she did. Her work made her the protector of agriculture
and the fruits of the earth, a beneficent Demeter of the nineteenth
century. She had, in fact, set up a self-appointed advisory service, and
as one of her biographers remarked, she carried on for years by her own
unaided means work that was done by government in other countries,
and now forms a substantial part of the National Agricultural Advisory
Service in this country.

Other examples of learned ladies are easy to recall, but Miss
Ormerod's work was so closely connected with farming that it deserves
special recognition here. And it was original and exceptional, far in
advance of the tepid interest in botany and natural history that the
average young lady reluctantly absorbed.

In the beginning of this half century "the lives of girls in well-to-do
families were often sheltered to an extent that cut them off from the
roots of life". It was an age of gentility, of much that was completely

valueless except as display. Young ladies were expected to acquire elegant accomplishments, and prideful menfolk swelled up as these pastimes were the more artistic. Their wives and daughters played the piano with varying degrees of skill, few very great, they danced with aplomb, they made wax flowers and different kinds of beadwork, they decorated mirror frames and other things with sea shells. A real lady had little knowledge of housewifery. She did not know one joint of meat from another. She might sometimes have been even more at a loss today.

Arthur Bryant has made devastating criticism of the age.

"Young ladies," he wrote, "artificially kept from all knowledge of the seamy and even normal side of life, grew up, in tight waists and voluminous skirts like flies in amber. The pursuit of wealth to the exclusion of almost every other worldly object was effecting changes in every department of English life, but in none more than in its tendency to rob the Englishwoman of useful occupation and of knowledge of the domestic arts and of the world in which she lived. The process was gradual, and so long as large families remained the fashion tempered by the discipline and give and take of communal home life. With the growth of commercial wealth and of the mechanical means of multiplying comforts and luxuries, its effects became even more insidious. For in the end it deprived many women of the upper and middle classes of the natural sources of vitality and strength, and the instinctive feeling for wise and balanced living, which as mothers, it should have been their lot to transmit to future generations. More of the ills of our present epoch of reckoning may be due to this cause than is yet realized."

By the end of the Victorian epoch a revolution had come about. The new public school type of girl's school had been widely established. At these, games were played, and soon the world was talking of the athletic performances of young ladies. In the early '70s these vaunted athletics were of a gentle order, greatly restricted by the long skirt and the confining corset. Twenty years later women's participation in games had become more real, but it was restricted to the classes. "Down among the masses," it has been said, "the female was so browbeaten by her conditions that she had only time for breeding and keeping alive."

Croquet, though still played at the end of the century, had given place to lawn tennis, a game that was necessarily only played on private lawns and by the intimates of those fortunate enough to own them. The few clubs that had been founded were the privilege of one social set. Golf was played by ladies at Westward Ho in 1873, and badminton and other games were played at the new schools. Fencing was popular, and ladies' cricket, though not treated with that high seriousness due to the game when played by men, was indulged in. Mixed hockey was first played about 1893 though some care was taken to see that players were of suitable equality in social status. A ladies' eight rowed at Marlow in 1891. The bicycle, especially after the invention of pneumatic tyres, was freely used as an aid to getting about. Mrs. Bloomer achieved an enviable fame by designing a suitable garment for this sport.

Ladies as a rule did not take an active part in shooting. They met the "guns" for lunch, an elaborate and alcoholic meal, after which they returned to the house for tea. They joined the gentlemen at the hunt breakfast, they danced at the annual hunt ball, they watched the "point to point", they skated on the large ornamental lake in the grounds, they graced the village flower show, and adorned each other's garden parties.

This change in habits, combined with easy travel on the railways, made for the disappearance of the great lady who habitually resided in the country. The family no longer resided on the estate only leaving it for the brief weeks of the London season. Other places were beginning to be fashionable, and soon it would be so necessary to be seen here and there about the earth's surface at the prescribed seasons that the class of great country ladies would be merged in a rather cosmopolitan type that only occasionally visited the country.

But the smaller landed proprietors continued to live in the country, and they and the larger tenant farmers were much of a class. Henri Taine met "a rich farmer's wife" in 1870. She was a woman of thirty who looked only twenty-six, graceful and accomplished, and wore a dress of small striped grey silk with one or two rings on her fingers. She had perfectly white hands, pink and cared-for nails, an admirable waist and was full of gaiety and vivacity. She rode on horseback and played the piano, none the less she was a good housekeeper, going every morning into the kitchen to give orders. Except for some slight shades in manners and talk she was a lady to this class-conscious writer. This class of country housewife has been even more eloquently described by Richard Jeffries in *Hodge and his Masters*.

Some of them had no experience of housekeeping before they married, and immediately found themselves confronted with difficult problems. Servants were liable to take advantage of a shy and diffident young wife. One such wrote to an elder and more established friend for advice in 1874. They were only two in family (as yet) and had two indoor servants, a cook and a housemaid. This young housewife wanted to know what were the proper rations for the maids. She gave them 1 lb. sugar and ¼ lb. tea each a week, and had been told they should have ½ lb. butter, but could not see how that could be given. The cook used the butter, and could help herself to what she chose. Any complaint was met by the answer, "The cooking takes so much." The maids were given 1s. 2d. a week each for beer money. But this young housewife was doubtful whether the cook should order sirloins of beef and legs of mutton at will for kitchen consumption. Plaintively she tells her friend and monitor that she and her husband live very plainly, but that she could not make the £20 a month allowed her pay for the food for four persons.

The reply was terse and to the point. Both these unprofitable servants should be dismissed and new ones engaged. The young housewife must go every morning to the kitchen, larder, scullery, etc., and make a real inspection. She must make up her mind what she was going to have for dinner, before she went into the kitchen. She must remember yesterday's, and remark upon any fault.

The servant's diet should be bread and butter for breakfast; hot meat and vegetables, or cold meat and pudding for dinner; bread and cheese for supper; and an occasional pot of jam for a treat, not as a right. Order the cook to leave untouched every dish from the dining-room table until she is given permission to consume it in the kitchen. Remnants of meat could be used for the master's breakfast as he gets so tired of bacon every day. Weekly rations for each maid should be ¼ lb. tea, ½ lb. sugar, ½ lb. butter, ½ lb. cheese, 1 quartern of bread, supplemented by a daily allowance of 1 pint of beer, ½ pint of milk and 1 lb. of meat (*sic*). Each maid's laundry should cost 1s. to 1s. 6d. a week.

The maid's duties were laid down. The cook should clean the dining-room, hall and steps besides the kitchen and its adjuncts. She should clear and wash up the breakfast things, help the housemaid make the beds, and wash all cloths used in the kitchen, except round towel and tablecloth. The housemaid must clean the windows weekly and wash glass-cloths, tea-cloths, antimacassars (a forgotten item) and get up collars and cuffs and the husband's collars. If this young house-wife did all that she was advised and kept a careful watch on the con-sumption of household stores, she would save her husband's money and gain the wholesome respect of her maids. Let us hope she was successful!

Taine had been told that many farmers' daughters were elegant, profuse, indolent, out of their sphere and unhappy. They were the daughters of the tenant farmers who in the golden age of farming of the '50s, '60s, and early 1870s, occupied substantial farmhouses and hunted. Their sons and daughters despised the old day of little things and the small but continuous profits they brought, the cheese and butter dairy, the henhouse and the acre or two of orchard.

The wife of such a farmer was the fine lady seen by Taine and described by Jefferies. She drove in a dandy dog cart at least, arrayed in a costly sealskin jacket. She wore kid gloves upon her hands and ostrich feathers in her hat. Her dress and petticoats were of silk and satin. She was not redolent of the dairy, but delicately perfumed. Her daughter was pale and interesting, a young lady who could interpret Beethoven, and paint the old mill indifferently well. But such an extravaganza could not last. A small farm of two or three hundred acres was no more sufficient to enable the housewife to play the fine lady then, than it was later or is today. A horrid fate was in store for all these. A farming depression decades long was to begin a few years later.

Many of these spoiled young women were to discover that, however much they might have sentimentalized over, once her father had lost his bank balance, her lot as a governess, supposing her to be qualified for such a genteel post, might well be an unhappy one. As a domestic servant her fate would be a trifle better because her status would be more definite; as an unskilled draper's assistant or sempstress, she would experience all the manifold miseries and few pleasures that the contem-porary novelists describe.

Not all farms were large then any more than now. Most were com-paratively small. Out of some three hundred or four hundred thousand holdings in the country only 582 farms of more than 1,000 acres were occupied in 1871. These were scattered over seventeen counties. The average size of a farm was about 152 acres and more than half of all the holdings in the country were smaller than 100 acres, many very small.

The wives of the occupiers of these farms were in no position to ape the great lady; they were interminably busy with household work, and the care of the family. It was still possible in 1866 for "An old Norfolk Farmer", Samuel Copland, to say that the dairy should be wholly in the charge of a man's wife and daughters, if only because they would be more likely than hired workers to attend to the essential cleanliness required there.

Some fifteen years later the Hon. G. C. Brodrick deemed the work and character of such a country housewife all that was praiseworthy. If there was a piano in her parlour it was a cheap one and was not often used. She was not too fine a lady to look after the fowl yard or to superintend, if she did not participate in, the making of butter and cheese. This skilled work was only done in the best style where superintended early and late by a skilled mistress who had the whole dairy under her eye, a job which few wives of the wealthier farmers would undertake. Much the same could be said for poultry keeping and egg production.

The best parlour, the pride of these housewives' hearts, was a good deal less attractive than the farm kitchen. The harsh horse-hair couch and chairs, supposedly easy, with their backs decorated with crocheted antimacassars, and fitted up with a monstrous collection of knick-knacks, were frightening places. The kitchen was bare enough, but it was warmed by being lived in. The heavy oaken table with its long benches and few chairs at least had the merit of being used daily. The old-fashioned dresser was loaded with china and polished dish covers. Inevitably a portrait of Queen Victoria adorned one wall at the side of the mantelpiece; on the other it might be balanced by almost any improbable thing; a portrait of Bismarck for example.

The housewife, the presiding genius of such a kitchen, worked almost as hard as her forbears, though any bread making, wine and cordial making and so on, was at her own choice rather than the severest of necessities as it formerly was. The profits on the butter and cheese making and the poultry were, however, just as important if not more important than they had been. For centuries they had been, except, of course, on specialist dairy farms, the perquisite and pocket money of the housewife. This traditional arrangement still held good on many farms until the beginning of the twentieth century, and to such housewives any disaster to cow or hen coop was more important than the politics of the Far East.

Butter making was the mistresses' part. Churning only was left to the maid, but she was painstakingly overseen lest she should churn too fast or too slow, or should change from fast to slow when the butter was long in coming, a difficulty that often arose in the days before the cream was kept at a definite temperature. Then much "elbow grease" had to be applied to the churning, and the butter when it did come was often very poor, but this was accepted as part of the general awkwardness of things then regarded as something that might not easily be overcome. Sometimes an ancient charm was recited in a sing-song. One was:—

> "Come butter, come,
> Come butter, come,
> Peter stands at the gate,
> Waiting for a buttered cake,
> Come butter, come."

There were tricks in the trade of poultry keeping too. One was to feed with hot food in cold weather and to give a small quantity of raw meat every day.

Cooking for the family, making beds, house-cleaning, dairy work and poultry cares made up a full day, but at the end of the day when "tea" had been disposed of this class of country housewife brought out her workbasket. She did not spend the evening "tatting" or doing ornamental and useless needlework though she owned some beautifully embroidered towels, tablecloths and sheets, made in her maiden days. Her marital evenings were spent in darning for the males of the family the long blue worsted stockings, very similar to those worn by Benjamin Stillingfleet from which the nickname "Bluestocking" was taken. She mended shirts and household linen and did other useful tasks of making and mending.

In the special dairying districts some of the more wealthy farmer's wives did supervise the dairy. S. G. Kendall tells a story of how once and again a Somersetshire farmer's wife, who was a careful housewife, would miss a half pound of butter from her dairy. The maids or the stepdaughter would be questioned, but no one ever seemed to know anything about it. By and by, however, and perhaps days later, it leaked out that her father had sneaked a half a pound of that special butter to grease his dogs' throats, and so help their wind before a day's coursing, a sport to which he was inordinately attached.

This was in a family that approximated in its habits to the country gentry who were commonly its associates. The daughters of such a family and the daughters of their friends were often educated by a local or resident young lady governess who either lived with the family or attended daily, or, it may be, received the pupils at her own home.

These apparent contradictions make it less than easy to generalize about the pursuits of the country housewife at that time. There must have been gradations of all kinds, some farm housewives having less of the actual housework and no farm work at all, through all degrees of responsibility and participation, even occasionally the actual direction of a whole farm by a spinster like Bathsheba Everdene, the heroine of Thomas Hardy's *Far From the Madding Crowd*, or a widow of a farmer. At the lowest end of the scale the wives on the smaller holdings lived in a fashion very little different from that of a labourer's wife.

It was the housewives that maintained whatever standard of refinement was possible and who insisted upon the kind of behaviour that they considered desirable. One lady, like Queen Victoria, or perhaps because of Queen Victoria's example, disliked tobacco smoke. The house was hers, she maintained, and she would not allow smoking in it. One night her husband came home from market, sober, but inoculated with the smoke of the cigars he was so fond of. His wife was asleep, but the fumes of the noxious weed were so offensive to her that she awakened, and was angry as anyone unpleasantly disturbed in the first sleep always is. She ordered the unfortunate husband to put his clothes outside the door as he took them off. Stubbornly he refused and disposed his garments upon a chair as usual before getting into bed. The wife got up and threw the clothes out of the window "to sweeten them". As a counter measure the husband rose, and in his turn, threw his wife's clothes out, although he found it a bit difficult to force the crinoline through.

His wife was no whit dismayed. She pointed out that her clothes were very shabby. Only consideration for him had prevented her from buying new ones; now she would have to. This defeated the husband who went down and collected both lots of clothing, his wife's first. Marjorie and C. H. B. Quennell, who recorded the story in *Everyday things in England, 1851–1934,* 1934, added the comment that men are very much what their mothers and wives make them; these women made fine men. Acceptance of this dictum we leave to the reader's judgement.

The day-to-day life of the less well-to-do country housewives can be collected from occasional remarks in Michael Home's *Autumn Fields,* 1944. In the nineties his mother was alone most of the time with a family to feed and even to clothe, for many of the children's garments were home made, or adapted to suit a younger child. There was the house to keep clean with a trifle of occasional help on washing days. In winter Mrs. Home rose at 6 a.m.; in summer at dawn. Her long day was spent in keeping bright and speckless a home with brick floors, blackleaded grates and ornamented with brass candlesticks, all of which seem specially designed to make more work. In the evening she read such works as *Mrs. Halliburton's Troubles,* or Marie Corelli, or Mrs. Humphrey Ward as an accompaniment to an everlasting basket of darning and needlework upon the family garments. Her husband's favourite reading was Thomas Hardy. Another occupation in the dark winter evenings was making rugs. Once a month, perhaps, Mrs. Home recreated herself by taking tea at a neighbour's and sometimes on winter afternoons she played a game of draughts. Her cooking was perfection in the recollection of her son, but she had no time to bake bread. When meat was scarce the family lived on bread and cheese, a necessary economy, and the infrequent rabbit brought home by the father had to serve as a dinner for two parents and six children.

This woman's daughters were brought up with no foolish snobbishness. They cooked and made and mended, and attending "Ouseland" Grammar School gave no exemption from scrubbing a brick floor. Training in these homely virtues was general in this class all over the country. Michael Home wrote about Norfolk, Douglas Fisher has written about Gloucester where the girl of the same sort had to do housework or help with it while she was still at school. Washing, cleaning and mending were her part and she was only allowed to go and play when she had finished her allotted task. It was good training if the mother was a good housewife and provided all that the State now supplies in its domestic science classes. Besides housework the mother and the girls looked after the flower garden. The men must grow something more useful in their allotment and garden, potatoes and other things that would help to fill the pot.

Reform a little later was anxious to provide small holdings and to encourage a return to the rural life that was, it was thought, being so rapidly abandoned before World War I. The Rt. Hon. Jesse Collings, no less, found that young women of the middle class and what are called the "leisured" classes had in 1906 of late years begun to attend agricultural schools and colleges, qualifying themselves by scientific and practical training to become agriculturists. Women were, he said, well suited for dairy work, for poultry and bee keeping, for fruit and flower growing and market gardening. This was profoundly original and discovered as new something that had been practised for centuries.

The daily life of Mrs. Home was not greatly different from that of the farm worker's wife. By the end of the nineteenth century these women had almost ceased to be employed as wage earners on the land, except in the north where the old-fashioned system of employment of women continued. There were, nevertheless, still about 40,000 women workers and about half that number of women farmers. The women themselves disliked the work, and did it in some measure only under direct or indirect compulsion. Hay and corn harvest they did not mind. It was hard work but it was done with a festive air that made it all rather enjoyable.

Frederick Clifford generalized rather too broadly in 1874 when he declared that the housewives stayed at home and looked after the house and their domestic work. An increasing number of them did, but by no means all. To his mind the reason for this change must be that there was less need for them to add to their husband's earnings by field work. The truth was that this work had never been really profitable to the family any more than had the tiny contribution to the common fund derived from the children's work. The farmers had been deprived of infant labour when the Education Acts began to operate. They could employ no one less than ten years old except when the school closed for harvest, and these hard-bitten employers declared time and again that they could not farm properly without the help of these tiny children. Both wives and children probably saved money by not going to work. They were paid so little and the wear and tear on their clothes and boots was so heavy that a loss was more probable than a net gain, although the few extra pence were welcome enough in a spending sense. Women working in the fields were almost obliged to neglect their homes, if they were married, or if single, they failed to learn the domestic jobs they would have to do when they did marry.

Francis George Heath emphasized the unprofitable character of women's field work in Devon in the same year, 1874. The advantage was so small as to be scarcely appreciable. The women's wage was 7d. or 8d. a day and on this ground alone many women would have refused to do field work at all, but for the fact that they were compelled to do so by the agreement made between their husbands and the farmers. The latter made the employment of the wife when called upon a condition of giving a job to the husband. On the other hand T. E. Kebbell deplored that the days of neat farming were at an end. A great deal of necessary work was not done for want of children to do it, and the increased cost of labour—men must be paid more than children or women though their wages were little enough—necessitated imperfect tillage. "We don't weed corn or pick stones as we did. The women must not work in the fields nowadays, and the children are at school. So the work is not done and we are glad of an excuse to curtail expense, however injurious it may prove to be hereafter."

One thing about the employment of housewives upon field work none of these writers remarks. It was the terrible dangers to which the children were exposed in the absence of their mothers. Many of them took tiny babies to the fields and bestowed them in a sheltered corner in the care of another child a year or two older, while they worked. This insured that the children were under their mother's eye at intervals during the day.

Other mothers of families of several children simply locked the whole lot up in the cottage. Consequently disastrous accidents sometimes happened. A cautious mother would, of course, leave no fire for the babies to tumble into, and the children must make out as best they could in summer heat or winter cold.

An example of the kind of thing that did happen was related to Major Gambier Parry by an old lady, Tabitha Stevens, in the early years of the present century. Her mother and father and elder sister, aged nine, all went out to work in "one of they gangs". They left

Tabitha locked up in the cottage at home with her three younger brothers and sisters to care for.

"Left alone, same as that, a pretty caddle us got into at times, and a pretty sight the housen were when mother came home in the dark, and set down to light the fire and take off the rags, all wet, as she did bind her legs with. She was wet to the middle times, and so were I, when it came to my turn to do as she done—or try to."

One day the children were famished. With all the natural improvidence of hungry children, they had eaten all the bread their mother had left them as soon as she was gone. There was a bit of gammon end hanging on a nail in a ceiling beam. It was the custom to have a bit of it for Sunday dinner. The boy Sammy determined to have a piece and pushed the table against the wall. He put a chair on the table in spite of all his sister could say, and climbed upon it. He reached the gammon, but the chair toppled over and he crashed down upon the stone floor. He laid there helpless but conscious until the parents came home. He had broken his back and later he died. It is easy to imagine the consternation of the family in face of such a disaster. We can only hope that such accidents were infrequent though constantly possible.

It was perhaps in the garden or on the allotment that the cottage housewife did the most outdoor work in the later years of the nineteenth century. A man who had done a long day in the fields did not relish, although often enough he felt compelled to it, exchanging the plough of his day's work for a spade in the evening. Where the men were regularly employed "it was the bent back of the women" which had to bear the brunt and burden of allotment tillage. This was especially so at harvest times when the men worked from dawn till dark and the women's labour was also wanted.

In spite of all the disadvantages of the system a large number of women were still employed in field work at the turn of the century. The number was large in itself though the women field workers were only a small proportion of the whole number of cottage housewives in the country.

An American, Clifton Johnson, observed that then all the heaviest farm work was done by men, but the lighter field tasks were often done by women, though he thought their employment was always intermittent and was never continuous throughout the year. In his travels through the countryside he first saw women workers on the newly ploughed grounds of early spring. They were going over the fields with forks and picking out all the witch grass (couch) roots. They were piled in little heaps and burned later. The women worked seven or eight hours a day and were then paid a shilling. They were, to Clifton Johnson, at first picturesque, but a closer view that showed them nearly all to be old, stumpy figured and slouchy in dress, left no room for romance.

He was perhaps fortunate in that his first glimpse of village maidens was not one of *Tess of the D'Urbervilles* and her companions on that May Day when they joined together in the club walking, a survival of a *Cerealia* that Thomas Hardy found singular in that the members were solely women. They must have been a pretty sight as he describes it. The banded ones were all dressed in white gowns, a gay survival of the old-style days when cheerfulness and May Day were synonyms. Walking two by two round the parish each woman carried a peeled willow wand in her right hand and a bunch of flowers in her left. After the procession there was dancing in a meadow.

But joyous occasions like these were all too infrequent and Tess was soon involved in the catastrophies that Hardy loved. Meanwhile she worked on different farms. On one she worked with other women and girls behind the reaper. Their job was to tie the sheaves, something the machine did not yet do. At this work in the heavy summer sunshine the women and girls wore drawn cotton bonnets with great flapping curtains to keep off the sun and gloves to prevent their hands being wounded by the stubble or the thistles that were cut with the corn. One wore a pale pink jacket, another a cream-coloured tight-sleeved gown, yet another a red petticoat, but most of them were content with the rough brown "wropper" or overall, a garment sanctified by tradition and utility. It was the most appropriate dress of the fieldwoman but the frivolity of the younger women demanded something gayer. The work was so regular and rhythmic that Hardy compared the women's movements to those of dancers in a quadrille.

Another job that Tess had was on a large dairy farm. Here the cows were milked in the yard if they were quiet, tied up in a long open-sided thatched shed if they were inclined to be restless. The milkers formed quite a battalion of men and maids, the latter walking on pattens through the mire of the yards. Each milker tackled from six to eight cows night and morning and sang pensive ditties while working to encourage the cows to give their milk readily. Many of the men and maids lived in on this farm. They took their meals all together in the kitchen, the dairyman and his wife and the men and maids, and the assembly at meal times was lively and cheerful.

Later Tess went back to field work on an arable farm. For this she wore the regular dress of a fieldswoman, a grey serge cape, a red woollen cravat, a stuff skirt covered by a whitey-brown wrapper and stiff leather gloves. Here she worked at hacking swedes, drawing reeds, turnip slicing and feeding the threshing machines. The worst of these jobs was perhaps the swede hacking. The leaves were often wet, the crop was grown on the bleak down where cold winds blew, a stooping position was necessary and the hours were long. The women worked shrouded in Hessian wrappers, sleeved brown pinafores tied behind to keep their skirts from blowing about, boots high up the ankles, and wore yellowish sheepskin gloves to protect their hands. Hardy described women doing similar work upon Dorset farms in *Far from the Madding Crowd*.

Taine had emphasized the disadvantages of women working in the fields so early as 1870. He found the female peasant lacking in address, which was not very surprising, but worse, she had no talent for keeping house. She could not make soup, a roast, a dish of any sort. She always went to the tradespeople and bought new bread, butter, tea, ham, and always at the highest prices. Everyone in the family he had in mind could hoe a field, but not one could cook a chop. It is doubtful whether she ever had the chance, but it is a commonplace that the labourers' wives were no longer baking their own bread, brewing their own beer, curing their own ham, or gathering fuel in the copse, or on the common. Nor was she practising any of those domestic economies that had been popularly sanctioned and proper in an earlier day.

Perhaps some of them had been dissuaded from baking their own bread by unfortunate results from using sprouted grain after a wet harvest. Both farm housewife and cottage housewife who baked their own bread of grain that had stood on the wet until it sprouted, as it did in 1860 for example, found it impossible to make good bread. S. G. Kendall's mother told him, and he had himself experienced the difficulty. Two knives were necessary when this dreadful bread had to be cut up into slices. One knife was used to tear up the loaf, the second was used to clean the first before trying to cut another slice. The dough made from sprouted grain did not rise after the yeast was added, nor would it bake properly. It simply ran into a glutinous sticky mass enclosed in a doubtful-looking crust. The finished product was, as one can imagine, quite unpalatable in appearance; in taste it had a sickly sweet flavour.

There was a partial remedy for this unfortunate state of affairs. The housewife sifted fine wood ash from the hearth, where little or no coal was used, into an earthenware crock. Boiling water was poured over the ashes, and left to settle covered by a clean cloth. After a day or so the ash had all sunk to the bottom of the crock, the water being clear and bright. This water was carefully skimmed off and used to mix the dough instead of water from the well or other ordinary source of supply.

Kendall believed that the alkaloid quality of this lye water acted as an antidote to the worst effects of sprouted grain, though his description of the improved product makes it sound less than appetizing.

Experiences like these were enough to discourage the most valiant housewife. It was easier to buy a better loaf from the village bakehouse than to go to all the trouble of baking bread and then to find it so nasty.

With greater facilities for mobility, better roads and the abolition of the toll gates, merchants from the towns invaded the villages and lonely cottages. "Johnny Fortnight", the tally man, used all his wiles to beguile and accommodate the village wives and maidens with his easy terms of fortnightly instalments of his elevated prices. Many of these women had been away from the village in domestic service for some years before marriage, and they looked for a trifle more grace in life than had been the lot of their mothers and grandmothers, who had never left the village of their birth. Some of their efforts to achieve it were rather misguided to a modern middle-class eye. The garish pair of vases sold by the ingratiating pedlar, the shrieking oleograph of still life, or some scene of heroism, storm and disaster, would not today be chosen as decorations for over the mantel and on the walls of a living-room, but they served their purpose of introducing a note of colour, possibly all too strident, into what were often dull and overcrowded interiors.

Some young wives, with memories of the grandeur of the houses where they had lived as domestic servants, would make a cosy corner out of old boxes and cretonne in imitation of the more ambitious efforts of their quondam employers. A gridiron might be covered with coloured wool and hung up to serve as a letter rack, to hold the infrequent correspondence. Cheap Japanese fans were brought by pedlars or purchased from the "fancy" shop in the town, window curtains were hung and tied back with bows of gaily coloured ribbon.

The young bride, too, wanted horsehair-seated chairs instead of the wooden Windsor chair common in her parents' cottage. A centre table, on which meals were taken, was usual, and this might be covered with a gay cloth between meals though American cloth, sometimes decorated with a pattern of flowers, was quite ordinary. A chest of drawers at one side could be used as a sideboard. The very ambitious might have a couple of wicker armchairs, one at each side of the fireplace.

The brightness of this new home dimmed as time passed and children came along. It became crowded and the humble furnishings worn. At Lark Rise, a lovely imagined village that Flora Thompson's memories have painted in such glowing colours, there was but one room downstairs in nearly all the cottages. Many of these rooms "were poor and bare with only a table and a few chairs and stools for furniture and a superannuated potato sack thrown down by way of hearth rug. Others were bright and cosy, with dressers of crockery, cushioned chairs, pictures on the walls, and brightly coloured home-made rugs on the floors." These last must have been those tenanted by the returned domestic worker who kept similar tiny homes going with such pride in all parts of the country.

Christopher Holdenby lodged in a rather good-class cottage when he was working as a farm labourer on the eve of World War I. A living-room, a parlour and three bedrooms was the accommodation. The living-room was very small. It was furnished with a home-made wooden bench, some of dad's own carpentry, a table and four chairs. A copper stood on one side of the stove, a cause of great discomfort on washing days, especially in hot weather. Meals then had to be eaten in that tiny room with a fire for cooking in the stove and amidst the heat and steam of the copper. Only half the window would open but probably the door gave directly to the open air and helped to ventilate in summer and create piercing draughts in winter. On the opposite side of the stove was the only cupboard in the house. The family boots and leggings were stored on its floor. The family nightgowns rested on the first shelf by day and day clothes by night. The bedrooms were too small to allow much washing and dressing upstairs. The children came down to breakfast in their nightgowns; at night they were undressed and bathed in a tin tub in the tiny kitchen. Adults could only get a bath when the rest of the family had gone to bed, and when water was scarce this was not only a nuisance but a decided luxury.

Besides the boots and leggings on the floor and the clothes on the first shelf, the groceries and crockery were also stored in this all-containing cupboard. Obviously there was a good deal of congestion in the living-room when "dad", the lodger, mother and the children were all in it. This congestion was the ordinary fate of the cottager all over the country. Holdenby does not identify the place where his cottage stood, but John Halsham, writing of a village in Sussex in 1898, said much the same thing.

"The new cottages built by speculators from Tisfield and owned by two or three small tradesmen in Arnington are detestable styes, with thin slate roofs, rubbishy doors and windows and scamped brickwork . . . internally a dull horror with their unused front par-lours, sacred to antimaccassars and wool work and the family Bible reposing cornerwise upon the table. The small kitchen-living-room at the back, with an impracticable little range (charged extra in the rent), perhaps a copper as well, is often inhabited at one time by a family of seven or eight souls, the dinner a-preparing, and the week's wash half dried. Up the breakneck stairs there are two or three little bedrooms, stifling in summer, bitter in frost. The whole building, whether Jacobean or Victorian, reeks with a thick warm smell, compounded nastiness, preserved within well-closed windows, save in the full dog-days."

All this is confirmed by the American, Clifton Johnson, and indeed by multitudes of cottages lived in at the present moment.

Personal cleanliness was not much followed. No doubt it was almost impossible to take a bath in the kitchen that was the common room of the house. Soap and water were hard to come by. In Lark Rise, for example, only three of the thirty cottages had their own water supply.

The rest used the well of a cottage that had fallen into ruin and disappeared. There was no public well or pump. The housewives had to get their water how they could. Much of it was secured from the rain that fell upon the roof, and was stored in an old barrel or iron tanks. "Babies," wrote Halsham, "are tubbed somewhat severely till they reach the knickerbocker age, when they gain their freedom, and thereafter achieve the low water mark conspicuously between collar and neck; below which soap seldom descends in after years."

The difficulty of water supply in a heathy district is shown by a story told by Louis J. Jennings, who explored the *Field Paths and Green Lanes* of Surrey and Sussex in 1875. Near Mr. Leveson-Gower's house at Holmwood Hill, Surrey, he met a poor woman walking inside a hoop with a pail of water in each hand. She looked to him very thin and miserable, as if it seldom fell to her lot to have enough to eat. The water was splashing all over her patched and worn-out gown, so Jennings suggested she should put a flat piece of wood on the top of each pail. Whether she was too lethargic to act on his advice or not does not appear. She told him she had to fetch all her water from a spring a quarter of a mile distant from her cottage. In a very dry summer she had to go two or three miles to Ewhurst for water. This was a large task because she had three children, a pig, and a husband who was a drunkard. This vice of the husband made it more than ever difficult to get the children a dinner. "They generally get a good slice of bread and sometimes a bit of treacle; and it is hard to get that."

It is easy enough to understand how hastily the clothes would be huddled on in winter when rising between 5 and 6 a.m. or perhaps earlier. Holdenby has described the actual difficulty of dressing in the minute bedroom he lodged in. When to restricted space the frosts of winter were added, speed in getting clad was the essence of the contract. Comfort in bed itself was impossible at a time when, as Hardy wrote, "in cottages the breath of the sleepers freezes to the sheets".

If it was difficult for the cottagers to maintain a high standard of personal cleanliness, it was by no means any easier for the housewife to keep the house clean. When she spent all her time at home she had the more time to spend upon the housework. The comparative few who worked in the fields at the end of the century had less. Miracles were achieved by some of these devoted women. Others gave up in despair or spent a lot of their time in gossip with their neighbours.

Caste feeling was very marked and friendships between women of different social standing, for example, the tradesmen's and the labourers' wives, was uncommon. Among equals cliques and gossips and formidable animosities existed just as they do today. A couple of labourers' wives, who lived in a pair of semi-detached cottages, known in some parts as a double-dweller, would for a while be particularly friendly with each other. If either wanted a pinch of salt, they ran to the other for it, or a loaf of bread, or a little tea, they ran for that. Instead of running back they would sit and talk for half the morning, and it was midday before the visitor thought of dashing home to get the dinner. Very soon each knew too much about the other, and at last a secret was let out. Then there was a row and each called the other "everything but their Christian names". After this they did not speak when they met, and might keep up such a feud for years. Others would forget the quarrel after a time, possibly upon an occasion when the enemy needed a helping hand, and very soon this pair of elementals would be as great friends as ever.

Housewives who tried to make a home for their families in these tiny cottages lived a life that was one long round of toil. They probably did not realize it because they had known nothing different. They, too, were often the managers, directing the activities of their husbands and sons. And at the turn of the century, if not a little before that, they had a weekly outing. On Saturday evening after the husband had come home from work at 6 p.m. they had a meal, and then set out to walk to the nearest town, possibly several miles, to do the week-end shopping. Though the spending of each penny of a wage of 10s. to 14s. a week was often a matter of anxious debate, the majority tried to make some sort of festivity of this weekly outing. It was indeed something quite outside the experience of their parents or forbears. They met friends, whom they may not have seen since the previous week, had a chat and dropped into the public for a glass which then cost only a penny. They endured the long walk home happily enough for they had been enjoying themselves with a touch of social life that was denied them in the formidable isolation of many of the cottages in which they lived.

Field work for cottage housewives, in spite of having been condemned as uneconomic for the women and their families, lingered on in the south-west and in Gloucestershire, and of course in the north. In Dorset the labourers' wives, though under no legal obligation to do so, must still in 1903 go out to field labour or "give offence". In a Cotswold Village of the 1890s the women worked in the fields at certain seasons of the year. This occasional employment brought them in a tiny sum of money and gave them a little change from the monotonous routine of housework. There was some change of companionship, too, because jobs like turnip hoeing were done in the company of other workers. Being only done at intervals, it did not lead to the neglect of the home or the loss of whatever domestic skill the housewife possessed. "Most of the cottages," wrote J. Arthur Gibbs, "are kept scrupulously clean; they have an air of homely comfort which calls forth the admiration of all strangers." Possibly, but it is doubtful whether any of these admiring strangers would have cared to live in these cottages for any length of time after practical experience of living in them.

The children, too, when they went to church on Sundays were dressed with a neatness and good taste that simply astonished Gibbs, when he remembered that the wages of a labourer in the Cotswolds were seldom more than 14s. a week.

In the next county, Wiltshire, at Corsham, women were no longer employed in farm work because, like so many more of England in those times, the land in the parish had largely gone down to grass. The women were no longer wanted to gather stones off the ploughland, to tie the sheaves of corn or to hoe roots for a wage of 10d. a day. The grass was cut by machine, a lot of the hay was made by horse-drawn tedders, etc., but hay making was nevertheless an occasion for everyone to turn out, if not for wages, then for the pleasure of being present. Mowing and reaping machines, binders and horse hoes were doing much of the work formerly done by women on the arable, and this was one more reason why fewer housewives were called away from their home duties.

Cooking in the cottages was a matter of boiling, stewing or pot roasting over the open fire as a general rule. Towards the end of the century some of the open hearths were fitted with an iron coal-burning stove with a small oven at one side and a hob on which saucepans could be boiled. This was often only to be found in the more modern cottages so bitterly complained of by John Halsham.

At Lark Rise fresh meat was a luxury only seen in a few of the cottages on Sunday. Then it might be only sixpennyworth of pieces used to make a pudding. Sometimes late on Saturday night in those days before refrigeration, the cheap butcher in the town would sell off the unsold meat at bargain rates by a sort of Dutch auction. Then perhaps the cottage housewife could secure a small joint as a special treat. It could be roasted in the oven if the cottage possessed a grate; if there was none it could be suspended from one of the pot-hooks and hangers in the chimney and turned by one of the children before the fire. For those villagers who kept a pig there was always a great feast on the Sunday after pig-killing, but this came only once, at most twice a year, and by no means all cottagers were able to keep a pig. Some employers categorically forbade them to do so in case they might be tempted to steal grain for feeding it.

Christopher Holdenby only gradually grew accustomed to cottage fare. The tea was so strong that it set his teeth on edge, and the only way he could drink it was after it had been sweetened with four lumps or two dessert spoonfuls of sugar. Bread and butter, cheese and pickles, and potatoes formed the main staples. The very cheapest scraps of meat were cooked to destruction to make a little gravy to moisten the potatoes. At the end of the week came the joint, but in some families they did not always have meat once a week. The other staple was bacon, fat beyond the taste of such a man, but tasty to the labourer's fat-starved body. It was eaten with the rind on so as to avoid waste. The great treat was tinned herrings on Saturday night.

In 1913 tins were already beginning to play an important part in the housewife's shopping however remote her cottage. The cheapest and pinkest brand of so-called tinned salmon, tinned sardines and herrings, tinned corned beef and tinned condensed milk were all amongst the benefits that civilization was bringing to the door of the cottage in the country as well as to the dwellers in the towns. They all helped her to solve some of her difficulties.

Other difficulties remained, as some of them still do. Water supply has now been provided in some places, but at the end of the nineteenth century a piped water supply was not even dreamed of by the majority of villagers. Just as there were no water mains there was no main drainage. Sewage disposal was as primitive in many villages and hamlets as it had been for hundreds of years. Lark Rise was particularly badly off in this respect. The cottages there had not even an earth closet, but used an arrangement such as can only be seen today in the more isolated mountainous regions of Middle Europe. It was simply a pit with a seat placed over it and was emptied twice a year. When this was being done the neighbours closed all their doors and windows. According to the talents of the housewife some of these places were horrible, others fairly decent. Those that were kept well cleaned were not too unpleasant. From this lowly level every primitive kind of arrangement was to be found in different parts of the country.

Superstition had not died out amongst rustic people, especially in the parts, and they were many, that were almost as isolated as they had ever been. In the Isle of Purbeck, for example, the women believed that a ride on a donkey's back to four cross roads, or wearing a bit of hair clipped from a donkey's shoulders, was an infallible cure for whooping cough. This was a mild kind of white witchcraft, but that gradually lost its power as the black art had done so long before, and at last all that the white witch could be expected to do was to charm away warts.

The First World War was but a few years in the future at the dawn of the twentieth century. It and the internal combustion engine were to introduce great changes in everyone's life. Some of these changes were already foreshadowed before the war. Although money wages only ranged from 10s. to 14s. a week upon the farms of those now remote days, life was becoming less, if only a trifle less, arduous for the cottage housewife than it had been for at least a century, and she was doing her best to make her cottage into a home for her husband and family.

It was the end of an epoch. The great ladies, who had been the caretakers of country life and the exemplars of how it should be lived, had deserted the countryside, or at the most, only spent a small part of their time there. For the rest the farm and cottage housewife were tied to their homes because of their husband's employment, and for many of them the conditions of their lives were little changed from what they had been for centuries.

Oil lamps had taken the place of rushlights and tallow dips for lighting. More coal was used in the farmhouse kitchens where new grates with ovens had been installed, though it was not yet the day of hot-water systems and bathrooms. The cottagers were mostly fain to be content with wood fires, many of them burning on open hearths. Water supply at farmhouse and cottage alike was from a well, or collected from a roof. In some places it was dipped from a murky pond, and in others there was a village pump. Sanitation was primitive in the extreme as it remains in some places.

In spite of all these primitive elements in the life of the country housewife, she went on doing her job as she had always so devotedly done, and she would have been happy indeed could she have foreseen how many of her children would benefit from rural electrification, piped water supply, and village sewage farms.

APPENDIX

*Authorities for Chapter One**

ASPINALL-OGLANDER, C., Nunwell Symphony, 1945.
BELLOC, HILAIRE, Elizabethan Commentary, 1942.
BYRNE, M. ST. CLARE, Elizabethan Life in Town and Country, 1925.
BYRNE, M. ST. CLARE, The Elizabethan Home, 1949.
BOAS, MRS. FREDERICK, In Shakespeare's England, 1903.
COX, J. CHARLES, Churchwarden's Accounts, 1913.
DAVIS, WILLIAM STEARNES, Life in Elizabethan Days, 1930.
DELONEY, THOMAS, The Pleasant History of Jack of Newbury, 1596.
FITZHERBERT, Boke of Husbandry, 1523.
GARVIN, KATHERINE, Great Tudors, 1935.
GOFF, LADY CECILIE, A Woman of the Tudor Age, 1930.
GOULD, S. BARING, Old Country Life, 1895.
HALL, HUBERT, Society in the Elizabethan Age, 1887.
HARRISON, WILLIAM, Elizabethan England (Scott Library), 1577.
LEE, SIR SIDNEY, Shakespeare's England, 1917.
LETTS, MALCOLM, As the Foreigner Saw Us, 1935.
MOTTRAM, R. H., The Corbells at War, c. 1946.
OVERBURY, SIR THOMAS, Works (ed. by Rimbault), 1890.
PLAT, SIR HUGH, Sundrie New and Artificial Remedies Against Famine, 1596.
PLAT, SIR HUGH, Delightes for Ladies, 1602 (ed. by G. E. and K. R. Fussell), 1949.
POLLARD, A. F., The Reign of Henry VII from Contemporary Sources, Vol. II, 1914.
RHODE, ELEANOR SINCLAIR, The Old English Gardening Books, 1924.
RHODE, ELEANOR SINCLAIR, The Story of the Garden, 1932.
ROWSE, A. L., The England of Elizabeth, 1950.
SALTER, EMMA GURNEY, Tudor England Through Venetian Eyes, 1930.
SALZMAN, L. F., England in Tudor Times, 1926.
STRACHEY, LYTTON, Portraits in Miniature, 1931.
THORNBURY, GEORGE WALTER, Shakespeare's England, 1856.
TUSSER, THOMAS, Five Hundred Points of Good Husbandry, 1573.
WEST, V. SACKVILLE, Knole and the Sackvilles, 1922.
WILLIAMS, C. H., England Under the Early Tudors, 1925.
WILLIAMS, CLARE, Thomas Platter's Travels in England, 1937.
WILSON, JOHN DOVER, John Lyly, 1905.
WILSON, VIOLET A., Society Women in Shakespeare's Time, 1924.
WOODWARD, MARCUS, The Countryman's Jewel, 1934.
WRIGHT, LOUIS B., Middle Class Culture in Elizabethan England, 1935.

Authorities for Chapter Two

ADDISON, WILLIAM, Epping Forest, 1945.
ADDISON, WILLIAM, Essex Heyday, 1949.
ASPINALL-OGLANDER, CECIL, Nunwell Symphony, 1945.
ASHTON, JOHN, Humour, Wit and Satire of the 17th Century, 1883.
BEST, HENRY, Rural Economy in 1641, Surtees Soc.
BRADLEY, ROSE M., The English Housewife in the 17th and 18th Centuries, 1912.

* A great deal of the current literature of the time has been consulted besides these books, most of which are secondary, but it is not desirable to expand this list unduly.

BRETON, NICHOLAS, The Court and Country, 1618.
CAMPION, THOMAS, Two Books on Airs (Muses Library), c. 1614.
CAMPBELL, MILDRED, The English Yeoman under Elizabeth, and the Early Stuarts, 1942.
CLARKE, ALICE, Working Life of Women in the 17th Century, 1919.
COATE, MARY, Social Life in Stuart England, 1924.
COKE, DOROTHEA, The Last Elizabethan, Sir John Coke, 1563-1644, 1929.
DAVIS, GODFREY, The Early Stuarts, 1603-1660, 1937.
DITCHFIELD, P. H., The Old English Country Squire, 1912.
EARLE, JOHN, Micro-Cosmographie, 1603.
ESTIENNE AND LIEBAULT, The Countrie Farm, c. 1600.
FANSHAWE, LADY ANNE, Memoirs, 1830.
FULLER, THOMAS, Holy and Profane State, 1642.
GODFREY, ELIZABETH, Social Life under the Stuarts, 1904.
GOOGE, BARNABY, The Whole Art and Trade of Husbandry, 1614.
HALSTED, CAROLINE, The Obligations of Literature to the Mothers of England, 1840.
HARRISON, G. B., England in Shakespeare's Day, 1929.
HUTCHINSON, LUCY, Memoirs of the Life of Col. Hutchinson, etc., 1907.
LAWSON, WILLIAM, The Country Housewife's Garden (Cresset Press, 1927), 1617.
MACKIE, J. D., Cavalier and Puritan, 1930.
MARKHAM, GERVASE, The English Huswife, 1615.
MARVELL, ANDREW, Poems.
MORLEY, HENRY, Character Writings of the 17th Century, 1891.
MORLEY, HENRY, Northamptonshire Past and Present, Vol. I, 1948.
OVERBURY, SIR THOMAS, Works (ed. by Rimbault), 1890.
PLAT, SIR HUGH, Delightes for Ladies, 1602 (ed. by G. E. and K. R. Fussell), 1949.
POWELL, WILLIAM, Tom of all Trades, or the Plain Pathway to Preferment, 1631.
REYNOLDS, MYRA, The Learned Lady in England, 1650-1760, 1920.
RHODE, ELEANOR SINCLAIR, The Old English Gardening Books, 1924.
RHODE, ELEANOR SINCLAIR, The Story of the Garden, 1932.
TIMBS, JOHN, Nooks and Corners of English Life, 1867.
TICKNER, F. W., Women in English Economic History, 1923.
THOMPSON, GLADYS SCOTT, Life in a Noble Household, 1641-1700, 1937.
TREVELYAN, G. M., England Under the Stuarts, 1904.
WEST, V. SACKVILLE, Knole and the Sackvilles, 1922.
WILKINSON, ROBERT, The Merchant Royal, 1607.

Authorities for Chapter Three

B.F., The Office of the Good Housewife, 1672.
BAXTER, REV. RICHARD, The Poor Husbandman's Advocate, ed. by F. J. Powicke, 1691.
BRADLEY, ROSE M., The English Housewife in the 17th and 18th Centuries, 1912.
BRYANT, ARTHUR, The England of Charles II, 1934.
BRYANT, ARTHUR, The National Character, 1934.
BRYANT, ARTHUR, Postman's Horn, 1936.
CARTWRIGHT, JULIA, Sacharissa, Dorothy Sidney, Countess of Sunderland, 1617-1684, 1901.
CLARK, ALICE, Working Life of Women in the 17th Century, 1919.
CLARK, G. N., The Later Stuarts, 1660-1714, 1934.
DELMEGE, J. ANTHONY, Towards National Health, 1931.
EVELYN, JOHN, Mundus Muliebris or the Ladies Dressing Room Unlock'd, 1690.
FIENNES, CELIA, The Journeys of Celia Fiennes, Cresset Press, 1949.
HAGGARD, HOWARD W., Devils, Drugs and Doctors, 1929.
HILL, GEORGIANA, Women in English Life, 1896.
MACAULAY, LORD, History of England, Chapter III, 1848.
OGG, DAVID, England in the Reign of Charles II, 1934.

PARKES, JOAN, Travel in the 17th Century, 1925.
PHILLIPS, M. AND TOMKINSON, W. S., English Women in Life and Letters, 1927.
REYNOLDS, MYRA, The Learned Lady in England, 1650–1760, 1920.
RHODE, ELEANOR SINCLAIR, The Story of the Garden, 1932.
RHYS, J. P., The Countryside of the 17th Century. Journal Land Agents Soc., December 1931.
RYAN, P. F. WILLIAM, Stuart Life and Manners, 1912.
SYDNEY, W. C., Social Life in England from the Restoration to the Revolution, 1660–1690, 1892.
SMITH, EDWARD, Foreign Visitors to England and What They Have Thought of us, 1889.
SUTHERLAND, JAMES, Defoe, 1937.
SWITZER, STEPHEN, Iconographia Rustica, 1718.
THOMPSON, GLADYS SCOTT, Life in a Noble Household, 1641–1700, 1937.
TICKNER, F. W., Women in English Economic History, 1923.
TRAILL'S Social England, Vol. V. Agriculture by R. E. Prothero, 1896.
WALTON, ISAAC, Compleat Angler (Macmillan Library of English Classics, 1900), 1653.
WARD, J. D. U., Dovecotes, Farmer's Weekly, 5th October, 1951.
WALLAS, ADA, Before the Bluestockings, 1929.
Besides the above some books have been mentioned in the text.

Authorities for Chapter IV

ADDISON, JOSEPH, Spectator, 1712.
ASHTON, JOHN, Social Life in the Reign of Queen Anne, 1882.
BOTSFORD, JAY BARRETT, English Society in the 18th Century as Influenced from Overseas, 1924.
BRADLEY, RICHARD, The Country Housewife and Lady's Director, 6th ed., 1736.
ELAND, G. (Ed.), Shardeloes Papers of the 17th and 18th Centuries, 1947.
EVELYN, CHARLES, The Lady's Recreation, 1718.
FIELDING, HENRY, Tom Jones, 1749.
FIELDING, HENRY, Amelia, 1751.
GARNIER, RUSSELL M., History of the English Landed Interest, 1893.
GARNIER, RUSSELL M., Annals of the British Peasantry, 1895.
GAY, JOHN, Rural Sports, 1711.
GAY, JOHN, The Shepherds Week, 1714.
GEORGE, M. DOROTHY, England in Transition, 1931.
GROSE, FRANCIS, The Olio, 1793.
HILL, GEORGIANA, Women in English Life, 1896.
LAWRENCE, JOHN, A New System of Agriculture, 1726.
LUCAS, JOSEPH (ed.), Kalm's Account of his Visit to England on his way to America in 1748, 1892.
POPE, Works.
REYNOLD, MYRA, The Learned Lady in England, 1650–1760, 1920.
RICHARDSON, SAMUEL, Clarissa, 1748.
RICHARDSON, SAMUEL, Pamela, 1741.
STRONG, L. A. G., English Domestic Life During the Last Two Hundred Years, 1942.
THOMPSON, GLADYS SCOTT, Letters of a Grandmother (Sarah, Duchess of Marlborough), 1732–1735, 1943.
TICKNER, F. W., Women in English Economic History, 1923.
TREVELYAN, G. M., The England of Queen Anne, 1934.
WORDSWORTH, CHRISTOPHER, Social Life at the English Universities in the 18th Centuries, 1874.

Authorities for Chapter V

ANON., The Farmer's Wife, or Complete Country Housewife, c. 1780.
BARKER, EILEEN, The Experienced Housekeeper of 150 Years Ago, Farmer's Weekly, 24th February, 1950.

BRADLEY, ROSE M., The English Housewife in the 17th and 18th Centuries, 1912.
BURNET, REGULA (ed.), Ann Cook and Friend, 1940.
CLARE, Shepherd's Calendar.
COLE, G. D. H. AND POSTGATE, RAYMOND, The Common People, 1746–1938, 1938.
DOBSON, AUSTIN, Eighteenth Century Studies, Wayfarers Lib.
GILBOY, ELIZABETH W., Wages in 18th Century England, 1934.
HILL, GEORGIANA, Women in English Life, 1896.
LANG, ELSIE M., British Women in the 20th Century, 1929.
MARSHALL, WILLIAM, Rural Economy of the Southern Counties (and other works), 1799.
MATON, WILLIAM GEORGE, Observations . . . of the Western Counties, 1797.
ORWIN, C. S., Agriculture and Rural Life in Johnson's England, 1934.
PASTON, GEORGE, Little Memoirs of the 18th Century, 1901.
PINCHBECK, IVY, Women workers in the Industrial Revolution, 1750–1850, 1930.
POPE-HENNESSEY, UNA, Durham Company, 1941.
QUINLAN, MAURICE, Victorian Prelude. A History of English Manners, 1700–1830, 1941.
RAFFALD, ELIZABETH, The Experienced English Housekeeper, 1769.
RICHARDSON, A. E., Georgian England (1700–1820), 1931.
SMOLLETT, TOBIAS, Humphrey Clinker, 1770.
STIRLING, A. M. W., Annals of a Yorkshire House, 1911.
STIRLING, A. M. W., Coke of Norfolk and his Friends, 1912.
STROUD, DOROTHY, Capability Brown, 1950.
TURBERVILLE, A. S., English Men and Manners in the 18th Century, 1926.
VANCOUVER, CHARLES, General View of Agriculture of the County of Devon (and other publications of the Board of Agriculture), 1808.
N.B. Some other books are mentioned in the text.

Authorities for Chapter VI

ANON., Farming for Ladies, 1844.
ARMSTRONG, HERBERT B. J. (ed.), A Norfolk Diary, 1850—1888, c. 1949.
AUSTEN, JANE, Pride and Prejudice (and other works), 1813.
BURTON, HESTER, Barbara Bodichon, 1827–1891, 1949.
CLAPHAM, J. H., Economic History of Modern Britain, The Early Railway Age, 1925.
COBBETT, WILLIAM, Rural Rides, ed. of 1893.
COBBOLD, RICHARD, Margaret Catchpole, 1845.
DICKENS, CHARLES, Martin Chuzzlewit (and other works), 1844.
DISRAELI, BENJAMIN, Sybil, 1845.
ELIOT, GEORGE, Felix Holt, 1866. Adam Bede, etc., 1859.
GASKELL, MRS., Cranford, 1853.
GOULD, S. BARING, Old Country Life, 1895.
GOULD, S. BARING, Kitty Alone, 1895.
HAM, ELIZABETH, by herself, intro. by ERIC GILLETT, 1945.
HAMMOND, J. L. AND BARBARA, The Village Labourer, 1911.
HAMMOND, J. L. AND BARBARA, Lord Shaftesbury, 1923.
HAZLITT, WILLIAM, The Round Table, ed. of 1869.
Hortense writes to Eloise in 1847, Farmer's Weekly, 27th July, 1945.
HOWITT, WILLIAM, Rural Life of England, 1838.
INGELOW, JEAN, Fated to be Free, 1900.
KINGSLEY, CHARLES, Works, c. 1850.
MITFORD, MARY, Our Village, 1824–1832.
PEEL, HON. MRS. C. S., A Hundred Wonderful Years, 1820–1920, 1926.
PEEL, HON. MRS. C. S., The Stream of Time, 1805–1861, 1931.
PINCHBECK, IVY, Women Workers and the Industrial Revolution, 1750–1850, 1930.
Report . . . on the employment of women and children in agriculture, 1843.
ibid, 1867.
STUART, D. M., Regency Roundabout, 1943.

THOMPSON, EDWARD G., Men of Branber, 1944.
WINGFIELD-STRATFORD ESMÉ, The Victorian Tragedy, 1930.
YOUNG, G. M. (ed.), Early Victorian England, 1830–1865, 1934.

Authorities for Chapter VII

BOURNE, GEORGE, Change in the Village, 1912.
BOURNE, GEORGE, Lucy Bettesworth and Other Works, 1913.
BRODERICK, GEORGE, English Land and English Landlords, 1881.
BRYANT, ARTHUR, English Saga, 1840–1940, 1942.
BURTON, HESTER, Barbara Bodichon, 1827–1891, 1949.
CLEPHANE, I. AND BOTT, A., Our Mothers, 1870–1900, 1932.
CLIFFORD, FREDERICK, Agricultural Lockout, 1874, 1875.
COPLAND, SAMUEL, Agriculture Ancient and Modern, 1866.
DAVIES, MAUDE, Life in an English Village, 1909.
FISHER, DOUGLAS, Little World, n.d. c. 1950.
GAMBIER-PARRY, MAJOR, Allegories of the Land, 1912.
GAMBIER-PARRY, MAJOR, The Spirit of the Old Folk, 1913.
GIBBS, J. ARTHUR, A Cotswold Village, 1899.
GREEN, F. E., A History of the English Agricultural Labourer, 1870–1920, 1920.
GREEN, JOHN RICHARD, Stray Studies in England and Italy, 1892.
HALSHAM, JOHN, Idlehurst, 1898.
HALSHAM, JOHN, Old Standards, South Country Sketches, 1913.
HARDY, THOMAS, Tess of the D'Urbervilles, ed. of. 1891.
HARDY, THOMAS, Far from the Madding Crowd, and other works, ed. of 1893.
HAYDON, E. G., Travels Round Our Village, 1905.
HEATH, FRANCIS GEORGE, The English Peasantry, 1874.
HEATH, RICHARD, The English Peasant, 1893.
HILL, GEORGIANA, Women in English Life, 1896.
HOME, MICHAEL, Autumn Fields, 1944.
HOME, MICHAEL, Spring Sowing, 1946.
JENNINGS, LOUIS J., Field Paths and Green Lanes, 1884.
JOHNSON, CLIFTON, Amongst English Hedgerows, 1899.
KEBBEL, T. E., The Agricultural Labourer, 1870.
KENDALL, S. G., Farming Memories of a West County Yeoman, 1944.
OLIVIER, EDITH, Four Victorian Ladies of Wiltshire, 1945.
P.T.F., Some Countryside Folk, 1911.
PANTON, J. E., County Sketches in Black and White, 1882.
PEDDER, LT.-COL., Contemporary Review, February, 1903.
PEEL, HON. MRS. C. S., Life's Enchanted Cup; an Autobiography, 1872–1933, 1933.
PINCHBECK, IVY, Women Workers and the Industrial Revolution, 1930.
QUENNELL, MARJORIE AND C. H. B., Everyday Things in England, 1851–1934, 1934.
TAINE, HENRI, Notes on England, 1871.
THOMPSON, FLORA, Lark Rise and other works, 1939.
TILTMAN, MARJORIE HESSELL, Fine Knacks for Ladies, *Farmer and Stockbreeder*, 24th July, 1945.
WARD, RUTH E., A Lesson in Housekeeping, 1874, *Farmer's Weekly*, 15th February, 1946.
WINGFIELD-STRATFORD, ESMÉ, The Victorian Sunset, 1932.

This list could be almost indefinitely extended. The literature describing country life during the past hundred years, both contemporary and reminiscent, is vast. Many books not mentioned in the above list have been consulted.

INDEX

A

Addison, Joseph, *Spectator*, 105, 106, 107, 110, 126

Albermarle, Lady, 132

Andrews, Pamela, 113, 114

Armstrong, Rev. B. J., Vicar of East Dereham, 166, 167, 174

Astell, Mary, 84, 105, 106

Austen, Jane, *Pride and Prejudice*, snobbery of Mrs. Bennett, 160

B

Banks, Lady, defends Corfe Castle, 55

Barker, Jane, 108

Baths and personal washing, 26, 27, 118, 119, 205, 206

Baxter, Rev. Richard, *The Poor Husband's Advocate*, 1691, 95, 98

Beaufort, Duke and Duchess of, household, 80, 81, 82, 89, 97

Becon, *The Boke of Matrimony*, 30

Behn, Aphra, 83, 84

Berkeley, Lady, 29, 182

Best, Henry, of Elmswell, 60, 61

"Bint Hannah", a character in Mitford's *Our Village*, 168, 169

Blackwell, Elizabeth, 108, 109

Bland, Mrs., of Yorkshire, 108

Bouverie, Mrs., 136

Boxer, Mrs., 136

Braithwaite, Richard, 62

"Bramble Matthew," in Smollett's *Humphrey Clinker*, 112

"Bramble, Miss Tabitha", 134, 135

Brank, 50

Breton, Nicholas, *Court and Country*, 1618, 64, 66

Bridgewater, Elizabeth, Countess of, 111

"Brown, Tom", his mother, 160

Bryant, Arthur, *The National Character*, 98

"Bustle, Lady", a character in Johnson's *Rambler*, 115, 116

Byrom, Mrs., 61, 62

C

Campion, Thomas, 67

Cantrey, Goodwife, 65

Capper sisters, 140, 141

"Cass Squire" character in George Eliot's *Silas Marner*, 166, 168; characters in her other works, 167

Catchpole, Margaret, 179, 180

Caudle's, Mrs., Curtain Lectures, 49

Centlivre, Susannah, 84

Chamberlain, John, on marriage, 57

Charlotte, Countess of Derby, 55

Child, Sir Josiah, 79

Chudleigh, Lady, 92

Churchwardens, Women, 41, 42

Churchyard, Thomas, *The Spider and the Goat*, 37

Clarendon, Earl of, 75, 76

Clare, John, 151

Clarke, Mrs., 136

Clifford, Lady Anne, 55, 56

Clifford, Frederick, on woman's work, 198

217

Clothes, 37, 38, 98, 104, 105, 122, 148, 149, 150, 165, 166, 201

Cobbett, William, 170, 171

Coke of Norfolk, 132

Coke, Lady, wife of Lord Chief Justice, 55, 63

Coke, Mrs., (afterwards Lady) Anne, 135, 136

Coke, Mrs., of Fishponds, 136

Coles, William, *The Art of Simpling*, 1656, 97

Collar, Maud, 94

Collings, Rt. Hon. Jesse, on young women, 198

Cooking: methods, 24, 89, 141, 142, 202, 203, 208; recipes, 31

Country Ferme, 54

Coventry, Lady, 136

Cowley, Abraham, 83

Cox, Mary, 173

Craven, Lady Elizabeth, 132, 134; her famous friends, 133

D

Dairy work, 39, 40, 66, 85, 96, 127, 128, 151, 152, 170, 194, 195, 201, 202

Darrell, Sir William, 29

Dawson, Isabell, 61

Defoe, Daniel, 88, 118; *The Compleat English Tradesman*, 1720, 115

Diet, 18, 21, 25, 26, 30, 31, 59, 60, 62, 68, 70, 79, 85, 98, 99, 102, 123, 124, 126, 127, 130, 142, 146, 147, 148, 174, 175, 176, 178, 183, 184, 192, 208, 209

Disraeli, on women's political position, 161

Domestic industries, 128, 172, 181

Donne, John, 78

Dovecotes, 65

Ducking stool, 50

E

Education: 20, 21, 51, 53, 58, 84, 107, 137, 138, 139, 159, 162, 188, 197, 202; Women writers of textbooks, 138

Elizabeth, Duchess of Rutland, 160, 161

Elstob, Elizabeth, 107, 108

Erasmus, on English Ladies, 27

Evelyn, John, *Mundus Muliebris*, 1690, 85, 86

Evelyn, Mary, 84, 86

"Everdene Bathsheba", character in Hardy's *Far from the Madding Crowd*, 196

F

Family Budget, 1880, 178

Fanshawe, Lady, 53

Farming for Ladies, 1844, 168

Feasts, 42, 60, 165, 179, 180

Fell, Sarah, of Swarthmore Hall, 82, 96

Female Spectator, The, a periodical of 1740, 106

Fiennes, Celia, 96

Firing, 99, 100, 101, 147, 156, 158, 210

Fitzherbert, 32, 40, 41

Flowers, 32, 33, 65, 98

Forests in Tudor days, xi

Four Victorian Ladies of Wiltshire, 186, 187

Fruit, 32, 33, 34

Fuller, Thomas, *Holy and Profane State*, 1642, 46, 47, 48

Funerals, 93

Furniture, 102, 123, 126, 127, 183, 194, 203, 204

Fyvie, Lady, 55

G

Gangs, Agricultural, 176, 177
Gardens, 32, 33, 65, 97, 98
Gardeners Professional, of Restoration, Mr. Rose, Mr. London, Mr. Wise, 97
Gaskill, Mrs., *Cranford*, 167
George III, (Farmer George), 131
Gibbs, J. Arthur, on cottage wives, 208
Gifts, 25, 93
Goldsmith, Oliver, *Vicar of Wakefield*, 99, 110
Googe, Barnaby, 32, 91
Grey, Agnes, 164
Grose, Francis, *The Olio*, 112
"Grym, Madame., of Grymstone", a character from Baring Gould, 160

H

Hale, Sir Matthew, 86
Halsham, John, on cottages, 205
Ham, Elizabeth, 162
Harington, Sir Joshua, his water closet, 22
Hayes, Miss, 136
Hazlitt, William, on fashionable women, 159
Heath, F. G., on women's work, 199
Heath land distribution in Tudor days, xii
Heber, Bishop, 90
Herbert, George, his mother, 44, 45
Hoby, Lady Margaret, 28, 29
Holdenby, Christopher, on cottage accommodation 204, 205; on cottage diet, 209
Home, Michael, *Autumn Fields*, 1944, 197
Horworthe, Isobell, 61
Howell, James, *Familiar Letters*, 62

Howland, Elizabeth, 79
Hurst, Anne, Life story from Eden's *State of the Poor*, 1797, 150, 151
Hutchinson, Mrs. Lucy, 51, 52, 83
Hyll, Thomas, *A Most Briefe and Pleasaunt Treatyse*, 1563, 32

I

Ingelow, Jean, 160
Isham, Lady, 56

J

Jack of Newbery, 38
Jefferies, Mrs., of Hereford, 58, 59
Jefferies, Richard, *Hodge and his Masters*, 192, 193
Jennings, Louis J., *Field Paths and Green Lanes*, 1875, 206
Johnson, Clifton, 200, 201, 205

K

Kalm, Pehr, on English women, 116, 117, 118, 124, 127, 137
Kebbell, T. E., 199
Kendall, S. J., 202, 203

L

Lark Rise, 205, 208, 209
Laundry, 90, 119
Lawson, William, *The Countrie Housewife's Garden*, 1617, 63
Lighting, 38, 120, 121, 210
Linday, Countess of, 97
Luxton, Roger, 164
Lyly, John, *Euphues and his England*, 25

M

Markham, Gervase, *The English Hus-wife*, 1615, 45, 46, 60, 65
Marlborough, Sarah, Duchess of, 110
Marriage, 57, 71, 77, 78, 91, 118, 124
Marshall, William, *Rural Economy of Gloucester*, 1788, 152
Marshes, distribution in Henry VIII's time, xi
Marvell, Andrew, 63
Mascall, Leonard, 29
Melbourne, Lady, 136
Midwifery, 93
Millbanks, Mr. and Mrs., of Seaham House, 133, 134
Milton, 44
Milton Abbas, Dorset, overcrowded cottages, 172, 173
Montague, Mrs., 105
More, Hannah, *Tales for the Common People*, 143, 144, 145
Murray, Anne, 55

N

Newcastle, Duchess of, 51, 52, 83
Norwich, 19

O

Ormerod, Eleanor, 188, 189
Osborne, Dorothy, 56, 57, 125
Overbury, Sir Thomas, 69, 70

P

Parker, Matthew, *The Milkmaid's Life*, 36
Philips, Katherine, the *Matchless Orinda*, 83, 97

"Pinch Tom" at Salisbury, 165
Pix, Mrs., 84
Plat, Sir Hugh, *Delightes for Ladies*, 26
Plattner, Thomas, a German tourist, on English Ladies, 27
Pope, 103, 104
Population, No. and class in Queen Elizabeth's day, xiii, xiv; No. and class by Gregory King, 1688, 94
Powell, William, *Tom of all Trades*, 1631, 57, 58
Prentice, E. Parmalee, *Hunger and History*, 1939, 26
Pringle, Andrew, 155

Q

Quennell, Marjorie, and C. H. B., *Everyday things in England*, 1851–1934, 197

R

Rambler, The, 109, 110, 115
Ravenscroft, *The Italian Husband*, 1698, 74
Reading matter, 56, 83, 88, 89, 197
Rich, Mary, Countess of Warwick, 76
Rumford, Count, his stoves, 143

S

"Sacharissa", Countess of Sunderland, 76
Sackville, Thomas, Lord Buckhurst, 1st Earl of Dorset, 27
Salisbury, Marchioness of, 136
Shadwell, Thomas, 84
Shakerley, Mrs. or Lady, 89, 90
Shakespeare, his noble ladies, 25; *Taming of the Shrew*, 49

Sidney, Sir Philip, *Arcadia*, 25
Sinclair, Sir John, 132
Soap, 26, 119, 120
Spencer, John, and servant trouble, 133
Spencer, Christiana, 133
Sport and Games, 20, 158, 187, 190, 191
Squatter's cottages, 125, 129, 181
Sleeping arrangements in Devon, Henry VII's reign, 22, 23
Stevens, Tabitha, described by Major Gambier Parry, 199, 120
Still room, 24
Stuart, Dorothy, *Regency Roundabout*, 162
Stuart, Francis, Duchess of Richmond, 82
Superstition, 180, 210
Surflet, Richard, 34
Switzer, Stephen, *Iconongraphia Rustica*, 1718, 97

T

Taine, Henri, on rich farmer's wife 1870, 191, 193; on field work for women, 202
Taylor, Jeremy, 83
Temple, Sir William, 78, 97
Tess of the D'Urbervilles, 201, 202
Thornton, Mrs., 158
Tooth brushes, 26
Travelling, difficulties of, xiv, 17, 94, 111
Trevelyan, G. M., *England under the Stuarts*, 1904, 44
Tusser, Thomas, 17, 18, 30, 32

V

Vancouver, Charles, 156
Vegetables, 33, 63, 98
Verney, Ralph, 53
Vesey, Mrs., 105
Vyner, Henry, 63

W

Wages, 35, 36, 60, 61, 71, 95, 115, 128, 145, 152, 153, 155, 170, 172, 181, 182, 183, 199, 207, 208
Walton, Isaac, 125
Washington, Anne, 56
Water supply, 205, 206, 209, 210
"Weston, Squire", and his wife, 116
White, Gilbert, *Natural History of Selbourne*, 121
Wilkinson, Rev. Robert, *The Merchant Royall*, 1607, 48
Williamson, Capt., saw women ploughing in 1810, 172
Willis, Mr., Life at Gordon Castle, 159
"Wilmot, Rebecca", 144, 145
Witchcraft, 100, 101, 180, 181
Woodward, Marcus, *The Countryman's Jewel*, 29
Woolley, Mrs. Hannah, her cookery books, 87, 88

Y

Young, Arthur, 131, 132